Knowledge and Knower

We live in 'knowledge societies' and work in 'knowledge economies', but accounts of social change treat knowledge as homogeneous and neutral. While knowledge should be central to educational research, it focuses on processes of knowing and condemns studies of knowledge as essentialist. This book unfolds a sophisticated theoretical framework for analysing knowledge practices: Legitimation Code Theory or 'LCT'. By extending and integrating the influential approaches of Pierre Bourdieu and Basil Bernstein, LCT offers a practical means for overcoming knowledge-blindness without succumbing to essentialism or relativism.

Through detailed studies of pressing issues in education, the book sets out the multidimensional conceptual toolkit of LCT and shows how it can be used in research. Chapters introduce concepts by exploring topics across the disciplinary and institutional maps of education:

- how to enable cumulative learning at school and university
- the unfounded popularity of 'student centred learning' and constructivism
- the rise and demise of British cultural studies in higher education
- the positive role of canons
- proclaimed 'revolutions' in social science
- the 'two cultures' debate between science and humanities
- how to build cumulative knowledge in research
- the unpopularity of school Music
- how current debates in economics and physics are creating major schisms in those fields.

LCT is a rapidly growing approach to the study of education, knowledge and practice, and this landmark book is the first to systematically set out key aspects of this theory. It offers an explanatory framework for empirical research, applicable to a wide range of practices and social fields, and will be essential reading for all serious students and scholars of education and sociology.

Karl Maton is Senior Lecturer in Sociology at the University of Sydney, Australia, and Honorary Professor at Rhodes University, South Africa.

Praise for *Knowledge and Knowers*:

'This tour-de-force will set the agenda for the future of the sociology of education. Maton's writing is always engaging and thought-provoking. The book offers nothing less than a new approach to the morphology of sociological knowledge itself – a "must-read".'

Michael Grenfell, Professor of Education at Trinity College, University of Dublin, Ireland, and internationally renowned expert on the sociology of Pierre Bourdieu.

'A truly majestic contribution that advances fundamentally the ideas of Basil Bernstein and Pierre Bourdieu. It is a formidable piece of work: imaginative, thought-provoking, intellectually out-reaching, and will surely constitute essential reading across the social sciences.'

John Evans, Professor of Sociology of Education and Physical Education at the University of Loughborough, UK, and author of numerous books in sociology of education.

'For decades sociology has been the missing link in discourse analyses of social context. Maton's inspirational volume consolidates a sociology of immense theoretical insight and undaunted analytical precision to make this blind-spot obsolete. Theory is every scholar's best friend; social theory of this order is a very best friend indeed.'

J.R. Martin, Professor of Linguistics at the University of Sydney, Australia, author of numerous books on language and education, and internationally recognized as a leading scholar of systemic functional linguistics.

Knowledge and Knowers

Towards a realist sociology of education

Karl Maton

Routledge
Taylor & Francis Group
LONDON AND NEW YORK

First published 2014
by Routledge
2 Park Square, Milton Park, Abingdon, Oxfordshire OX14 4RN

Simultaneously published in the USA and Canada
by Routledge
711 Third Avenue, New York, NY 10017

First issued in paperback 2014

Routledge is an imprint of the Taylor and Francis Group, an informa business

British Library Cataloguing in Publication Data
A catalogue record for this book is available from the British Library

Library of Congress Cataloging in Publication Data
Maton, Karl.
Knowledge and knowers: towards a realist sociology of education / Karl Maton.
pages cm
Includes bibliographical references and index.
1. Educational sociology. 2. Education—Curricula. 3. Constructivism (Education) I. Title.
LC191.M17 2014
306.43'2—dc23
2013008156

ISBN 978-0-415-47999-8 (hbk)
ISBN 978-1-138-90305-0 (pbk)
ISBN 978-0-203-88573-4 (ebk)

Typeset in Galliard
by Book Now Ltd, London

For my mother, Rosemarie

Contents

Illustrations

Figures

Tables

Acknowledgements

The ideas articulated in this book were developed over a long period, so my accumulated gratitude is great. The advice, encouragement and inspiration of Basil Bernstein echoes throughout – Legitimation Code Theory (LCT) aims to keep his approach alive and vital and so begin repaying my debt. For the longest time I have enjoyed the best of intellectual conversations with Rob Moore. His belief during my years of isolation and our synchronicity have been priceless. In recent years I have been lucky enough to work with Jim Martin, a model intellectual. Talking with Jim is a workout, an education, and the most wonderful fun. I cannot thank them enough.

I am extremely grateful for encouragement from the late Pierre Bourdieu and gained immeasurably from working with Alexandra Lamont, Sue Bennett, and Peter Freebody, and discussions with Mike Grenfell and Brad Shipway. Three overlapping groups of scholars have given stimulation and support. First autobiographically was the community centred on past International Basil Bernstein Symposia. I should particularly like to thank Madeleine Arnot, John Evans, Gabrielle Ivinson, Ana Morais, Joe Muller, Isabel Neves, Alan Sadovnik, Susan Semel, Parlo Singh, Bill Tyler, and Leesa Wheelahan. Special hugs are due to Brian Davies, Gemma Moss and Sally Power for decisive advice and encouragement. More recently, I have enjoyed a genuinely inter-disciplinary dialogue with systemic functional linguists. Sue Hood provides unwavering support, for which I am eternally grateful. I also wish to thank Frances Christie, Beverley Derewianka, Alexanne Don, Yaegan Doran, Jing Hao, Jo Lander, Mary Macken-Horarik, Lucy Macnaught, Erika Matruglio, Len Unsworth, Trish Weekes, Peter White and Geoff Williams. Last but not least, LCT is a friendly community who make this a joyous field activity rather than individual labour. In addition to those already mentioned, I am grateful to Sharon Aris, Lucila Carvalho, Jenni Case, Rainbow Chen, Anna David, Andy Dong, Tristan Enright, Helen Georgiou, Christine Lindstrøm, Kathy Luckett, Jodie Martin, Bec O'Brien, Célia Poulet, Gina Roach, Anna-Vera Sigsgaard, Sophia Stavrou, and Eszter Szenes. I owe special (semantic) waves of appreciation to Martin McNamara, Suellen Shay, Philippe Vitale, and Jo-Anne Vorster, Chrissie Boughey and Sioux McKenna.

I learn enormously from opportunities to teach or present LCT and so extend my gratitude to everyone who invited me to do so. In addition to those already mentioned, my thanks go to Roy Bhaskar, Rosemary Clerehan, Daniel Frandji, Peter Gates, Jenny Gore, Pauline Jones, Ahmar Mahboob, Jean-Yves Rochex, Siyabulela Sabata, Manjula Sharma, and Geoff Whitty. I am proud to be associated with my colleagues at the Centre for Higher Education Research, Teaching and Learning at Rhodes University (South Africa) as a Visiting Professor, and at Départment de Sociologie de lUFR Civilisations et Humanités, Université de Provence (France) as an Elected International Professor during 2012.

The code novelist Milan Kundera wrote: 'Being in a foreign country means walking a tightrope high above the ground' (1984: 71). Without Sarah Howard I would be far more battered and bruised from falling, if not fatally done for. Sarah provides support, advice and encouragement throughout every part of my life – without her this book would not now be in your hands. Thanks also to my longest-lasting friends, Alex and Ian. My sister Helen and her extended family – Kelvin, Kim, Alex, Abbie, Kieran, Jamie and Ethan – are an inspiration to me, as is my mother's husband, Tony.

This book is lovingly dedicated to my mother, Rosemarie Shirley Ann Bathew. Words would belittle what I owe to you.

Last, this book is an invitation to its readers to collaborate in creation. As it emphasizes, knowledge-building is an open-ended process. The book as a product represents a compromise between desires for definitive exposition and demands for timely release. These ideas will continue to develop. Knowledge-building is also a social activity and not confined to the writings of any one person. So, for both what is useful and for the inevitable omissions, errors and shortcomings in what follows, I should not be held solely responsible – after all, we're in this together.

Karl Maton
Sydney, 2013

1 Seeing knowledge and knowers

Social realism and Legitimation Code Theory

Seeing what is hidden by a blind spot requires a new gaze, a different insight.

The knowledge paradox

Knowledge is everything and nothing. This paradox marks the heart of debate over social change. For over fifty years, successive accounts have proclaimed the birth of a new era in which knowledge is paramount to a new kind of society. The names of eras are legion: 'late capitalism', 'postmodernity', 'the information age', among many others. The roll call of new societies is voluminous: 'post-industrial society' (Touraine 1971; Bell 1973), 'information society' (Masuda 1981), 'knowledge society' (Drucker 1969; Stehr 1994), 'network society' (Castells 2000), and so on. These countless proclamations of profound change differ in their choice of labels and the specific changes they emphasize. However, all foreground knowledge as reshaping every aspect of social life.

'Knowledge economies' based on the creation, circulation and consumption of information rather than material goods are said to require workers to engage in 'lifelong learning' to keep pace with the resulting fluidity of labour markets. Politics is characterized as concerned with information management and public relations rather than parliamentary procedure and policy enactment. Exponential growth in the volume, complexity and sources of knowledge is proclaimed as undermining traditional notions of authority and expertise. In particular, the rise of new information and communication technologies are heralded as democratizing the creation of knowledge and allowing anyone with Internet access to have 'all the world's knowledge at their fingertips' (Friedman 2005: 178). At the same time, these potentially all-knowing citizens are themselves said to be subject to unparalleled levels of information-gathering in a 'superpanopticon' (Poster 1990) managed by a growing army of professionals whose disciplining gaze reaches into every minutiae of everyday life.

Such claims are commonly found and repeatedly made across the social sciences. Their shared import is to proclaim knowledge as everything. Never has knowledge been viewed as so crucial to the nature of society. Yet, ***understanding knowledge*** is not viewed as crucial to ***understanding society***. For what unites accounts of social change is not only their emphasis on the centrality of knowledge but also their lack of a theory of knowledge. Knowledge is described as a defining feature of modern societies, but what that knowledge is, its forms and its effects, are not part of the analysis. Instead, knowledge is treated as having no inner structures with properties, powers and tendencies of their own, as if all forms of knowledge are identical, homogeneous and neutral.

There resides a further irony here. Writing of how social change is reshaping education, Bernstein argued that:

> there is a new concept of knowledge and of its relation to those who create it and use it. ... Knowledge should flow like money, to wherever it can create advantage and profit. Indeed knowledge is not like money, it *is* money.
>
> (Bernstein 2000: 86; original emphasis)

This view of knowledge is held by many sociological accounts to characterize contemporary advanced societies. However, in a circular manner, this conception is also *adopted* by those accounts: they treat knowledge as interchangeable tokens, like money. The central concern of research has thus become exploring the extent, intensity and comparative value of flows of knowledge, rather than its forms and their effects. For example, in Manuel Castells' seminal and otherwise brilliant three-volume work on *The Information Age*, 'a definition of knowledge and information' is relegated to a footnote in which Castells declares:

> I have no compelling reason to improve on Daniel Bell's (1976: 175) own definition of *knowledge*: 'Knowledge: a set of organized statements of facts or ideas, presenting a reasoned judgement or an experimental result, which is transmitted to others through some communication medium in some systematic form. Thus I distinguish knowledge from news and entertainment'. As for *information* ... I would rejoin the operational definition of information proposed by Porat in his classic work (1977: 2): 'Information is data that have been organized and communicated'.
>
> (Castells 2000: 17, n25; original emphases)

This way of defining knowledge represents what Popper (2003a: 29) terms 'methodological essentialism': it attempts to establish universal definitions or demarcation criteria between 'knowledge' and 'not-knowledge' (such as 'news and entertainment'). Such asociological and ahistorical essentialism offers little insight into the knowledge held to be central to society. It invariably leads to broad descriptions of generic attributes that obscure differences *within* 'knowledge'. As Stehr argues, 'our knowledge about knowledge remains unsophisticated ... knowledge is treated as a black box' (1994: x). Knowledge is thus one of the most discussed *and* one of the least discussed issues in academic debate. Knowledge is everything to society but nothing to social science.

This book contributes towards resolving the knowledge paradox by introducing a conceptual framework, Legitimation Code Theory (LCT), that enables knowledge practices to be seen, their organizing principles to be conceptualized, and their effects to be explored. Since LCT first emerged in the late 1990s, it has evolved into a sophisticated toolkit. Research using LCT is growing rapidly. Having begun with a focus on knowledge practices in education, studies are embracing a widening range of fields and practices (Chapter 10). LCT is far more than a sociology of knowledge or education – it is a sociology of possibility. Nonetheless, education and knowledge remain key points of departure and central foci of studies for the framework.

Accordingly, in the course of unfolding two dimensions of LCT, this book addresses a range of educational issues. Concepts are introduced in the context of analyses of: the peculiar position of British cultural studies in higher education (Chapter 2); proclaimed 'revolutions' in social science (Chapter 3); what is at stake in the 'two cultures' debate, why school qualifications in Music are so unpopular, and what relates such different issues (Chapter 4); the role of canons in the humanities and how these fields can develop cumulatively (Chapter 5); the conditions for cumulative learning at school and university (Chapter 6); the conditions for cumulative knowledge-building in research (Chapter 7); how ideas with little empirical basis, such as 'student-centred learning', become so powerful in education (Chapter 8); and why seemingly minor differences in intellectual fields can have major effects on their development (Chapter 9).

What these diverse topics share is a concern with knowledge-building: all chapters explore how powerful and cumulative knowledge can be built in research or learning (Chapter 10 explores the development embodied by concepts from and studies using LCT). A theme running through this book is building knowledge about knowledge-building. However, exploring these diverse topics (denoted by the subtitle of each chapter) is not the book's sole purpose: they occasion the unfolding of the framework. Each chapter introduces new concepts (indicated by its main title) that build cumulatively into a conceptual toolkit and analytic methodology for substantive research. The book is thereby intended to contribute towards developing a realist sociology that resolves the knowledge paradox. In this chapter I begin with why this is necessary by discussing knowledge-blindness in educational research, a field ostensibly concerned with knowledge. Second, I introduce 'social realism', a school of thought that takes knowledge seriously as an object of study. Third, I briefly sketch the contours of LCT, highlighting its relations to social ontologies and research studies and introducing its conceptual architecture.

Knowledge-blindness in education

The knowledge paradox extends to the intellectual field one might expect to explicitly address knowledge: educational research. Knowledge is the basis of education as a social field of practice – it is the creation, curricularization, and teaching and learning of knowledge which make education a distinctive field. Yet a *subjectivist doxa* in educational research reduces knowledge to knowing, and a deep-seated tendency towards constructivist relativism, based on a long-established but false dichotomy with positivist absolutism, reduces knowledge to power. The result is ***knowledge-blindness***, leaving knowledge under-researched, the study of education underdeveloped, and the sociology of knowledge unaware of its ostensible object of study.

The subjectivist doxa

'I am,' Popper remarked, 'a great admirer of, and believer in common sense. But common sense is sometimes seriously mistaken. It is so in connection with the theory of knowledge ... For the commonsense theory of knowledge is subjectivist and sensualist' (1994a: 132). Popper was referring to the widespread belief that 'knowledge' entirely comprises a state of mind, consciousness or a disposition to act, is wholly sensory in source, and must be inextricably associated with a knowing subject. This subjectivist account of knowledge is also a doxa of educational research: it goes without saying that the study of 'knowledge' is exhausted by exploring processes of and influences on knowing. Indeed, this subjectivist view is so taken for granted across the field that what Popper (1979, 1994a) called 'objective knowledge' – including intellectual problem-situations, theories, critical discussions and arguments – has become almost entirely suppressed as a potential object of study.

The specific forms taken by the doxa in research depends on their underlying disciplinary influences. Psychologically informed approaches, for example, typically construe 'knowledge' as subjective states of consciousness and mental processes or, in more 'social' versions (such as activity and situated cognition theories), as aggregates of the workings of individual minds or communities of practice. In short, 'knowledge' represents processes of knowing within the minds of knowers. This perspective has been widely propagated by the rise of constructivist ideas which hold that:

> knowledge, no matter how it be defined, is in the heads of persons, and that the thinking subject has no alternative but to construct what he or she knows on the basis of his or her own experience.
>
> (von Glasersfeld 1995: 1)

Over recent decades, the theory of learning offered by constructivism has become propagated as a theory of everything, including teaching, curriculum, and research. Different knowledge practices have thereby been reduced to a logic of learning, based on the belief that 'the more basic phenomenon is learning' (Lave and Wenger 1991: 92). From this perspective, ***what*** is being learned is of little significance. Accordingly, research typically focuses on generic processes of learning and sidelines differences between the forms of knowledge being learned. An influential text, for example, states that:

> scientific understanding of learning includes understanding about learning processes, learning environments, teaching, socio-cultural processes, and the many other factors that contribute to learning. Research on all of these

> topics ... provides the fundamental knowledge base for understanding and implementing changes in education.
>
> (Bransford *et al.* 2000: 233)

Research into knowledge as an object, into *what* is being learned, is thus not viewed as integral to 'the fundamental knowledge base' of educational research and policy. Indeed, while 'knowledge' is reduced to knowing, 'what is being learned' (that which is being mentally processed) is typically understood as the world rather than a system of knowledge about the world – the physical world rather than physics, the social world rather than sociology, etc. Bypassing knowledge, this subjectivist empiricism thereby commits what can be called the *learning fallacy* of confusing 'epistemology' with learning (see, for example, diSessa 1993).

Though couched in less explicitly mental terms, sociologically informed approaches to education offer a similar picture. Dominant approaches share a subjectivist account of knowledge, whether externalist analyses of relations between education and social structures or internalist studies of practices within education. From Hegel, through Marx, Mannheim, reproduction theories and onto standpoint theories, externalist sociologies have focused on how nationality, social class, gender, ethnicity, sexuality, geographic region, or other socio-historical factors shape actors' ways of viewing, being and acting in the world. In short, they foreground the effects on knowing of the social circumstances of knowers (cf. Popper 2003b; Moore 2009). Internalist accounts typically focus more on relations among knowers but similarly view knowledge in terms of thinking, acting and being. From phenomenological studies of classroom practice underpinned by symbolic interactionism during the 1970s to discursively focused Foucauldian, Deleuzian and other 'critical' theories in recent years, research has explored how actors' identities are shaped by interactions with others, or, in current parlance, the capacity for discursive practices to form, construct or assemble subjectivities.

Despite their many and significant differences, most sociological approaches to education thereby share a subjectivist understanding of knowledge – they offer sociologies of knowing. From this perspective, *what* knowledge is being created, pedagogized, taught and learned is of little significance. Rather, research typically explores the social influences on how different kinds of knowers act, think and feel. This subjectivist doxa is further reflected by the psychotherapeutic solutions proffered for overcoming such influences, including 'socioanalysis' (as mocked by Popper in 1945 [2003b], and later heralded by Bourdieu [1994]), 'reflexivity', consciousness raising, and 'auto ' methods of self reflection (Maton 2003). Moreover, as I shall now discuss, where knowledge itself enters the picture, it is engulfed by the question of *whose* knowledge it represents, as part of revealing the social interests these influences serve.

Knowledge-aversion

Knowledge represents not simply a blind spot for educational research, it is also taboo. Studies of the intrinsic features of knowledge are typically stigmatized as ahistorical, asociological, idealist, positivist, and conservative. These associations follow from the application of methodological essentialism, the search for universal definitions, to the subjectivist understanding of knowledge. Historically, an influential result was the conviction that, as Moore summarizes,

> to count as knowledge beliefs must be grounded directly in ***unmediated*** sensory experience and, hence, outside of history and detached from power and the social. Positivism was assumed as *the* model of knowledge and also of science.
>
> (Moore 2009: 2; original emphases)

Crucially, positivism has repeatedly served as a touchstone against which approaches define themselves. The identification of a positivist mainstream, its denunciation, and the announcement of a more humanist and social approach has recurred in the guise of progressivism, standpoint theories, 'critical' theories, 'post-' theories, social constructivism, among others (Moore 2009). Despite their fundamental differences, such approaches all construct what Alexander (1995) terms an 'epistemological dilemma': a false dichotomy between positivist absolutism and constructivist relativism. That is, they posit a choice between understanding knowledge either as decontextualized, value-free, detached and certain or as socially constructed within cultural and historical conditions in ways that reflect vested social interests. Of these options, they then choose the latter, and thereby dissolve knowledge.

In other words, having (re-)discovered the obvious point that 'knowledge is socially constructed', many approaches take this to also mean '... rather than related to something real'. By committing the 'epistemic fallacy' of confusing epistemology with ontology (Bhaskar 1993: 397), social construction is extended from knowledge to reality. Berger and Luckmann (1966), for example, influentially declared the sociology of knowledge to be concerned with *The Social Construction of Reality*. At the same time, knowledge is reduced to nothing but an arbitrary reflection of a social position, standpoint, culture, 'form of life', 'language game', and so on. The key issue for research then becomes unmasking the social power underpinning the standpoint, culture, form of life, etc., to reveal 'knowledge' as the disguised interests of dominant social groups. Though highlighting the coupling of power/knowledge, knowledge is thereby reduced to social power.

The notions that knowledge practices may be more than arbitrary reflections of power, and that their forms possess properties and tendencies that are worthy of study, have thus become associated with positivism and the interests of dominant social groups. The central preoccupation of the sociology of education has accordingly been with what Bernstein (1990) called 'relations to', such as the relations of social class, gender and ethnicity to research, curriculum and pedagogy. In contrast, what he termed 'relations within', the 'intrinsic features' of knowledge, have rarely been analysed, for to do so, Bernstein argued, 'would most likely lead to a charge of essentialism reinforced by a secondary, more heinous charge of fetishism' (1996: 170). A well-known example of this stigmatization accompanied the emergence of the 'new sociology of education' in the early 1970s. Previously, a dominant approach to knowledge and curriculum had been the 'London line' in the philosophy of education (Peters 1967; Hirst and Peters 1970) that analysed academic subjects in terms of distinctions into logical 'forms' and development into 'indisputably logically cohesive disciplines' (Hirst 1967: 44). Advocates of the 'new sociology of education' portrayed this tradition as embodying a positivist model that essentialized, desocialized and dehistoricized knowledge, and proclaimed a 'new', social and more politically radical understanding of knowledge (Jenks 1977). Such negative connotations have dogged any focus on knowledge itself ever since.[1] Knowledge has become the silenced Other in education.

Knowledge-blindness

The 'epistemological dilemma' limits what Bourdieu (1991) termed 'the space of possibles' within the field: the range of stances actors see as viable and legitimate. It posits a false choice between either positivism or relativism, so that the only *visible* option for seeing knowledge is ontologically untenable and morally undesirable. However, the 'space of possibles' is even more restricted than it might appear, for both sides of this false dichotomy share a subjectivist understanding of 'knowledge'. As Moore highlights, both 'are committed to the fundamental principle that truth is that which is given within the immediate consciousness of a knowing subject ... issues of knowledge are, for both, reduced to an epistemology of the knowing subject' (2013a: 341). For example, Berger and Luckmann, whose ideas have influenced generations of scholars, argued against a 'neo-positivist' focus on 'theoretical thought' and proclaimed that:

> the sociology of knowledge must first of all concern itself with what people 'know' as 'reality' in their everyday, non- or pre-theoretical lives. In other words, commonsense 'knowledge' rather than 'ideas' must be the central focus for the sociology of knowledge.
>
> (Berger and Luckmann 1966: 27)

The opposition they present is between two approaches that both construct knowledge (whether 'theoretical thought' or 'commonsense') as knowing. The 'epistemological dilemma' is thus embedded in a subjectivist doxa.

The resulting knowledge-blindness has implications far beyond epistemology. In research it focuses attention on processes of learning and whose knowledge is being learned, but obscures what is being learned and how it shapes these processes and power relations. Indeed, by reducing knowledge to knowing *and nothing but*, or to power *and nothing but*, the subjectivist doxa limits our understanding of knowing and power, for the crucial role played in these issues by 'relations within' knowledge is ignored. In teaching and learning, knowledge-blindness is reflected by oscillations between 'traditional' and 'constructivist' pedagogies that are generalized across the curriculum. In educational policy, knowledge is widely viewed as undifferentiated, as 'generic' skills (such as 'critical thinking') or interchangeable packets of information, and the basis of its selection, sequencing and pacing in a curriculum considered arbitrary. Indeed, knowledge-blindness has manifold consequences across education. For example, debates over educational technology, in which considerable budgets are at stake, obscure differences between everyday and educational knowledges, and between different forms of the latter. The resulting tendency is to deprofessionalize, if not denigrate (as resistant or uninformed) and attempt to bypass teachers who fail to adopt technologies in constructivist ways (Howard and Maton 2011).

This is not to suggest knowledge-blindness is universal. An incipient awareness of knowledge can be found within a range of specialisms, including applied psychology (Biglan 1973a, b; Bereiter 2002), studies of school subjects (Goodson 1997), higher education studies (Becher and Trowler 2001), educational technology (Scardamalia and Bereiter 2006), philosophy (Boghossian 2006; Frankfurt 2006), and science education (diSessa 1993), as well as popularly aimed publications (Benson and Stangroom 2006). However, recognizing the need to analyse knowledge is not realizing the analysis of knowledge, for this requires the right kind of conceptual tools. Three characteristics of these disparate fields of scholarship still leave educational research with, at best, knowledge-myopia. First, many arguments remain at the stage of calls to arms – they highlight the significance of knowledge but do not provide the means for its analysis. Second, where analytic tools are offered, the subjectivist doxa often reasserts itself in models of knowing, such as Bloom's taxonomy (Krathwohl 2002), Shulman's 'PCK' (1986), and diSessa's 'phenomenological primitives' (1993). Third, among accounts which do analyse knowledge, models are often restricted to segmental typologies and taxonomies of limited explanatory power. As I discuss in Chapter 7 (and Maton 2013), this kind of theorizing offers a first step towards seeing knowledge but must be developed to conceptualize the organizing principles of knowledge if their properties and powers are to be explored.

The cumulative effect of the subjectivist doxa, epistemological dilemma and myopic modelling is to foster a belief that knowledge is only the knowing of knowers, that studying 'relations within' knowledge is subscribing to conservatism and positivism, and that, if studied, knowledge must be endlessly typologized. The result of these seductive illusions is the knowledge paradox: our understanding of contemporary society, in which knowledge is held to be key, and of education, a field based on knowledge, are afflicted by knowledge-blindness. Pointing to what is hidden by a blind spot is, however, difficult, for seeing it requires a new gaze and different insight. Social realism, a diverse school of thought to which Legitimation Code Theory is allied, lays the foundations for a new way of seeing that overcomes this blind spot. It demonstrates that exploring knowledge is neither positivist nor conservative, that analyses of 'relations to' and 'relations within' knowledge can be brought together, and that knowledge is not reducible to knowing.

Taking knowledge seriously: Social realism

Coalescence of a coalition

'Social realism' is the label for a variety of movements. Here I refer to a 'coalition of minds' in the sociology of education that emerged during the late 1990s (Maton and Moore 2010a). Like any 'school of thought', social realism is heterogeneous in terms of its constitutive intellectual contributions. These can be described by using the three criteria offered by Deleuze for determining 'a worthwhile book':

> (1) you think that the books on the same or a related subject fall into a sort of general *error* (polemical function ...); (2) you think that something essential about the subject has been *forgotten* (inventive function); (3) you consider that you are capable of creating a new *concept* (creative function). Of course, that's the quantitative minimum: an error, an oversight, a concept.
>
> (quoted in Villani 1999: 56; original emphases)

Worthwhile books may serve these functions, but usually not all three equally. The principal concerns of most social realist work have been 'polemical' and 'inventive': the essential groundclearing and foundational functions of diagnosing general errors of educational thinking and highlighting the neglect of knowledge. Indeed, social realism emerged from scholars coalescing around the need to see knowledge as an object of study, as illustrated by emblematic early publications that aimed at *Reclaiming Knowledge* (Muller 2000), 'Recovering pedagogic discourse' (Maton 2000a), arguing 'For knowledge' (Moore 2000) and 'Founding the sociology of knowledge' (Moore and Maton 2001).

This initial impulse rippled out to include further protagonists. For example, an analysis of standpoint theories in cultural studies in Maton (1998, 2000b) (revised here as Chapter 2) helped influence an analysis of the sociology of education by Moore and Muller (1999) that prompted Young to respond (2000), resulting in a host of papers by various combinations of these scholars and others. Subsequently a succession of landmark works have set about *Bringing Knowledge Back In* (Young 2008), moving *Towards the Sociology of Truth* (Moore 2009), showing *Why Knowledge Matters in Curriculum* (Wheelahan 2010) and exploring *The Politics of Knowledge in Education* (Rata 2012). More widely, a series of international conferences and edited collections have enabled this concern with taking knowledge seriously to become a vibrant, inter-disciplinary endeavour embracing, among others, systemic functional linguists, educationalists of a wide range of subjects, and philosophers.[2]

Stronger knowledge

In identifying errors and blind spots in educational thinking, social realism argues for a stronger theory of knowledge. Put simply, social realism shows knowledge to be not only social but also real (hence its name) in the sense of possessing properties, powers and tendencies that have effects. Accordingly, research aligned with social realism explores the organizing principles of (or 'relations within') different forms of knowledge, their modes of change, and their implications for such issues as social inclusion, student achievement, and knowledge-building (e.g. Maton and Moore 2010b). Space precludes discussing the scrupulous arguments of social realist scholars – they deserve to read in the original. Moreover, like any non-doctrinaire 'school of thought', social realism is heterogeneous in terms of influences, modes of argument, and concepts.[3] Thus, rather than attempt to definitively summarize or speak on behalf of a school of thought, I shall introduce stances fundamental to social realism using ideas I find particularly illuminating. Specifically, I draw on critical realism to explain how the 'epistemological dilemma' can be denied, and on critical rationalism to illustrate how the subjectivist doxa can be defied.

Denying the dilemma

Social realism has made the 'epistemological dilemma' a central concern. Following Bernstein (1990), social realists have typically focused on combating the sociological reductionism endemic to studies of 'relations to' education. In short, social realism holds that analyses of 'relations to' and 'relations within' education and knowledge can be brought together to offer greater explanatory power, thereby denying the dilemma. To illustrate how, I shall begin by drawing on notions of 'ontological realism', 'epistemological relativism' and 'judgemental rationality' from critical realist philosophy, as pioneered by Bhaskar (see Archer *et al.* 1998).

'Ontological realism' recognizes that knowledge is about something other than itself, that there exists an independently existing reality beyond discourse that helps to shape our knowledge of the world. This is *not* to suggest knowledge is an unmediated reflection of reality but rather that knowledge is more than the arbitrary expression of power relations, and that reality may react back on knowledge. 'Epistemological relativism' acknowledges that our knowledge of the world is not universal, invariant, transhistorical and essential Truth. Rather, we can only know the world through socially produced knowledges that change over time and differ across social, historical and cultural contexts. Crucially, epistemological relativism does not entail judgemental relativism, the notion that judgements among different knowledges are not possible. Instead, 'judgemental rationality' highlights that there are intersubjective bases for determining the relative merits of competing claims to insight. It is not contradictory to argue *both* that definitive Truth has not been and, indeed, may never be attained *and* that there exist means of judging among knowledge claims, for critical preference does not entail transhistorical belief (cf. Popper 1959).

Together these ideas highlight that we construct knowledge of the world but not just as we please (or at least not free of worldly consequences), not perfectly, and not simply by ourselves. Put another way, actors construct knowledge but not under conditions or in ways entirely of their own making, and not entirely alone. Rather, knowledge is about something other than itself, draws on existing knowledge, and is produced and judged by socially situated actors. Social realism develops these ideas sociologically to deny the 'epistemological dilemma' in educational research.[4]

Against positivism, knowledge is understood as inescapably social and historical but, against constructivism, knowledge is not reduced to social power alone, as some knowledge claims have greater explanatory power than others. Social realism is thus concerned neither with essentialist definitions of 'knowledge', 'truth' or 'belief', nor with proclaiming all definitions equal. Rather, it highlights the need to explore how knowledges come to be defined in particular social and historical contexts, their forms, and their effects. Accordingly, this perspective views intellectual and educational fields as comprising *both* relational structures of knowledge practices *and* actors situated within specific social and historical contexts. In so doing, it shows that knowledge practices are *both* emergent from *and* irreducible to their contexts of production – the forms taken by knowledge practice in turn shape those contexts.

Social realism also reveals that analysing the intrinsic features of knowledge is not asocial; indeed, the converse holds: studies that overlook knowledge are not social enough. Though emphasizing their focus on the 'social' nature of knowledge, constructivist approaches and 'strong' programmes in the sociology of knowledge obscure a critical feature shaping the communities engaged in its production. As Popper argued, '*What the "sociology of knowledge" overlooks is just the sociology of knowledge*'; it 'shows an astounding failure to understand precisely its main subject, the *social aspects of knowledge*' (1957: 144; 2003b: 240; original emphases). By overfocusing on one social aspect, namely 'relations to' knowledge, these approaches neglect another social aspect: 'relations within' knowledge, which are socially generated, maintained and changed. They fail to grasp that knowledge is not constructed by individuals as each sees fit but rather produced by actors within social fields of practice characterized by intersubjectively shared assumptions, ways of working, beliefs and so forth. The philosophical term 'judgemental rationality', reflecting a focus on natural science, does not capture the wide array of different forms taken by these 'rules of the game'. Chapter 8, for example, shows the field of educational research to be more axiological than epistemological in basis – less 'rationality' than 'sentimentality'. Nonetheless, the broader notion of intersubjective judgement that the term highlights is not itself an article of faith: the existence of social fields of practice such as higher education, law and medicine demonstrates there *are* such bases for judging knowledge, however fallible, contested and subject to change they may be.

Crucially, social realism does not hold an empiricist view of social fields of practice as comprising direct social interactions. Actors sharing an epistemic community may never meet personally; their knowledge practices are

> the product of an immense cooperation that extends not only through space but also through time; to make them, a multitude of different minds have associated, intermixed, and combined their ideas and feelings; long generations have accumulated their experience and knowledge.
>
> (Durkheim 1912/1967: 15)

However, to fully understand these social aspects of knowledge one must first overcome the subjectivist doxa.

Defying the doxa

Dissolving the 'epistemological dilemma' does not by itself overcome knowledge-blindness, for one can construe the above in terms of knowing. One also needs to defy the subjectivist doxa by seeing knowledge as more than the mental states, mental processes or dispositions to act of knowers. To help grasp this difficult, even counterintuitive notion, I shall draw on ideas from critical rationalism, as pioneered by Popper.

Consider Popper's heuristic distinction between three metaphorical 'worlds': *world 1* refers to physical bodies and their physical and physiological states; *world 2* refers to mental states or processes; and *world 3* refers to the products of our human minds, such as architecture, art, literature, music, scholarship, educational knowledge, etc. (1979, 1994a, b). Key here is Popper's distinction between world 2, which includes 'subjective knowledge' or what I term 'knowing', and world 3, which includes 'objective knowledge' (meaning it has an objective existence and *not* that it is certain) or what I simply term 'knowledge'.[5] Popper highlights that things may participate in more than one 'world'; for example, this book is physical, the product of my human (all too human) mind, and elaborates an explanatory framework. Though a *product* of world 2 and *made manifest* in the materials of world 1, the framework itself is a member of world 3. It is 'objective knowledge' and, though the product of mental processes, is not reducible to my 'subjective knowledge' – it comprises knowledge not knowing.

As Popper (1979, 1994a) emphasizes, the three 'worlds' are not an axiomatic ontology but rather metaphors for making a simple point. The point here is that though knowledge is the product of our minds, it has relative autonomy from knowing – knowledge has emergent properties and powers of its own. This can be seen in the ways knowledge mediates: creativity; learning; and relations among knowers. First, creativity involves not simply an unfolding of something already existing within us but rather 'give and take' between the creator and the evolving object of creation; the products of our minds 'react back' on our thoughts, ideas, aims and dispositions. Anyone who creates scientifically or artistically will have experienced this 'give and take' and the reality of ideas: once formulated as knowledge, 'objectified', our ideas can reshape our knowing. We can both improve and be improved by what we create. That it can be argued knowledge originates in our minds thus does not necessitate reducing the former to the latter: a symbolic product is not identical with the mental and physical processes of its genesis.

Second, against the *learning fallacy* propagated by empiricist understandings of knowing, we do not learn about the world in an unmediated and direct fashion but rather in relation to existing and objectified knowledge about the world. We can 'plug into' existing knowledge and so do not have to start from scratch or attempt by ourselves to recreate what has taken, in the case of 'academic' knowledge, thousands of years and even more minds to develop. As Popper argues, we can each gain far more from this heritage than we contribute. Thus studies of learning that overlook knowledge fail to grasp one of the most significant dimensions shaping the development of actors' forms of knowing.

Third, returning to its social aspects, knowledge also mediates relations among knowers in fields of practice. As Popper (1994a) argued, Einstein said 'My pencil is cleverer than I am' because explicitly formulating his ideas enabled him to 'plug into' a world of ideas beyond his own mind, relate the products of his mind to those of other minds, and thereby achieve results beyond his intentions or hopes. Similarly, Paul Dirac said 'My equation is smarter than I am' (Farmelo 2002: xvii) because it had 'the strangest and most startling consequences' (Wilczek 2002: 133) that were unintended, unanticipated and inexplicable in terms of his own consciousness. (Dirac declared: 'It gave just the properties one needed for an electron. That was really an unexpected bonus for me, completely unexpected'; quoted, ibid.: 132). As knowledge the 'Dirac equation' could also be extended, related to ideas and applied by other actors. Thus, to offer a properly social account of knowledge, one must see knowledge itself.

One could argue these examples describe interactions between the mental states of knowers. Knowledge practices could be described as symbolic or linguistic expressions of subjective mental states or dispositions that evoke mental states or dispositions in other actors. However, whatever their veracity, such claims do not license viewing knowledge, the medium of these interactions, as a homogeneous and neutral relay for messages between minds. Collins describes how intellectual production involves creating 'coalitions in the mind':

> The intellectual alone, reading or writing: but he or she is not mentally alone. His or her ideas are loaded with social significance because they symbolize membership in existing and prospective coalitions in the intellectual network.
>
> (Collins 2000: 7, 51–52)

However, minds do not connect directly via a mental aether. 'Coalitions in the mind' occur via ***knowledge beyond the mind***, and the nature of that knowledge shapes the kinds of 'existing and prospective coalitions' that are possible. As this book demonstrates, the organizing principles of knowledge shape the spatial and temporal reach, modes of engagement, and forms of development of social fields. They are key to social inclusion and social justice, in both education and civic life. Though made by us, knowledge possesses properties and tendencies of which we may be unaware and which may lead to consequences that are unintended, even contrary to our aims and beliefs; Chapters 2, 5 and 9, for example, explore the deleterious effects of fragmentation on cultural studies caused by tendencies intrinsic to its knowledge claims. Chapter 6 and other research studies (e.g. Chen *et al.* 2011) explore how forms of knowledge enacted in pedagogic practices differentially affect the educational achievement of social groups of knowers. Thus, any social justice agenda that excludes analysis of relations within knowledge is unlikely to succeed, for our knowledge practices are anything but neutral.

From seeing to analysing

For social realism, studies of knowledge and education have ignored their ostensible objects of study. Against the reductionism engendered by the 'epistemological dilemma', social realism holds with Alexander (1995: 129) that 'the sociology of knowledge can never substitute for the analysis of knowledge'. Against the subjectivist doxa, social realism would proclaim with Popper that 'no theory of subjective knowledge will be able to account for objective knowledge' (1994a: 13). In short, knowledge itself needs to be taken seriously. To do so requires not only the right way of seeing but also the right conceptual tools for analysing this object of study.

Social realist work predominantly establishes the need to see knowledge. It is thanks to this pioneering work in what Deleuze termed 'polemical' and 'inventive' functions that the current book is able to focus on the 'creative function' of developing new concepts. This is not to say this book does not itself also highlight errors and oversights. The work collected here has formed part of social realism's critical engagement with educational research to recover knowledge as an object. Moreover, it also critically engages with social realism itself, to overcome a tendency intrinsic to this endeavour of overfocusing on explicit structures of knowledge at the expense of practices more concerned with developing knowers. As subsequent chapters will highlight, when arguing for knowledge to be seen it is easy to valorize the kinds of knowledge most easily seen: explicit, abstract, condensed, hierarchical forms that visibly announce themselves. This tendency can drift towards offering a deficit model of the arts, crafts, humanities and many social sciences, as well as everyday understandings, where knowledge may be less explicit and more concrete, context-dependent, embodied, and axiological. At this point, knowledge-blindness gives way to seeing nothing but knowledge and obscuring practices for socializing or cultivating knowers. Accordingly, this book serves the polemical and inventive functions of avoiding both the Scylla of knowledge-blindness and the Charybdis of knower-blindness. However, its *principal* concern lies with the corresponding *creative* function of developing concepts for analysing both knowledge and knowers.[6] I shall now begin to introduce the conceptual toolkit and analytic methodology that is Legitimation Code Theory.

Analysing knowledge and knowers: Legitimation Code Theory

What kind of 'theory'?

We have one word for 'theory' – we need many. As Merton (1957) highlighted, 'theory' is used in manifold ways, a polysemy that, Boudon (1980) suggested, results partly from failing to distinguish theories from paradigms. Given several '-isms' have been mentioned, it is thus worth clarifying what *kind* of 'theory' is referred to by 'Legitimation Code Theory' (LCT) before sketching its conceptual contours and how they are related within this book.

I must emphasize: my aim is *not* to describe the intellectual pedigree of LCT – 'epistemological botany', as Bernstein (2000: 92) put it – but simply to orient the reader to the kind of thing they will encounter in subsequent chapters.

To do so I shall revise a schema from Archer (1995) to describe *social ontologies* (SO), *explanatory frameworks* (EF), and *substantive research studies* (SRS), as heuristically depicted in Figure 1.1. One can thereby analytically distinguish three kinds of 'theories' based on different problematics: meta-theories of ontologies; theories (in the sense used in 'LCT') of frameworks; and substantive theories of studies. Arrows in Figure 1.1 indicate ideal relations among these kinds of theories for building cumulative and powerful knowledge: social ontologies offer meta-theoretical implications for explanatory frameworks (SO→EF); frameworks inform social ontologies by mediating their access to the social world (SO←EF); frameworks inform substantive research studies (EF→SRS), as all research involves a theory, whether explicit or tacit, that defines data; and studies inform frameworks by 'speaking back' to theory in the light of what data reveal (EF←SRS).

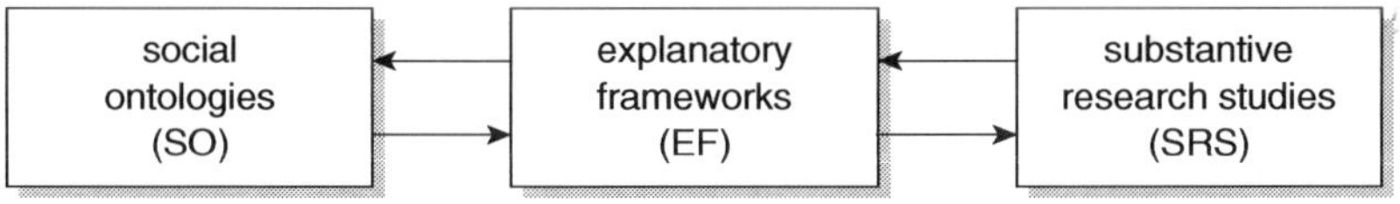

Figure 1.1 Meta-theories, theories and substantive theories

LCT can be described as an explanatory framework for enactment in and (re-)shaping by substantive research studies: in Figure 1.1, LCT embraces 'EF' and interrelations with 'SRS' (both arrows). LCT develops from and for research into substantive problems. A defining characteristic is its evolution through research into a growing range of topics, where data 'speak back' to the theory, demanding clarifications, refinements and new developments. In short, LCT is a practical theory rather than a paradigm, a conceptual toolkit and analytic methodology rather than an '-ism', and sociological rather than philosophical.

This helps clarify what LCT is not. First, it is not a specific substantive account of knowledge or education. Studies using concepts from LCT generate conjectures concerning problem-situations, such as the basis of fragmentation in intellectual fields (Chapters 2, 5 and 9), choice of school qualifications (Chapter 4), or practices enabling cumulative knowledge-building (Chapters 6 and 7; Maton 2013). However, these explanations are not the framework itself but rather outcomes of its creative enactment. This is not to describe legitimation code research as separate to Legitimation Code Theory – indeed, studies are a principal driver of the theory's development. Rather, it is to distinguish between a conceptual framework and the explanations, arguments and conclusions concerning substantive issues generated using that framework.[7] As Archer (1995: 6) states, 'an explanatory framework neither explains, nor purports to explain, anything'. One could say that LCT invites use to generate explanations.

Second, LCT is not an epistemology or ontology. This is not to suggest it is without epistemological or ontological assumptions and implications. LCT is characterized by, *inter alia*, depth ontology involving stratification and emergence, relational analysis, generative theorizing, and a non-empiricist exploration of the organizing principles of practices. However, it is not a meta-theory of why such characteristics are ontologically necessary. In short, LCT is *realist* rather than *a realism*. In contrast, much social realist work explores relations between frameworks and ontologies, quarrying what must be the case about knowledge and education given what studies using frameworks such as code theory reveal and, conversely, exploring the kinds of frameworks required to explore phenomena established by a realist understanding of knowledge and education. Philosophies being engaged with by this work include critical realism, whose meta-theoretical implications appear compatible with code sociology (Wheelahan 2010; Moore 2013a), critical rationalism (above), and Cassirer (Young and Muller 2007).

Social ontologies, explanatory frameworks, and substantive research studies enjoy relative autonomy from each other. On the one hand, studies using LCT are not cookie-cutter applications; they involve creative enactment in dialogue with the specificities of their objects of study. Conversely, LCT does not comprise segmented and empiricist models of particular contexts. There exists what Bernstein (2000) called a 'discursive gap' between theory and data that is traversed through 'external languages of description' for translating between them (Chapters 6 and 7; Maton *et al.* 2014). On the other hand, while they are compatible, LCT did not arise solely from working through the sociological implications of critical realist or critical rationalist philosophies, any more than they arose from exploring the ontological implications of LCT. They each have their own logics, trajectories, objects of study, problem-situations, concepts, methodologies, and data. One can thus extend Bernstein to describe a second 'discursive gap' between meta-theories and theories that is traversed through the kind of work exemplified by social realism. These discursive gaps between ontologies and frameworks, and between frameworks and the data of studies, allow for reality to speak back to theories and to meta-theories. Failure to recognize or to traverse both these gaps creates obstacles for powerful and cumulative knowledge-building.

Explanatory frameworks, however, often explore one gap more than the other, either more clearly articulating their ontological basis or better developing the practicality of their concepts for research. This shapes their reception, easing philosophical acceptance as, for example, 'critical realist', or providing more explanatory power for researchers. LCT is primarily driven by problem-solving and its exposition in this book is concerned with the first discursive gap. (For example, relations between theory and data are explicitly discussed in Chapters 6, 7 and 8). However, LCT is a social realist approach, and social realism's greater focus on the second discursive gap provides a valuable connection with ontologies. Space precludes discussion here. I will simply note that realist ontologies themselves establish the need for specialized explanatory frameworks to engage with distinctive objects of study (which can work together to better capture the complex nature of reality). Accordingly, Bhaskar (1989) describes critical realism as an 'under-labourer' rather than overlord. In contrast, philosophical failure to recognize this gap can lead to ontological policing (based on the fallacy that frameworks and studies cannot work without philosophical accreditation), reductionism (where explanatory frameworks are viewed as concerned with ontology), and substitutionism (where meta-theories are 'applied' in substantive studies consequently characterized by bifurcated discourses of ontological axioms and empirical descriptions – the return of the repressed discursive gap).

LCT and Knowledge and Knowers

LCT is more than *Knowledge and Knowers*. Substantively, the book begins from the knowledge paradox, addresses a diversity of educational issues, and contributes towards a realist sociology of education. However, LCT itself is more accurately described as a *sociology of legitimacy* or a *sociology of possibility* with broader application. As a growing range of studies reveal, its concepts enable the exploration of social fields beyond education and of practices other than knowledge (Chapter 10). Theoretically, as discussed above, the principal focus of this book lies not with philosophical discussions nor with empirical descriptions but rather with unfolding an explanatory framework in relation to substantive research studies. However, LCT comprises more than the concepts introduced here. I shall thus briefly locate this book within the broader contours of the framework as multidimensional, cumulative and evolving.

Multidimensional

LCT includes a multidimensional conceptual toolkit for analysing actors' dispositions, practices and contexts, within a variegated range of fields. For LCT, society comprises an array of relatively autonomous social universes that are neither wholly separate from nor reducible to others. Each field has its own distinctive ways of working, resources and forms of status that are specific in terms of their realizations yet similar in terms of their underlying generative principles. Within each field, actors cooperate and struggle to maximize their relational positions in its hierarchies by striving both to attain more of that which defines achievement and to shape what is defined as achievement to match their own practices. LCT highlights that actors' practices thereby represent competing claims to legitimacy, whether explicit or tacit (such as routinized ways of working) – they are *languages of legitimation* (Chapter 2). These strategies to shape the 'rules of the game' are themselves shaped by relations between actors' dispositions (which are in turn shaped by previous and ongoing experiences in fields) and the current structure of the field. The organizing principles of dispositions, practices and fields are conceptualized by LCT in terms of *legitimation codes*, each 'code' representing in effect a currency proposed by actors as the ruler of the field. Underlying the structuring of fields, and acting as a kind of exchange rate mechanism among currencies, is the *Legitimation Device* (Chapter 3). Whoever controls this 'device' establishes specific legitimation codes as dominant and so defines what is legitimate, shaping the social field of practice as a dynamic field of possibilities. To analyse legitimation codes is thus to explore what is possible for whom, when, where and how, and who is able to define these possibilities, when, where and how.

Table 1.1 Basic summary of legitimation codes

Codes	*Concepts*	*Principal modalities*
Autonomy	positional autonomy, relational autonomy	PA+/–, RA+/–
Density	material density, moral density	MaD+/–, MoD+/–
Specialization	epistemic relations, social relations	ER+/–, SR+/–
Semantics	semantic gravity, semantic density	SG+/–, SD+/–
Temporality	temporal position, temporal orientation	TP+/–, TO+/–

Thus far, the conceptual toolkit of LCT comprises five 'dimensions': Autonomy, Density, Specialization, Semantics, and Temporality. Each dimension includes concepts for analysing organizing principles as specific kinds of *legitimation codes*, such as *specialization codes* and *semantic codes*. Table 1.1 lists the principal concepts generating different legitimation codes. Each dimension also explores an 'aspect' to the Legitimation Device (the generative mechanism of social fields of practice), such as the *epistemic–pedagogic device* (Specialization) and the *semantic device* (Semantics). Figure 1.2 summarizes the five dimensions of LCT, devices and codes in a simplified and synoptic manner.

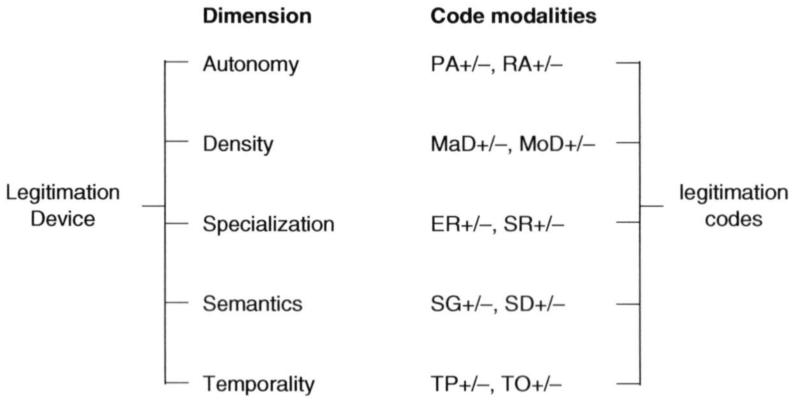

Figure 1.2 Synoptic view of five dimensions of LCT

Crucially, each dimension explores not different empirical practices but rather different organizing principles of practices. Thus, more than one dimension can be utilized in research into a specific object of study. However, in research you only need as much theory as the problem-situation demands, no more and no less. Thus, not all these concepts are required for all substantive studies. Moreover, in publishing, you only need as much theory as space will allow. Accordingly, this book is limited to explicating two dimensions of LCT: Specialization, the first developed, most elaborated and most enacted in studies; and Semantics, the newest but fastest growing in research. (Other dimensions are articulated in Maton 2005a, b). Each dimension comprises a set of concepts. Specialization includes ***specialization codes*** (Chapter 2), ***the epistemic–pedagogic device*** (Chapter 3), ***knowledge–knower structures*** (Chapter 4), ***gazes*** and ***insights*** (Chapters 5 and 9); and Semantics includes ***semantic gravity*** (Chapter 6), ***semantic density*** (Chapter 7), and ***condensation*** (Chapter 8). Using dimensions together also generates further concepts, such as different forms of condensation (Chapters 8 and 9). As well as not discussing other dimensions, the book is not an exhaustive account of these two dimensions: for example, if space allowed I would add 'Making semantic waves' (Maton 2013), which develops Semantics further. Nonetheless, the book offers an introduction to key landmarks in the unfolding of the two most widely used dimensions of LCT thus far.

Cumulative

Knowledge-building is a theme of the book, both as focus and form. Chapters explore the bases of cumulative progress in a range of intellectual and educational fields. The theory itself also extends and integrates concepts from established approaches. Intellectual influences on the development of LCT are manifold, for its ongoing evolution is concerned less with maintaining a pure intellectual lineage than with generating explanatory power. The theory thus embodies what Bernstein (1977) called an allegiance to a problem rather than to an approach, and the belief, as Bourdieu (1994) put it, that being Marxist, Weberian, Durkheimian, etc., are religious rather than social scientific choices. Nonetheless, its most central foundations are Pierre Bourdieu's 'field theory' and Basil Bernstein's 'code theory'. LCT develops rather than displaces these frameworks, though in different ways that themselves feature to different degrees within this book. In short, chapters typically begin from code theory, as its concepts are the most directly built upon by those of LCT.

Concepts are not all created equal: they can do different things. Earlier I described a division of conceptual labour among ontologies, frameworks and studies. Concepts from different frameworks also offer different qualities: some provoke thought, others orient one's gaze, less offer analytic power in empirical research. Bourdieu's field theory is widely described as 'good to think with' and offers what he called 'a sociological eye' that involves 'a mental revolution, a transformation of one's whole vision of the social world' (Bourdieu and Wacquant 1992: 251). Specifically, field theory calls for a relational and realist gaze: 'To think in terms of field is to *think relationally*'; one must see that '*the real is the relational*' (ibid.: 96, 97), something which 'requires a conversion of one's entire usual vision of the social world, a vision which is interested only in those things which are visible' (Bourdieu 1994: 192). Moreover, Bourdieu's key concepts of 'field', 'capital' and 'habitus' highlight issues for understanding practice and emphasize the need to move beyond surface features to explore their organizing principles and emergent properties (Grenfell 2004).

However, while highlighting what needs to be analysed and how, Bourdieu's 'thinking tools' do not fully enable what he called for. As relational concepts, they are intentional rather than operative (Boudon 1971). For example, the internal structuring of a habitus cannot be described separately from a description of the practices it gives rise to (Bernstein 2000, Maton 2012) – 'relations within' habituses remain untheorized as relational systems. Similarly, while calling for 'a realist theory of knowledge' (2004: 3), Bourdieu's concepts reduce knowledge practices to epiphenomena of the play of positions among actors within a field (Chapter 2). Thus, while enabling a 'mental revolution', field theory is an unfinished conceptual revolution: the framework does not reveal the organizing principles of practices, dispositions and fields.

LCT embodies the relational mode of thinking of field theory to develop operative relational concepts and to enact realist knowing as realist knowledge. However, after Chapter 3, theoretical development in this book does not begin from Bourdieu's concepts. Their influence becomes that which he emphasized as the framework's most significant feature: the 'gaze' it exemplifies. This is not to say LCT concepts cannot be explicitly developed from field theory; Maton (2005a), for example, extends Bourdieu's notion of autonomy to introduce *autonomy codes* (though this concept can also be developed from Bernstein's concepts of 'singulars' and 'regions'). Nonetheless, this book does not extensively elaborate relations to field theory, for its principal focus lies with a closer and more direct launching pad for theoretical innovation: Bernstein's code theory.

As I shall elaborate, where Bourdieu's field theory provides a new *gaze*, Bernstein's code theory provides a different *insight* (Chapter 9); where Bourdieu offers a 'mental revolution', Bernstein enables a conceptual evolution that is required to democratize that gaze (Chapter 7). That is, code theory provides a *conceptual* basis for cumulatively building a relational and realist sociology as an extended epistemic community (Chapter 3). Code theory not only provokes thought and orients one's gaze, its central notions of 'codes' and 'devices' also provide templates for enabling analytic power in substantive research. I shall not elaborate here on code theory (see Atkinson 1985; Moore 2013b) or its relations to LCT: Bernstein's concepts provide the explicit starting point for subsequent chapters, and these relations are revisited in Chapter 10. I shall only highlight that LCT works *within* Bernstein's problematic and approach to extend and integrate existing concepts in ways he described as the basis for cumulative knowledge-building, so as to enable greater fidelity to more phenomena with conceptual economy. As I emphasize in Chapter 10, there is more to Bernstein's framework than the concepts built upon in this book. Nonetheless, subsequent chapters illustrate how the framework inherited from Bernstein can be developed to overcome both knowledge- and knower-blindness in educational research and to resolve the knowledge paradox in social science.

Evolving

Bernstein (2000) insisted code theory represents a work-in-progress. Accordingly, LCT is always evolving, in relations with data, inherited frameworks, and other approaches (Chapter 10). As concepts are used to explore new problem-situations, these objects of study 'speak back' to the theory, raising questions and necessitating theoretical development. Moreover, as repeated throughout this book, answers to questions beget new questions: cumulative knowledge-building is an unending process. Accordingly, *Knowledge and Knowers* presents not a finished theoretical system as a fully formed and baroque edifice but rather a cumulative set of papers that unfold an explanatory framework as it evolved through time. Chapters are arranged in chronological order of the development of the concepts they introduce, based on ideas first publicly aired in 1998 (Chapter 2), 2000 (Chapter 3), 2004 (Chapter 4), 2006 (Chapter 5), 2007 (Chapter 6), 2008 (Chapters 7 and 8), and 2012 (Chapter 9). Each chapter builds on both concepts from code theory and preceding chapters, whose main points I briefly summarize, creating some repetition but enabling, I hope, each chapter to be understood independently and underlining how LCT concepts extend and integrate existing ideas.

Where chapters are based on published papers, they have been revised for this book, sometimes extensively.[8] For example, the notion of extending Bernstein's 'pedagogic device', undertaken in Chapter 3, was originally inspired by work with Rob Moore (Moore and Maton 2001), but is now radically different in its theorization (and written in 2012). If time allowed, I would revise many of these chapters further, especially older ones. The reason is simple and salutary: I have learned more about LCT and have learned more from LCT. It is because knowledge is not knowing that working with the framework and preparing this book have taught me much about LCT I did not previously know. At the same time, the social reality of knowledge also advanced my understanding: LCT is being rapidly adopted across a range of countries and disciplines to explore an ever-widening array of issues, posing questions that continue to reshape the framework. This has been above all a process of creative evolution, of both LCT as knowledge and me as a knower. It is in that spirit of open-ended and social creativity that the following chapters are offered, with the aim of contributing towards a better understanding and better forms of knowledge, education and society.

Notes

1 Chapter 8 conceptualizes the basis of this process as an *axiological cosmology* whereby a knower code creates binary constellations of stances that are condensed with axiological meanings and charged positively and negatively.

2 The biennial 'International Basil Bernstein Symposium' was one key venue for developing social realist ideas (Morais *et al.* 2001; Muller *et al.* 2004; Moore *et al.* 2006; Singh *et al.* 2010; Ivinson *et al.* 2011; see also Frandji and Vitale 2010). International conferences in Sydney on 'Reclaiming Knowledge' (2004) and 'Disciplinarity, Knowledge and Language' (2008) brought together social realists with systemic functional linguists (Christie and Martin 2007; Christie and Maton 2011); and a symposium on 'Social Realism in Education' in Cambridge (2008) also involved critical realist philosophers (Maton and Moore 2010b).

3 An example of this 'similarity in difference' is that I shall adopt ideas from Popper more extensively here than is found in extant literature.

4 These arguments do not flow directly from the preceding ontological premises; they employ sociological concepts, such as 'social fields of practice' and 'rules of the game'. I discuss relations between ontologies and frameworks, further below.

5 I prefer 'knowledge' and 'knowing' over Popper's terms because 'objective' and 'subjective' invite misconstrual as 'certain, universal, disinterested' and 'partial, situated, vested' – that is, they are likely to reinforce the 'epistemological dilemma'.

6 This highlights the 'difference in similarity' of social realism that the label may disguise. For example, in claiming social realists focus on knowledge at the expense of ideal knowers projected by practices, critics (e.g. MacKnight 2011) unwittingly repeat arguments fundamental to developing the LCT concepts of *social relations* (Maton 1998, 2000a, b, 2005b), *knower structures* (Maton 2006, 2007), *gazes* (Maton 2004, 2009, 2010a), and *axiological cosmologies* (Maton 2008; Martin *et al.* 2010), among others. Moreover, these longstanding arguments are being absorbed by social realism (e.g. Muller 2007, 2012), which is beginning to bring knowers back in.

7 Maton (2013), for example, includes the concept of 'semantic waves' and a conjecture concerning the significance of enacting semantic waves in classroom practice. If the conjecture is shown to be false, the concept may remain productive; indeed the concept may be the basis for revealing that falsity and offering an improved model. The concept and the conjecture are thus not identical. The former is part of the framework of LCT; the latter is an outcome of its enactment within a specific research project.

8 The analytic outlines of Chapters 2 and 6 originate in Maton (2000a, b) and Maton (2009). Chapters 4 and 5 are revised versions of Maton (2007) and Maton (2010a), respectively, both by kind permission of Continuum International Publishing Group.

2 Languages of legitimation

The curious case of British cultural studies

The medium is also *a message.*

Introduction

Studies of education tend towards knowledge-blindness (Chapter 1). As Bernstein (1990) argued, sociological analysis has overwhelmingly focused on *relations to* knowledge practices, such as relations of social class, ethnicity and gender to research, curriculum and pedagogy. *Relations within* knowledge practices, their intrinsic features, have been largely neglected. Consequently, knowledge has been treated as if it is 'no more than a relay for power relations external to itself; a relay whose form has no consequences for what is relayed' (Bernstein 1990: 166). In effect, the focus has been on the message at the expense of the medium. This chapter argues that the medium – the structuring of knowledge practices – is itself also a message. The aim is to illustrate the significance of analysing knowledge practices for understanding intellectual and educational fields. To do so, the chapter introduces the beginnings of an explanatory framework that register the messages this medium tell us, one which overcomes the divide between studies of 'relations to' and 'relations within' knowledge.

As Chapter 1 highlights, the foundations for such an integrating framework can be found in the approaches of Pierre Bourdieu and Basil Bernstein. Bourdieu's 'field theory' describes social fields in terms of struggles over status and resources; Bernstein's 'code theory' additionally conceptualizes the structuring of knowledge. Bourdieu's approach raises questions of 'who', 'where', 'when' and 'how'; Bernstein's framework additionally emphasizes the neglected issue of 'what' (1996: 169–181). In short, field theory highlights how social fields of practice structure knowledge, whilst code theory highlights the structuring significance of knowledge structures for those fields. Bringing together these approaches suggests knowledge is a structured and structuring structure. The question, then, is how to conceptualize these features in an integrative manner.

Here I begin that task by analysing knowledge practices as embodying claims made by actors. When actors engage in practices they are at the same time making a claim of legitimacy for what they are doing or, more accurately, for the organizing principles embodied by their actions. Practices can thus be understood as ***languages of legitimation***: claims made by actors for carving out and maintaining spaces within social fields of practice. These languages propose a ruler for participation within the field and proclaim criteria by which achievement within this field should be measured. That is, they offer messages as to what should be the dominant basis of achievement. Languages of legitimation thereby represent the basis for competing claims to limited status and material resources; they are strategic stances aimed at maximizing actors' positions within a relationally structured field. Languages of legitimation are thus also situated – the forms taken by strategic stances are shaped by actors' positions and thus viewpoints within their fields (cf. Bourdieu 1988). At the same time, the knowledge comprising these claims may be more or less legitimate (cf. Bhaskar 1975; Popper 1959). That is, knowledge practices are not merely a reflection of actors' positions within relations of power but also comprise more or less powerful claims to legitimacy, including (but not exclusively) claims to truth – they are languages of possible legitimacy. Moreover, these practices assume forms that have powers and tendencies of their own which shape the play of power in fields (cf. Bernstein 2000). Languages of legitimation embody organizing principles that have effects – their instrinsic structures are neither homogeneous nor neutral; the form taken by a language shapes what it is possible to convey.

Conceiving of knowledge practices in terms of 'legitimation' brings together awareness of these features: it embraces the nature of practices as *structured*, their potentially legitimate nature, and their *structuring* significance, by virtue of their intrinsic *structures*, for fields. In other words, thinking in terms of 'legitimation' embraces issues raised by analyses of both 'relations to' and 'relations within' knowledge practices within a realist approach.

However, as Chapter 1 insists, it is one thing to highlight and suggest ways of thinking about an issue, and another thing to provide concepts capable of enacting that intention. This requires, among other things, engaging with data. To introduce concepts capable of enacting this approach I shall explore the curious case of British cultural studies. It is 'curious' because the position of the subject area appears contradictory (Maton 2002). Institutionally, cultural studies seems to be booming, with proliferating journals, textbooks and conferences, yet as a named subject area it has a limited presence in British higher education. Intellectually, it is often portrayed as cutting-edge, radical and progressive, yet also as fragmented, insular and politically disengaged. British cultural studies would seem to be everywhere yet nowhere, vibrant and radical yet in decline and isolated.

To explore these apparent contradictions I begin by briefly sketching the institutional and intellectual histories of British cultural studies. Viewing its knowledge practices as embodying a language of legitimation, I analyse the organizing principles of this language in terms of *legitimation codes*. Specifically, I focus on the dimension of Specialization to outline a generative conceptualization of *specialization codes of legitimation*. This framework is then employed in analyses of 'relations to' and 'relations within' cultural studies. First, I analyse relations to the specialization code of British cultural studies, showing how its history can be partly explained in terms of its social and institutional positions. Second, I outline the tendencies generated by relations within its specialization code, including proliferation of 'voices', fragmentation, knower wars and recurrent schismatism. These intrinsic features, I argue, have also shaped the field's intellectual and institutional trajectories in ways that contribute to its seemingly contradictory positions. I conclude by suggesting how the concepts introduced here may contribute towards overcoming knowledge-blindness within the sociology of education.

Cultural studies in British higher education

Institutional trajectories

During research into the institutionalization of cultural studies, I constructed a database of every course, option and module in cultural studies, media studies and communication studies offered in post-war British higher education until the mid-1990s, collected archival sources detailing the development of courses, and collated statistical information on the social profile of its student population.[1] Analysis of this data revealed several general patterns of institutionalization, including the sustained marginality and the relative invisibility of cultural studies as a distinct, named area of study within British higher education.

British cultural studies can be characterized as occupying institutional positions of relatively low status throughout its history (Maton 2005b). Indeed, educational interest in commercial or 'mass' culture first arose outside the field. The earliest professional associations (The Society of Film Teachers, from 1950), journals (*The Film Teacher*, from 1952), conferences (National Union of Teachers 1960) and courses (Mainds 1965) in Britain were based in primary and secondary schooling. Within this nascent formation universities were considered only in terms of the need for training schoolteachers and research on schooling (Harcourt 1964). When courses in cultural studies did emerge within higher education during the late 1950s, they were located in extra-mural departments of adult education (Steele 1997), technical colleges (Hall 1964), colleges of art (Burton 1964) and teacher training colleges (Knight 1962). Similarly, the 'founding texts' of cultural studies (typically listed as Hoggart 1957, Williams 1958, 1961, and Thompson 1963) were written by tutors of English in adult education.

During the 1960s several research centres emerged on the margins of existing university departments. The best-known example is the Centre for Contemporary Cultural Studies at Birmingham University (CCCS), founded in 1964. Although the CCCS later became renowned as having been a site of intellectual pioneering, University of Birmingham (1964–1974, 1975–1989) and CCCS (1964–1981) annual reports show its institutional standing was less impressive. The CCCS had limited staff (2.5 full-time equivalent staff supervised well over 220 postgraduate students during 1964–1980) and endured low status among actors within established disciplines (CCCS 1964–1981; Hall 1990). The Centre survived financially through outside funding from the publishing company Penguin and sporadic projects commissioned by external bodies such as UNESCO. At first Birmingham University offered only furniture and accommodation, the nature of which is amusingly illustrated by directions given to prospective students in the late 1960s:

> The new Centre hut may be found by taking the main entrance to the Administration building; left along the corridor, first stairs down on the right; left at the bottom and left again into the back courtyard. The hut is at the far end of the outer courtyard, overlooking the parapet.
>
> (CCCS 1968: 4)

The main expansion of cultural studies occurred after the late 1970s, when it established a foothold within degree courses in colleges, the Open University (part-time distance learning) and polytechnics. These institutions bore the brunt of successive educational expansions since the early 1960s and the social profile of the student body of cultural studies reflected this position. Bolstered by arguments that the less educated the student, the more susceptible they are to media influence (Newsom Report 1963), the study of mass culture often first entered curricula for the purposes of cultivating critical discrimination amongst students deemed of lower ability or providing a liberal education that would engage non-traditional students (Hall and Whannel 1964). In addition, the status of the central intellectual figures of the field as social outsiders to higher education is oft-noted (Turner 1990). Cultural studies has, in short, been associated with low-status institutions and dominated social groups.

Cultural studies is considered to have been a growth area within higher education since the 1980s and new journals, textbooks, conferences and courses which claim cultural studies among their concerns have proliferated. However, in terms of numbers of departments, degree courses and students, cultural studies as a ***named*** area of study remains a relatively small-scale phenomenon. If it has found a place in the sun, this has largely been ***within*** other academic subjects. The institutional history of cultural studies is one of origins in the interstices of the curriculum and infiltration via existing subject areas. Its emergence within British higher education was within courses of 'liberal studies', 'social studies', 'general studies' and 'complementary studies' (Kitses 1964); the CCCS was established within an English department; and today much of what is commonly referred to as 'cultural studies' teaching and research is conducted within departments and by actors with professional titles displaying a variety of nomenclature. Cultural studies is often visible more as an adjunct or adjective to more established disciplines (e.g. 'English and cultural studies', 'cultural geography') than as a distinct entity within higher education.

Even where cultural studies has carved out institutional spaces of its own, its position has been anything but secure. The first full degree course offered in Cultural Studies (at Portsmouth University in 1975) was closed down in 1999 and its teaching staff retired or dispersed despite a healthy student intake. The CCCS was seriously threatened with closure at least twice prior to the mid-1970s and only saved after concerted campaigns by international scholars proclaimed its intellectual significance (CCCS 1964–1981). Despite its later renown, it was closed in 2002. Such institutional vulnerability has been reinforced by the scattered nature of the field. Courses and departments of cultural studies often resulted from individual initiatives (Mainds 1965) and professional associations were for a long time *ad hoc*, limited or short-lived; the first national organization embracing intellectual and institutional responsibilities (the Media, Communication and Cultural Studies Association) had its first annual conference in 2000.

This marginal institutional presence has been reflected in the status of the subject area. Cultural studies has long been the subject of attacks from both within and without higher education. From inception, it has been depicted as unacademic, politically pernicious and undermining academic standards (e.g. Watson 1977), a famous example being the eagerness with which the 'Sokal Hoax', perpetrated in the American journal *Social Text*, was embraced in Britain (Osborne 1997). In summary, cultural studies as a specialized academic subject has generally emerged within the dominated pole of the field of British higher education.

Language of legitimation: The voice of cultural studies

Focusing on its main period of institutionalization in British higher education, analysis of the knowledge practices of cultural studies reveals a number of overarching themes. These include: breaking down boundaries, an unlimited object of study, recurrent 'breaks', the 'view from below', radical pedagogies, and subjectivist epistemologies (Maton 2000a). These themes coalesce around two principal issues, which I address in turn: questions of disciplinarity and notions of 'giving voice'.

The vexed question of discipline

Proponents have often legitimated cultural studies as 'multi-', 'cross-', 'inter-', 'post-', 'trans', or even 'anti-disciplinary' (Nelson and Gaonkar 1996). Perceived signs of impending disciplinary status, such as named degree courses, have evoked warnings that its defining oppositional status is endangered (Johnson 1983; Hall 1992). Cultural studies has remained committed to breaking down boundaries between: established disciplines, 'official' educational knowledge and everyday experience, 'high' and 'low' culture, inside and outside higher education, and teachers and learners. As 'undisciplined', cultural studies is also characterized by advocates as free from disciplinary notions of a delimited object of study and specialized procedures of enquiry (Turner 1990). Although nominally 'cultural studies', the definition of 'culture' and how it should be studied are often explicitly renounced or held open (Milner 1994). When defined, its object of study is conventionally boundless in scope – typified by the influential definition of 'culture' as 'a whole way of life', following Williams (1961) – and specialized procedures are eschewed in favour of celebrating diversity of theories, methodologies and methods (McGuigan 1997). Indeed, that there is no defining 'cultural studies' approach is conventionally the opening remark of accounts (Turner 1990). In summary, its objects of study and procedures of enquiry are (at least hypothetically) uncircumscribed.

Another central characteristic of cultural studies is its proclaimed anti-canonical stance. Practitioners regularly announce its rebirth and their own originality or decentre its intellectual tradition (Wright 1998). Accounts of its development typically highlight: a theoretical landscape of recurrent rupture and renewal (Hall 1971), illustrated by enthusiasm for 'post-' theories; 'interventions' on behalf of silenced voices that declare new beginnings; and a rapid turnover of substantive issues, reflecting a preoccupation with the contemporary and new (Pickering 1997). Cultural studies is thus typically described as developing through radical disjunctures, and progress is measured by the addition of new voices or 'theories of the break'.

'Giving voice to'

Proponents often identify cultural studies with a radical educational project committed to offering an oppositional pedagogy capable of empowering dominated social groups (Canaan and Epstein 1997). It has become associated with student-centred learning, participatory forms of evaluation, and flexible curricular structures, as well as pioneering innovative research practices such as collective authorship and publishing unfinished student work. The unifying thrust of these initiatives is the aim of 'giving voice to' the experiences of actors said to be silenced by official knowledge. This notion of 'giving voice to' has become a central theme in the legitimation of cultural studies, associating its raison d'être with the dominated social positions of those whose interests it claims to serve. Correspondingly, the curricular history of cultural studies is conventionally schematized as the successive study of social class, race, ethnicity, gender and sexuality. In such accounts, key texts first focus upon giving voice to the experiences of working-class men (e.g. Willis 1977), turn to address the silenced voice of women (Women's Studies Group 1978) and then of ethnic minorities (CCCS 1982), before highlighting marginalized voices of sexuality (McRobbie 1997).

Cultural studies has thus been a key site for 'interventions' by feminism, race studies and queer theory. Common to these interventions is a critique of the capacity of existing voices to represent a new voice, underpinned by (often implicit) notions of standpoint epistemology (Carby 1982); that is, a privileging of claims to unique insight based upon one's subjective experiences as a member of a specific social category. Cultural studies is also legitimated as having advanced anti-positivist ideas through employing contextualist and perspectival epistemologies and emphasizing the multiplicity of truths and narratives. These various theories share the contention that knowledge claims are reducible to the social characteristics of the group voicing them and a critique of notions of the possibility of a neutral voice or objective truth. Cultural studies has thus tended to valorize primary experience over the detached viewpoint. For example, studies of youth subcultures (Thornton and Gelder 1996) and of audiences (Morley 1992) typically valorize participants' experiences, highlight the active construction of meanings 'from below', and explore subjectivity and identity. Similarly, the self-labelling of qualitative audience reception studies as 'ethnographic', despite typically involving limited contact time with research subjects, unnatural settings for this contact, and a focus upon only one aspect of their lives, highlights the guiding principle of giving voice to the viewpoint 'from below' (McGuigan 1997).

Specialization codes of legitimation

Bringing together ideas from Bourdieu and Bernstein highlights that knowledge is a structured and structuring structure. However, as Boudon (1971) argued, unless one can state what that structure comprises and how it differs from other possible structures, this view remains intentional rather than operative. Moreover, if knowledge practices are not only a medium but also a message, a 'language of legitimation' concerning the basis of achievement within a field, the question is how to understand this coded message. Both these points highlight the organizing principles underlying practices. These principles can be conceptualized as *legitimation codes*, of which two dimensions are outlined in this book (Chapter 1). Here I shall focus on analysing legitimation codes using Specialization.

Specialization can be introduced via the simple premise that practices and beliefs are about or oriented towards something and by someone. They thus involve relations to objects and to subjects.[2] One can, therefore, *analytically* distinguish: *epistemic relations* between practices and their object or focus (that part of the world towards which they are oriented); and *social relations* between practices and their subject, author or actor (who is enacting the practices). For knowledge claims, these are realized as: epistemic relations between knowledge and its proclaimed objects of study; and social relations between knowledge and its authors or subjects.

These relations highlight questions of: *what* can be legitimately described as knowledge (epistemic relations); and *who* can claim to be a legitimate knower (social relations). To analyse the answers cultural studies gives to these questions, I shall build upon Bernstein's concepts of 'classification' and 'framing' (1977). The strength of *classification* (+/–C) refers to the relative strength of boundaries *between* contexts or categories; and the strength of *framing* (+/–F) refers to the locus of control *within* contexts or categories (where stronger framing indicates greater control from above).

Epistemic relations (ER) between cultural studies and its objects of study are realized in its language of legitimation as, *inter alia*, opposition to notions of disciplinarity, an uncircumscribed object of study, open procedures of enquiry, and a commitment to problematizing categories, boundaries and hierarchies between and within forms of knowledge. In other words, cultural studies exhibits relatively weak classification and framing of epistemic relations: ER(–C, –F) or ER–. In contrast, its social relations (SR) exhibit relatively stronger classification and framing: SR(+C, +F) or SR+. Here the emphasis is on 'giving voice to' the primary experience of knowers, where legitimate knowledge or 'truth' is defined by and restricted to the specific 'voice' said to have privileged understanding by virtue of their attributes. In other words, the language of legitimation of cultural studies has placed different strengths of boundaries around and control over the definitions of *what* can be claimed knowledge of and *how* (ER–), and of *who* can claim knowledge (SR+).

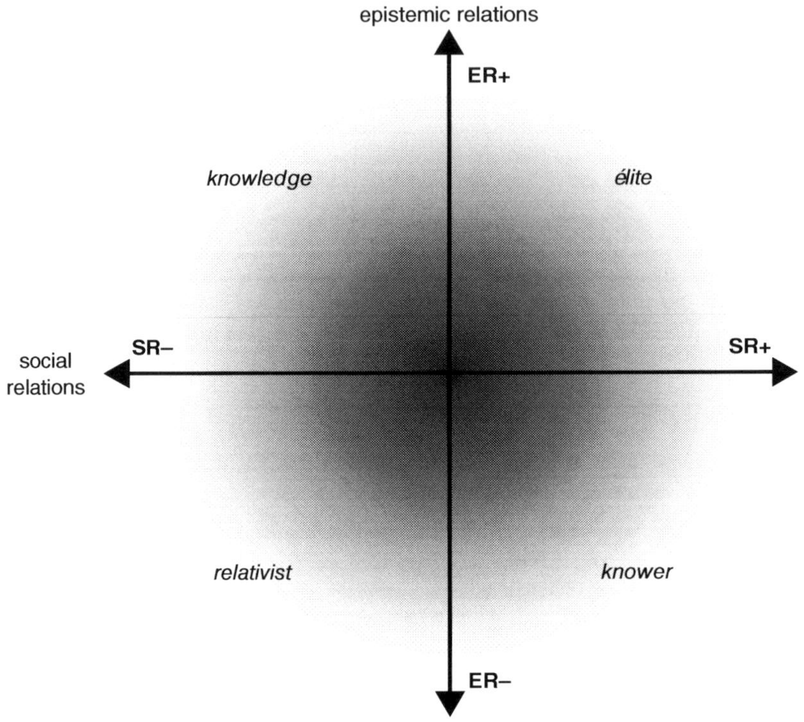

Figure 2.1 Specialization codes

From this one may generatively conceptualize the organizing principles of practices as *specialization codes*. The relative strengths of (classification and framing for) epistemic relations and social relations can be varied independently from stronger (+) to weaker (–) to generate a range of specialization codes (ER+/–, SR+/–). These continua of strengths can be visualized as the axes of a Cartesian plane to create a topological space with both infinite capacity for gradation and four principal modalities (see Figure 2.1):

- *knowledge codes* (ER+, SR–), where possession of specialized knowledge of specific objects of study is emphasized as the basis of achievement, and the attributes of actors are downplayed;
- *knower codes* (ER–, SR+), where specialized knowledge and objects are less significant and instead the attributes of actors are emphasized as measures

of achievement, whether these are viewed as born (e.g. 'natural talent'), cultivated (e.g. artistic gaze or 'taste') or socially based (e.g. the notion of gendered gaze in feminist standpoint theory);
- *élite codes* (ER+, SR+), where legitimacy is based on both possessing specialist knowledge and being the right kind of knower (here, 'élite' refers not to social exclusivity but rather to possessing *both* legitimate knowledge *and* legitimate dispositions); and
- *relativist codes* (ER–, SR–), where legitimacy is determined by neither specialist knowledge nor knower attributes – a kind of 'anything goes'.

Epistemic relations and social relations can be used both to describe the *focus* and to analyse the *basis* of practices. In terms of knowledge claims, this is to say they can:

(i) map the *focus* of knowledge claims, such as whether they refer to theories, methods, actor's social categories, dispositions, etc. – this describes the *content* of languages of legitimation; and/or
(ii) conceptualize the *basis* of knowledge claims to legitimacy – this describes the *form* of languages of legitimation, that is, their specialization codes.

For example, I may make claims concerning my own physical experiences (a *focus* on social relations to a subject) based either on specialist knowledge, such as a medical report (a *basis* of stronger epistemic relations), or on being the person to whom the experiences occurred (a *basis* of stronger social relations). Crucially, the *strengths* of epistemic relations and social relations, and thus *specialization codes*, refer to the *basis* of practices. Thus, while *focus* offers an additional mapping feature, it is *basis* with which Specialization is concerned.

Knowledge codes and knower codes

I shall now briefly introduce two of the four principal specialization codes: *knowledge codes* and *knower codes*. Table 2.1 presents the relative strengths of classifications and framings of their epistemic relations and social relations (cell numbers refer to the order of discussion). I begin by discussing knowledge codes, to illustrate a contrasting form of legitimation, before introducing the code exhibited by cultural studies.

Table 2.1 Classification and framing strengths for knowledge codes and knower codes

	Epistemic relations	*Social relations*
Knowledge codes	(1) +C, +F	(2) –C, –F
Knower codes	(3) –C, –F	(4) +C, +F

Knowledge codes

(1) Intellectual fields characterized by knowledge codes are legitimated by reference to specialized knowledge purported to provide insight into a determinate object of study. Knowledge-code practices thereby emphasize differences between their legitimate object and other possible objects, and/or between their legitimate theoretical or methodological approaches for accessing that object and those of other fields – relatively strong classification of epistemic relations. The field's focus and forms of study are thus not unbounded, and strong controls exist to ensure its objects are not appropriated by actors using different procedures and/or its approaches are not applied to inappropriate objects. There is thus relatively little personal discretion for actors in the choice of legitimate objects, procedures, and criteria – relatively strong framing of epistemic relations. An adequate grasp of these specialized forms of knowledge and their legitimate uses serves as the basis of professional identity within the field.

(2) These more or less consensual, relatively formal and explicit principles and procedures are said to transcend personal differences among members of the field. In terms of their subjective characteristics, actors are neither strongly differentiated nor strongly controlled in their relations to legitimate practices. Everyone is said to be equally positioned in relation to the field's practices, and it is claimed anyone can produce legitimate knowledge provided they comply with these defining practices. Knowledge codes thus exhibit relatively weak classification and weak framing of social relations.

Knower codes

(3) Knower codes base claims on a legitimate kind of knower. This knower may claim unique knowledge of more than a delimited object of study; the object of their claims may be boundless, difficult to define, or encompass a host of disparate and seemingly unconnected objects of study – relatively weak classification of epistemic relations. The procedures of enquiry and criteria of validation prevalent within the field are thereby not deemed appropriate/inappropriate according to a defined object of study, enabling more personal discretion in the choice of topics and methods. Procedures and principles of knowledge are thus relatively tacit, and adjudication of competing claims on strictly epistemological grounds is deemed problematic if not renounced. In short, knower codes display relatively weak framing of epistemic relations.

(4) Based on the unique insight of a particular kind of knower, claims to knowledge by actors are legitimated by reference to this ideal knower's attributes, which serve as the basis for professional identity within the field. These attributes may include biological or social categories and socialized or cultivated dispositions generating different kinds of knower codes (born, social and cultivated), each with their own properties and tendencies (Chapters 5 and 9). Here I shall discuss a ***social knower code***, one based on social categories, such as class, gender and

ethnicity. For social knower codes the aim is to 'give voice to' experiences of the knower, with 'truth' being defined by the 'voice'. This unique knowledge is specialized to the privileged knower such that actors with different subjective characteristics are unable to make claims, and attempts to do so risk censure from the field. Knower codes thus exhibit relatively strong classification and strong framing of social relations.

The specialization plane and codes

Knowledge codes characterize languages of legitimation with relatively strong epistemic relations and relatively weak social relations (ER+, SR−); and knower codes refer to languages with relatively weak epistemic relations and relatively strong social relations (ER−, SR+). Before enacting these concepts, it is worth highlighting several features of the above descriptions of these codes.

First, they are introductory and will be refined through the book: Chapters 5 and 9, in particular, explore different kinds of knowledge codes and knower codes. Second, the lack of empirical examples is intentional. The codes are not ideal types – they conceptualize organizing principles rather than gather empirical characteristics. Moreover, their realizations as *languages of legitimation* are a function of the context; for example, stronger epistemic relations may be empirically realized differently in curriculum, pedagogy, textbooks, classrooms, subject areas, etc. (Chapter 7 will discuss how this is resolved by 'external languages of description'). Third, though I have focused on two codes for contrast, they are not dichotomous types. As Chapter 3 will elaborate, the *specialization plane* of Figure 2.1 provides both a typology of four principal modalities (see Chapter 4 on élite codes) and a topology of infinite positions in which epistemic relations and social relations are continua of relative strengths: 'strong*er*'/'weak*er*' or 'relatively strong'/'relatively weak', rather than simply 'strong'/'weak'. Fourth, describing a field as characterized by a code is not portraying that field as homogeneous. A set of practices may represent a kind of scatter pattern across the plane, with some points falling within quadrants other than the dominant code. As I discuss in subsequent chapters, there is often more than one code present in a context. Last, codes have different powers and tendencies, such as the degree to which they enable or constrain cumulative knowledge-building – they shape their fields. Exploring how these are realized in any particular instance requires substantive research.

Analysing relations to and relations within social knower codes

British cultural studies during its expansion from the late 1970s can now be redescribed as dominated by social knower codes. This begins to address how relations within knowledge practices may be conceptualized; the question remains, however, of whether this can be enacted in both 'relations to' and 'relations within' analyses. I shall thus briefly outline two illustrative analyses of the development of cultural studies in terms of: (i) relations to its social positions; and (ii) relations within its knowledge practices, exploring the ramifications of the social knower code for the field's trajectories. The aim is to illustrate how the structures of knowledge practices are both structured by and in turn structure intellectual fields.

Relations to social knower codes

Drawing upon Bourdieu (1984), one can characterize society as structured into, first, dominant and dominated classes, and then, within each class, into dominant and dominated fractions. As Figure 2.2 highlights, higher education is located in the dominated fraction of the dominant class (Bourdieu 1988). That is, the social positions of actors in higher education are based upon the possession of cultural capital (knowledge and know-how) which is subordinate relative to economic capital. As outlined earlier, cultural studies emerged and developed within relatively low-status institutions associated with the teaching of marginalized social groups. It has thus occupied dominated positions within the dominated fraction of the dominant class. According to Bourdieu's approach, intellectuals are prone to perceiving their dominated position within the dominant class as homologous to that of the dominated class in society as a whole: in Figure 2.2, the homologous relation of dominant-dominated of top-bottom and right-left. That cultural studies has occupied positions of multiple domination suggests the field is particularly vulnerable to regarding hierarchical relations within the field of higher education as applicable to wider society, generating a perception of shared interests with dominated social groups.

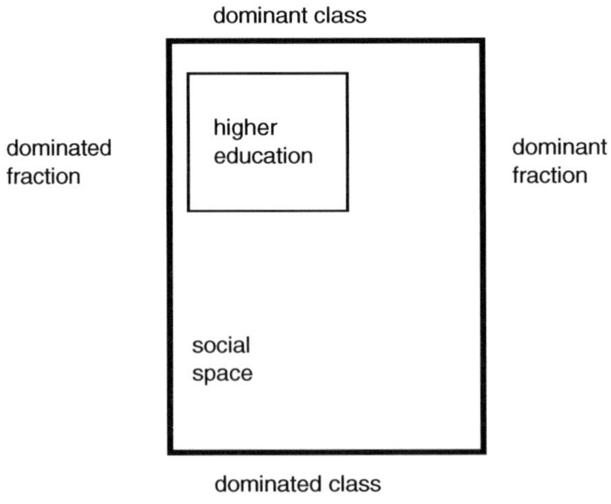

Figure 2.2 Social position of the field of higher education

One does indeed finds this logic reflected in the language of legitimation of cultural studies. The subject began with the working class as a dominant focus of enquiry and emerged out of attempts, via the involvement of its 'founding fathers' in the New Left and adult education, to forge alliances with the working class (Kenny 1995). A perception of common interests, however, was cemented more firmly during the mid-1970s. At this time a feminist 'intervention' in cultural studies claimed that the working class had served not only as the *focus* but also as the *basis* of knowledge claims. Highlighting that many of the pioneers of the field were working-class 'scholarship boys' (Hoggart 1957), the intervention claimed that working-class membership effectively operated as the social category upon which claims to privileged insight had been made – a ***social knower code***.[3]

Social mobility through prolonged education, however, makes claims to membership of or shared interests with the working class increasingly hard to sustain. One accordingly finds attempts within cultural studies to construct a theoretical basis for overcoming the distance between social origins and current position, such as Gramscian notions of the 'organic intellectual' in the late 1970s. As Stuart Hall, Director of the CCCS during the 1970s, later described:

> there is no doubt in my mind that we were trying to find an institutional practice in cultural studies that might produce an organic intellectual. ... The problem about the concept of an organic intellectual is that it appears to align intellectuals with an emerging historic movement and we couldn't tell then, and can hardly tell now, where that emerging historical movement was to be found.
>
> (Hall 1992: 281)

However, despite educational expansion, the proportion of working-class students within higher education remained relatively small, restricting the supply of potential organic intellectuals. The 'emerging historic movement' was not emerging. One then finds attempts to develop further theories of structural homology, such as the academic as 'intellectual proletarian'. These become the basis of what can be termed ***imaginary alliances*** (such as between the 'intellectual' and 'proletarian'). As Hall goes on to admit:

> More truthfully, we were prepared to imagine or model or simulate such a relationship in its absence ... We never produced organic intellectuals (would that we had) at the Centre. We never connected with that rising historic movement; it was a metaphoric exercise. Nevertheless, metaphors are serious things. They affect one's practice.
>
> (Hall 1992: 282)

Similarly, Richard Johnson, CCCS Director during 1979–88, stated:

> My best practices, I imagine, seek out and ally with marginal positions, their agenda of study, and critical intellectual projects ... I see the history of Cultural Studies ... as a story of such alliances
>
> (Johnson 1997: 48)

Paradoxically for cultural studies, such imaginary alliances downplay the role of *cultural* capital because it is the principal difference between the social positions of intellectuals and dominated classes. Similarly, social class tends to be suppressed as a marker of difference (between academic and non-academic members of the privileged knower category) when membership or representation claims are based upon other characteristics, such as race, ethnicity, gender, sexuality or region. It is thus perhaps not entirely unrelated that social class was eclipsed within cultural studies during the rise to prominence of these 'interventions'.

The idea of imaginary alliances, however, (like Bourdieu's notion of field on which it builds) is rather static. To explore the development of academic subjects over time, it must be set in motion. In the case of cultural studies, its history comprises a *procession of the excluded*: the working class, women, ethnic minorities, and so on. In other words, the field takes on the characteristics of a queue: once one group enters higher education (usually within legitimating discourse rather than as staff or students), then another group appears to take its place outside the door demanding (or having demands made on its behalf for) entry. Until everyone and/or their experiences are included within higher education, there is always scope for a new excluded group to emerge. This may help explain the restless search for a new 'proletariat' (based on class, race, ethnicity, gender, sexuality) which has characterized cultural studies (Harris 1992).

Thus far, I have focused on exploring relations between the social position of cultural studies and broader social structures. However, Bourdieu's 'field theory' offers a further level of analysis. Bourdieu (1984, 1988) argues that 'externalist' approaches that reduce practices to the social positions of actors are too crude and highlights the significance of social fields in mediating relations between their constitutive practices and wider social structures. Bourdieu's framework is arguably the most sophisticated form of 'relations to' analysis; nonetheless, it remains itself 'externalist' in relation to practices (see Maton 2005b). According to this approach, the relational practices or 'position-takings' of actors within a specific field are determined by their relational positions within that field. Positions and position-takings are 'methodologically inseparable' and 'must be analyzed together', but '*the space of positions tends to command the space of position-takings*' (Bourdieu and Wacquant 1992: 105, original emphasis). Basically, actors are held to be inclined towards conservative/subversive strategies, depending upon whether they occupy dominant/dominated positions, respectively, within the field.

The discursive practices of cultural studies would thus be explained in terms of actors' strategies reflecting their institutional and social positions. In short, actors from dominated social positions (the working class, women, etc.) tended to occupy dominated institutional positions within higher education (colleges, polytechnics, etc.). By virtue of these positions of multiple domination, they were inclined to adopt subversive 'position-takings' in an attempt to maximize their positions: against dominant notions of disciplinary specialization, cultural studies celebrated non-disciplinarity; against traditional pedagogy was set a radical educational project; against positivism, subjective experience was privileged; and so forth. Thus, given the perceived dominance of knowledge codes within higher education during the development of cultural studies, social knower codes provided an oppositional means for actors occupying dominated positions to attempt to subvert the hierarchy of the field. A form of this explanation can indeed be found within cultural studies itself; Epstein (1997), for example, emphasizes the subversive potential of marginal academic positions.

The whole story?

To conclude here would be to have undertaken an (albeit simplistic) analysis of 'relations to': the relations of a language of legitimation to its social and institutional positions. As briefly illustrated above, this approach explores issues of who, where, when, how and why. However, it also constructs the form taken by knowledge as arbitrary and historically contingent, and views an analysis of its structural history as irrelevant for an understanding of its development. From this perspective, actors tend to adopt (subversive) practices which reflect their (dominated) relational positions, regardless of the form taken by these practices. The implication is that if relativism had been dominant at the time of its institutionalization British cultural studies would now be associated with positivism or realism. In other words, the *function* of languages of legitimation, as strategic 'position-takings', is abstracted from their *form*, which is described only in terms of being oppositionally defined to other possible position-takings. The point for such 'relations to' analyses is to describe actors' relational positions within the field, from which their practices can then be 'read off'. The knowledge practices of an intellectual field are thereby viewed as epiphenomena of its play of positions. Such analyses thus have a blind spot: the issue of 'what'. This blind spot obscures much of the basis of the contradictory positions of cultural studies. For example, though one may attribute its institutional positions to dominant social power marginalizing dominated social groups, this would not account for the subject's apparent ubiquity. Similarly, exploring the field's social and institutional positions highlights the potential for 'imaginary alliances' and a 'procession of the excluded' but does not by itself account for the oft-noted fragmentation and withdrawal from wider political engagement of the subject area.

This approach, then, offers much but provides only part of the story. I shall now illustrate how analysis of the intrinsic dynamic of social knower codes highlights the significance of relations within practices to both the development of those practices and their institutional trajectories. Additionally, by using the same concepts of specialization codes to consider the structurings of these 'position-takings', the aim is to extend and integrate rather than displace the above analysis.

Relations within social knower codes

During its expansion in the late 1970s and 1980s, British cultural studies was characterized by a particular kind of knower code, one based on a social category. This *social knower code* involves actors claiming to represent the interests of a social group, to whom they 'give voice'. Such knower codes thus base their legitimation upon the privileged insight of a particular category of knower and work at maintaining strong boundaries around their definition of this knower. They celebrate difference where 'truth' is defined by the 'knower' or 'voice'; that is, they exhibit relatively strong social relations. Such discourses are often legitimated on the basis of the inability of existing knowledge to articulate the voice of this knower. However, one intrinsic dynamic of this code is that once its proponents have succeeded in carving out an institutional or intellectual position within higher education, they are likely to become prone to the same legitimating strategy; it is difficult to deny new voices what one has described as denied to one's own. Such a strategy thus tends to evoke its own disrupter, a new voice – 'interruptions interrupted' as Brunsdon (1996: 179) characterizes feminist work in cultural studies – enabling a procession of the excluded.

If this dynamic is considered over time, then as each new voice is brought into the academic choir, the category of the new privileged knower becomes ever smaller, each strongly bounded from one another, for each voice claims its own privileged knowledge inaccessible to other knowers. The range of knowers within the intellectual field as a whole thus not only proliferates but also fragments, each client knower group having its own representative. For example, this may begin with 'the working class'; then, as the category of the working class fragments under the impact of the procession of the excluded (as the knower's ability to speak for other voices is critiqued), it may develop as follows:

social class	– the working class
gender	– working-class men
race	– white, working-class men
sexuality	– white, heterosexual, working-class men
	– English, state-schooled, Cambridge-educated, white, heterosexual men of working-class origin, currently living in Australia
	... and so on, until you reach me, at this moment in time.[4]

Thus, whilst carving out a discursive space for itself, the knower critique of existing voices enables the possibility of being critiqued in turn by the same specialization code. Cultural studies itself has often illustrated the multiplicities of subjectivity and identity – the potential categories of new knowers are hypothetically endless. The procession of the excluded thus becomes, in terms of the privileged knower, an accretion of adjectives or 'hyphenation' effect. This intrinsic dynamic of social knower codes, fragmenting the focus and basis of knowledge claims, also tends towards methodological individualism and hermeneutic narcissism, a spiralling inwards from large social categories, such as social class, towards ever-smaller categories, culminating in oneself and autobiographical reflection (Maton 2003). Thus, whilst social knower codes can be understood (from a Bourdieuan perspective) as strategies of capital maximization, the dynamic of their *intrinsic* structure enables the proliferation of new positions that leads to fragmentation within the field and progressively inward-looking and individualized stances.

This dynamic also helps explain the field's schismatic nature and neophilia. Where new knowledge is defined according to the criteria of articulating a knower's specialized voice, and truth is defined as whatever may be said by this voice, then it is not *what* has been said before that matters, it is *who* has said it. It is thus likely that, with each addition of a new adjective or hyphen, existing work within the field will be overhauled – old songs will be sung by new voices in their own distinctive register. Rather than building upon previous knowledge, there is a tendency for new knowers to declare new beginnings, re-definitions and even complete ruptures with the past – an anti-canonical, iconoclastic and parricidal stance generating recurrent schisms. The intellectual field then gives the appearance of undergoing permanent cultural revolution. However, although the names and faces featured regularly change, the underlying form of these recurrent radical 'breaks' is the same: they represent realizations of social knower codes.

Proliferation and fragmentation also reduces the social bases for political action: social knower codes emphasize *difference from* rather than *similarity with*, leading to ever-smaller categories of knowers. The procession of the excluded may quickly become the site of ***knower wars***, both between and within various 'voices', as to who is the most legitimate knower. Such infighting problematizes collective action. It is notable that threats to the CCCS prior to the rise of social knower codes in the mid-1970s were countered by international action, but that in 2002 the Centre was closed down by the University of Birmingham. (This closure came two years after the original version of this chapter conjectured the difficulty of maintaining such an institutional presence; Maton 2000b.) Furthermore, lacking an explicit and strongly defined notion of specialized knowledge of an object of study leaves the intellectual field's knowledge and actors vulnerable to poaching by other fields. Rather than design and develop a named course in or department of 'cultural studies', institutions are able to add a module or unit onto existing courses or a lecturer into established departments. Similarly, in research the field's name can be annexed as an adjective: cultural geography, cultural history, even perhaps cultural physics. Thus, proliferation and fragmentation results in the paradoxical situation of an intellectual field appearing to be both blossoming and in decline, both everywhere and nowhere to be seen.

Social knower codes also leave intellectual fields vulnerable to criticism from beyond higher education; after all, if only a specific knower can know, then professional academics are dispensable (unless they research only themselves, the hermeneutic narcissism of 'auto-' methods). The tendency of social knower codes to emphasize the multiplicity of truths and argue against the adjudication of competing knowledge claims (by virtue of their weaker epistemic relations) renders them particularly vulnerable to utilitarian policy climates. One possible response is to highlight the significance of one's object of study. As an example of this strategy in reverse, one could relate Margaret Thatcher's declaration that 'society' does not exist to the targeting of social sciences for funding cutbacks in Britain during the 1980s. Social knower codes, however, are not primarily based upon claims to provide specialized insight into a discrete foundational object. Instead they tend to emphasize the significance of their *subjects* of study. Whilst the marginalized position of a specific group of knowers may be highlighted, the vitality of this strategy varies inversely with its success – once a voice begins to be heard, claims to marginality begin to lose their force (as well as evoking its own disrupter, as outlined above). In addition, with proliferation and fragmentation of knowers, the question of to whom the intellectual field is 'giving voice' becomes increasingly problematic. Social knower codes may, therefore, problematize attempts to carve out spaces within higher education by enabling a process of 'divide and be conquered'.

Conclusion

British cultural studies is a curious case: it appears to be both everywhere and nowhere institutionally, both blossoming and in fragmented disarray intellectually. Viewing its knowledge practices as languages of legitimation enables them to be conceptualized as particular kinds of legitimation codes. Specifically, analysing its specialization code brings to light one reason for the subject's apparently Janus-faced position: the rise of social knower codes during the late 1970s. This specialization code tends towards proliferation, fragmentation and segmentation. The resultant schismatic intellectual field problematizes the ability of actors to establish or maintain discrete institutional spaces: they are vulnerable to utilitarian criticism from beyond higher education, poaching of actors and knowledge from within higher education, and knower wars within the field itself. Thus, the academic subject can seem both everywhere and nowhere in particular, both vibrant and in decline, both radical and insular. Of course, these are not the only tendencies of social knower codes (see Maton 2000a). Moreover, tendencies may be unexercised (because of a lack of enabling conditions), exercised unrealized (due to countervailing pressures), or realized unperceived (because of a lack of suitable concepts) (Bhaskar 1975). For example, papal infallibility and 'the divine right of kings' can also be characterized as social knower codes (Maton 2002), but the positions of Popes and monarchs as privileged knowers have remained relatively stable (in terms of the position rather than specific occupants) over relatively long periods of time because of countervailing pressures such as monopoly of the means of violent coercion or manufacturing consent. In other words, the status of the powers and tendencies of relations within knowledge practices is always a matter for substantive research. Nonetheless, the conceptual development presented here enables investigation of specific realizations of knowledge practices in determinate conditions and so helps bring to light these powers and tendencies.

More generally, the concepts introduced represent a first step towards addressing both knowledge-blindness and the false dichotomy between analysing 'relations to' and 'relations within' knowledge that bedevil studies of education. At the outset of this chapter I drew on Bernstein's argument that the sociology of education typically treats knowledge as a neutral relay for external power relations and so focuses on the messages relayed by this medium. By showing how relations within knowledge practices impact upon the institutional and intellectual trajectories of an intellectual field, the analysis demonstrates their significance for understanding knowledge and education. In other words, this medium is *also* a message. The emphasis is deliberate: this is not to claim the medium is *the* message. Analyses of 'relations to' knowledge practices should not be displaced by but rather complemented with analyses of 'relations within'. Conceiving practices in terms of languages of legitimation aims to help extend and integrate ideas from both these approaches. In addition to showing the socially and historically located nature of knowledge practices, the way power shapes knowledge, one needs also to show how knowledge shapes power and that the power of knowledge is not just social but also epistemic. The notion of legitimation highlights both the sociological nature of knowledge practices, as comprising strategies by actors socially positioned within a field of struggle over status and resources, and its epistemological nature as potentially legitimate knowledge claims. Conceptualizing relations within knowledge practices as specialization codes highlights one dimension of their structure and allows its effects to be explored. All these features must be embraced by a realist sociology which is to avoid the false 'epistemological dilemma' of asocial essentialism or reductionist relativism (Chapter 1).

British cultural studies may be a curious case but is by no means unique (see Chapter 3). Many tendencies of social knower codes are found in the sociology of education, which has been periodically dominated by similar intellectual stances since the early 1970s (Moore and Muller 1999). The concepts introduced in this chapter aim to contribute towards establishing knowledge practices as an object of study with its own specialized principles and procedures. The analysis suggests such a strengthening of epistemic relations is necessary to avoid the proliferation, fragmentation, segmentation and schismatism of social knower codes that have recurrently characterized the sociology of education. This conceptualization of languages of legitimation is, however, only a first step towards overcoming knowledge-blindness, hearing the messages this medium has to tell us, and so creating a realist sociology of education.[5] Nonetheless, as will become clear in subsequent chapters, this first step towards providing a language about legitimation enables the possibility of cumulative knowledge-building about knowledge.

Notes

1 Most of this work has yet to be published. My focus changed from cultural studies to its contextual field of higher education (Maton 2005b). I hope to return to this data in future.

2 The distinction is analytic rather than empirical: one may analytically distinguish between a subject and an object of discussion even when discussing oneself.

3 Previous work in cultural studies is more accurately described as a *cultivated knower code*. A social knower code was attributed to that work retrospectively as part of the feminist 'intervention' (see Chapters 5 and 9).

4 More specifically, the son and the heir of a shyness that is criminally vulgar (see Maton 2010b).

5 I return to consider how specialization codes also helps avoid knower-blindness within social realism in Chapters 4 and 5.

3 The epistemic–pedagogic device

Breaks and continuities in the social sciences and mathematics

In sociology 'revolutionary science' has become normal and 'normal science' would be revolutionary.

Introduction

In recent decades sociology has been characterized by proclamations of radical breaks with the past and declarations of new beginnings. During the early 1970s 'new' sociologies were announced, including the 'new sociology of education' (Young 1971) and 'new sociology of deviance' (Taylor *et al.* 1973). In the later 1970s and 1980s 'interventions' by a series of standpoint theories declared rebirths of sociology when 'giving voice' to previously silenced social groups. In the 1980s and 1990s, 'post-' theories, such as post-modernism, declared fundamental breaks with past approaches. At the same time, there have been recurrent announcements of profound 'crisis' in the discipline (e.g. Gouldner 1971; Lemert 1995). Sociology regularly experiences revolutionary change, renewal and rebirth. How can we understand such schisms and crises?

Chapter 1 argued that most sociological approaches exhibit knowledge-blindness and would reduce such intellectual developments to issues of social power. Though offering insights into the effects of social structure and institutional politics on knowledge practices, they occlude how knowledge practices shape both social and institutional power and their own positions and trajectories. Such approaches hold what LiPuma (1993: 17) called an 'absolute substantive theory of arbitrariness' in which symbolic forms are entirely interchangeable and their internal structurings deemed insignificant, so that anything could have served the same function as anything else. They thereby cannot explain why *these* kinds of beliefs, ideas and practices have undergone schisms and crises and other kinds have not.

Chapter 2 began outlining the basis for a conceptual framework that brings together insights from such analyses of 'relations to' knowledge with an understanding of 'relations within' knowledge. The practices of actors were described as representing ***languages of legitimation*** in struggles for the status and resources at stake within social fields of practice. Such strategic stances embody rulers for achievement within their fields and thereby aim at maximizing actors' positions. The organizing principles underlying these languages were conceptualized as ***legitimation codes***, of which Chapter 2 introduced one dimension: ***specialization codes***, comprising ***epistemic relations*** and ***social relations***. These concepts begin to bring the internal structuring of symbolic practices into the picture and enable their powers and tendencies to be analysed. Chapter 2, for example, explored the social knower codes underlying British cultural studies in the late 1970s, revealing their tendencies towards proliferation, fragmentation and recurrent schisms. However, these concepts also raise questions of their own.

First, if actors' practices represent strategies in struggles, then what is the ground over which these struggles are being fought? This is to ask questions of the nature of the social field being studied, such as whether it is undifferentiated or comprises specialized contexts and practices. How such questions are answered has implications for knowledge-building in research. To enable an integrated account of, for example, education requires a ***theorization*** of the field, because empirical descriptions of educational levels or institutions vary over time and across national contexts. Moreover, this framework must avoid the Scylla of universalizing specific contexts or practices as the whole, and the Charybdis of proliferating segmented models of specific contexts or practices. The former homogenizes the field, leading to ideas inapplicable to most of its activities; the latter fragments the field, leading to ideas incapable of reaching beyond their context; both limit cumulative knowledge-building.

Second, if actors are engaged in struggles, what are they struggling over? This is to ask how relations are established among the differing measures of achievement embodied by actors' languages of legitimation. Specialization codes analyse one dimension of the 'messages' of these languages but leave open what generates both the codes themselves and their relational positions within the hierarchies of social fields. Thus, how some actors and practices come to be higher or lower status than others needs to be explored and (to avoid reductionism) in a way that captures the role of knowledge practices in this process.

Last, the issue of schisms and crises draws attention to how these new concepts relate to their foundational frameworks. Is Specialization another 'break'? Is LCT a 'new new sociology of education'? Chapters 1 and 7 briefly discuss the different roles played in LCT by ideas from Bourdieu and Bernstein; Chapters 4–9 begin from existing concepts from code theory, discuss their limitations, and demonstrate how they can be enhanced to enable greater fidelity to more phenomena with conceptual economy; and Chapter 10 draws these together to show how LCT extends and integrates inherited concepts. However, Chapter 2 was concerned with illustrating how using 'specialization codes' integrates *analyses* of 'relations to' and 'relations within' knowledge rather than with explicating how they develop existing concepts. So, how they relate to inherited ideas requires explication.

This chapter addresses these questions by elaborating the *epistemic–pedagogic device*, one aspect of a *Legitimation Device* that conceptualizes the means whereby symbolic control is created, maintained, transformed and changed in society. I begin by explaining the necessity of theorizing the Legitimation Device for understanding social fields of practice. I then introduce the epistemic–pedagogic device, or 'EPD', to explore the Specialization aspect of this ruler of power, knowledge and consciousness. Second, I outline the arena created by the EPD when applied to education to theoretically map the ground over which struggles are fought, and the intrinsic grammar of the EPD to describe what actors are struggling over. Third, I discuss how specialization codes conceptualize the realizations of the device in the practices and dispositions of actors. Last, I briefly illustrate the effects of different settings of the EPD for knowledge-building by considering breaks and continuities in social science and mathematics.

At the same time, the chapter reveals how Specialization relates to its foundational frameworks. I begin by establishing the need to develop field theory, elaborating how code theory addressed such issues in terms of 'the pedagogic device', and outlining the need to extend this framework. Second, I show how the EPD selectively develops Bernstein's model to more fully conceptualize contexts of education, and how 'specialization codes' extend and integrate Bernstein's 'pedagogic codes' to analyse their practices. I conclude by highlighting how the evolutionary intellectual development embodied by LCT offers genuinely critical potential for research.

Devices

The key to understanding both the ground over which actors struggle and what they struggle over is the *Legitimation Device*. As outlined above, *languages of legitimation* conceptualize the practices of actors as strategic stances that proclaim measures of achievement, and *legitimation codes* conceptualize their organizing principles. The Legitimation Device conceptualizes, in turn, the means whereby these principles are created, maintained, transformed and changed. It is the condition for practices which are, in turn, both realizations of its logics and resources for the creation, maintenance and change of code modalities. In terms of struggles among actors, the Legitimation Device establishes the relative values of legitimation codes and thus the basis of achievement in and relational structure of social fields. This abstract description reflects the nature of the Legitimation Device: it is not observed directly but rather known through its effects in shaping the organizing principles (legitimation codes) of practices.

The Legitimation Device is the overarching generative mechanism underlying social fields of practice and, I shall argue, the necessary foundation for, and multi-faceted, fundamental theoretical object of study for sociology. As yet not all of its 'aspects' have been theorized. (The dimensions of Autonomy, Density, Semantics, Specialization, and Temporality each explore an aspect of the Device; see Chapter 1.) Indeed, given the variety and complexity of social fields, it is likely the Legitimation Device is analytically inexhaustible. Here I shall conceptualize *one aspect* of this Device, revealed by the dimension of Specialization. Bernstein's model of 'the pedagogic device' (1990, 2000) is the inspiration behind the Legitimation Device. In this chapter I develop his model in directions suggested by the concepts of Chapter 2 to theorize its Specialization aspect: the *epistemic–pedagogic device.*

Why the notion of 'devices' is necessary can be illustrated by considering Bourdieu's field theory. As will become obvious, Bourdieu's approach foregrounds issues of strategies, status hierarchies and fields in ways that resonate with the theorization of struggles over the Legitimation Device. Indeed, it is arguably the best developed framework for analysing 'relations to' practice of social power. Moreover, Bourdieu's ideas were developed through studies of education. It is thus an exemplary illustration of the limitations of 'relations to' analyses, such as those adapting ideas from Foucault, Deleuze, Butler, and so forth. Principal among these limitations is that, though premised on the notion that actors struggle for control over the means of symbolic domination in order to impose a viewpoint as legitimate, such approaches offer little insight into the object of such struggles and the ground over which they are fought. Ironically, the proclaimed inheritors of the mantle of 'conflict theory' offer little theory of conflict.

For example, Bourdieu's toolkit neither differentiates specialized contexts and practices within the field nor accounts for its underlying generative principles. Bourdieu's concepts that explicitly address education, such as 'pedagogic work', 'pedagogic authority' and 'cultural arbitrary' (Bourdieu and Passeron 1977) cannot generate descriptions of any specific agencies or kinds of practice. Similarly, his 'thinking tools' of 'field', 'capital' and 'habitus' enable relational structures of power to be described but cannot generate descriptions of what comprises education. Moreover, as highlighted in Chapter 1, these concepts highlight what needs to be conceptualized but need development to capture the organizing principles of practices.

Second, field theory offers no account of what generates fields. According to Bourdieu, the structure of a field is given by the rate of exchange among the species of capital (kinds of status and resources) active within it; their relative values reflect the relational positions of actors possessing them. This leaves open how the relative statuses of capitals are established at any moment in time. If actors attempt to impose one species of capital as the dominant measure of achievement within a field, then what enables that measure to dominate? This question does *not* imply intentional orchestration by specific actors but rather highlights the need to theorize the basis of exchange rates among capitals. Here, Bourdieu offered a flat ontology: the limits of legitimate participation in the field are at once what is at stake in struggles, the ground over which struggles are fought, and what is used in struggles (1994: 143). Though Bourdieu criticized 'substantialist' accounts that grasp only the empirical, the framework lacks the notion of an underlying generative mechanism over which agents are struggling and which articulates their strategies. Thus, to develop field theory requires theorizing the means whereby the evolving system of possibilities constituting a field is generated, maintained, transformed and changed.

To capture this mechanism, I shall build on Bernstein's notion of 'the pedagogic device' (1990, 2000). Bernstein's model is ambitious in scope, reaching from social structure to individual consciousness, and comprises a complex web of relations among finely differentiated series of agents, contexts and practices. It has inspired studies whose foci range from macro-processes of national curriculum formation to micro-processes of classroom interaction (e.g. Singh 1993, 2002; Christie 1999; Neves and Morais 2001; Tyler 2001). Here, I *selectively* build on this model. I extract and develop a key element – the arena – *to address the specific questions* of the ground over which struggles are fought and what actors are struggling over in social fields of practice. I do so in two stages. First, I build on Bernstein's account of the 'arena of struggle' created by the device and the 'rules' of its intrinsic grammar to elaborate the *epistemic–pedagogic device*. Second, I discuss how 'specialization codes' provide concepts for analysing the effects of this device on practices. To address the question of how these concepts relate to their foundations, I begin each step from their nearest 'take-off' point in Bernstein's concepts and highlight how the epistemic–pedagogic device and specialization codes extend and integrate these ideas.

Fields and logics

Bernstein's 'pedagogic device'

To analyse the 'intrinsic grammar of pedagogic discourse' (2000: 28), Bernstein posited the 'pedagogic device'. This device, he argued, creates an 'arena of struggle' (Bernstein 1990: 206) comprising three fields of practice, as heuristically portrayed in Figure 3.1:

- a *field of production* where 'new' knowledge is constructed, modified and positioned;
- a *field of reproduction* where pedagogic practice occurs; and
- a *field of recontextualizing* where discourses from the field of production are selected, appropriated and transformed to become *pedagogic* discourse available to be taught and learned within the field of reproduction.[1]

This is obviously not an empirical map of different levels of education systems but rather analytically distinguishes practices and contexts that shape pedagogic discourse. As Bernstein (2000) emphasized, their locations may differ empirically but are typically sited primarily in: universities (production); schools (reproduction); and specialized state agencies ('official recontextualizing field') and/or education departments of tertiary institutions ('pedagogic recontextualizing field').

Field of production	**Field of recontextualizing**	**Field of reproduction**
sites where 'new' knowledge is created	sites where knowledges from the field of production are selected, rearranged and transformed to become pedagogic discourse	sites of teaching and learning
distributive rules	recontextualizing rules	evaluative rules

Figure 3.1 Arena created by the 'pedagogic device'

Bernstein's distinction between the three fields highlights key issues often neglected by accounts of knowledge and education. The quotidian responsibilities of university academics typically combine knowledge production, curriculum construction and pedagogy. Suffering from what Bourdieu (2000) termed 'the scholastic fallacy', they often conflate these practices: models of research (e.g. Becher and Trowler 2001) are used to study learning; constructivists apply models of learning to curriculum and research; philosophies reduce everything to ontology; among many others. In contrast, Bernstein emphasized that each field has its own structure and logic which should not be reduced to those of other fields. Educational knowledge, for example, does not simply reflect the practices of knowledge producers within a discipline; one cannot understand school physics by studying the research practices of physicists, and vice versa. Once these differences are recognized one can then agree with Bruner (1960: 14) that '[i]ntellectual activity is anywhere and everywhere, whether at the frontier of knowledge or in a third-grade classroom', without succumbing to the fallacy that these activities are identical in form.

Pedagogic discourse, Bernstein (1990) stated, is a principle for appropriating other discourses from the field of production and subordinating them to a different principle of organization and relation – they are *pedagogized*. The three fields are thus hierarchically related: reproduction of educational knowledge depends upon the recontextualization of knowledge which, in turn, depends upon its production. This is not, however, a conveyor belt: meanings from intellectual fields are transformed by recontextualizing fields, and the resulting pedagogized knowledge is transformed again within classroom practice, where teachers may also recontextualize discourses from the family, community and student peer groups (Bernstein 1990: 199).

As illustrated in Figure 3.1, Bernstein described the 'intrinsic grammar' constituting the pedagogic device as comprising three rules, each regulating the activities of a field: 'distributive rules' specialize forms of knowledge, consciousness and practice to social groups through regulating access to the field of production and thus the 'unthinkable' or means of producing 'new' knowledge; 'recontextualizing rules' regulate the delocation, relocation and refocusing of knowledge to become pedagogic discourse in the field of recontextualizing; and 'evaluative rules' regulate pedagogic practices in the field of reproduction. As I discuss further below, these 'rules' are, as intrinsic grammar, not available empirically but rather known through their realizations in practices that provide resources for the construction of code modalities (Bernstein 2000: 188).

From 'pedagogic' to 'epistemic–pedagogic'

This brief summary highlights several features of the model that will serve as foundations for addressing the morphology and basis of education. However, the model first requires development, primarily due to its peculiarly pedagogic perspective on knowledge production. This reflects Bernstein's explicit focus when introducing the *pedagogic* device: 'My question is: are there any general principles underlying *the transformation of knowledge into pedagogic communication*' (2000: 25; emphasis added). It also reflects the trajectory of Bernstein's theory, which he described as a movement from exploring the organizing principles of pedagogic contexts (as 'pedagogic codes'), through theorizing the construction of this pedagogic discourse (as 'the pedagogic device'), to analyses of the 'knowledge structures' subject to such pedagogic transformation (2000: 155). In short, theorization began from the right-hand side of Figure 3.1 and advanced towards the left: from reproduction through recontextualizing towards production. This focus and trajectory are reflected in a portrayal of knowledge production from the viewpoint of its role in pedagogic discourse rather than on its own terms. Thus, for Bernstein, 'evaluative rules' regulate the practices of the reproduction field, and 'recontextualizing rules' regulate the practices of the recontextualizing field, but 'distributive rules' regulate *access* to the field of production rather than its practices. This creates a contradiction in the framework. On the one hand, the model states that each field has its own specialized practices; indeed, Bernstein emphasized that the 'field [of production] and its history are created by the positions, relations, and practices arising out of the *production* rather than the reproduction of educational discourse and its practices' (1990: 191; original emphasis). On the other hand, the 'rules' regulating the specialized practices of the field of production are not conceptualized. This absence remained: though the forms taken by intellectual fields were subsequently conceptualized as 'knowledge structures' (Bernstein 2000), the 'pedagogic device' model was unchanged.

Analysing the field of production on its own terms foregrounds issues that are typically secondary to pedagogic concerns in recontextualization and reproduction fields: the epistemological and ontological bases of knowledge claims. Bringing these issues into view has three principal implications for developing the inherited model of the arena. First, it highlights the need to theorize the 'rules' regulating the practices of production fields. Knowledge is socially produced by means of antecedent knowledge and how this is done forms the specific (though not monopolistic) concern of intellectual fields. The 'rules' regulating these practices thus need to be included in a model of the basis of knowledge practices. Second, the 'rules' regulating the field of production are not, as the model suggests, primarily distributive. Put another way, Bernstein stated that 'distributive rules mark and distribute who may transmit what to whom and under what conditions, and they attempt to set the outer limits of legitimate discourse' (2000: 31). I argue that Bernstein's definition suggests, contrary to his own model, that these rules concern *all* fields of the arena rather than regulating solely the field of production.

The third implication is a broader need to rethink the device itself. To explore how 'new' knowledge is created is to explore how it articulates the arbitrary and non-arbitrary (Moore and Maton 2001). It is to ask questions of relations between arbitrary influences on knowledge practices, such as social relations of power, and such non-arbitrary considerations as ontological necessity. Though most explicit in intellectual fields, such questions are relevant to practices across the entire arena. Bernstein highlighted how recontextualization 'creates *a space for the play of ideology*' (1990: 189; original emphasis); in other words, it creates a space for the influence of the arbitrary alongside the non-arbitrary. 'No discourse,' he stated, 'ever moves without ideology at play' (Bernstein 2000: 33). Thus, both the pedagogization of new knowledge and the enactment of pedagogized knowledge in classroom practice involve spaces for re-articulating the arbitrary and non-arbitrary. As well as addressing pedagogic issues, a developed theorization of the device must, therefore, also embrace epistemological and ontological issues. This is not to suggest the model should explicate an epistemology or ontology; it forms part of a sociology of knowledge practices, not a philosophy of knowing or being (Chapter 1).[2] Rather, it highlights that the model must embrace analysis of how the arbitrary and non-arbitrary are articulated within knowledge practices across all three fields. This point is particularly pertinent to conceptualizing practices as codes: Bernstein's concept of 'pedagogic codes' must be developed to address these articulations in order to explore the play of ideology. I discuss this further below. My point here is that such developments entail a different way of thinking about the device. In one of his final papers Bernstein (2001: 367) described the term 'pedagogy' as having 'restrictive references', including that it does not 'point to the phenomena to be described', and advocated moving 'from pedagogies to knowledges'. Similarly, I am arguing that we need to move from 'pedagogic device' to 'epistemic–pedagogic device'.

The epistemic–pedagogic device

Building on Bernstein's model, the arena of struggle created by the epistemic–pedagogic device or 'EPD' comprises fields of production, recontextualization and reproduction. This arena is heuristically portrayed in Figure 3.2. As Figure 3.2 shows, the EPD model develops the inherited model in several

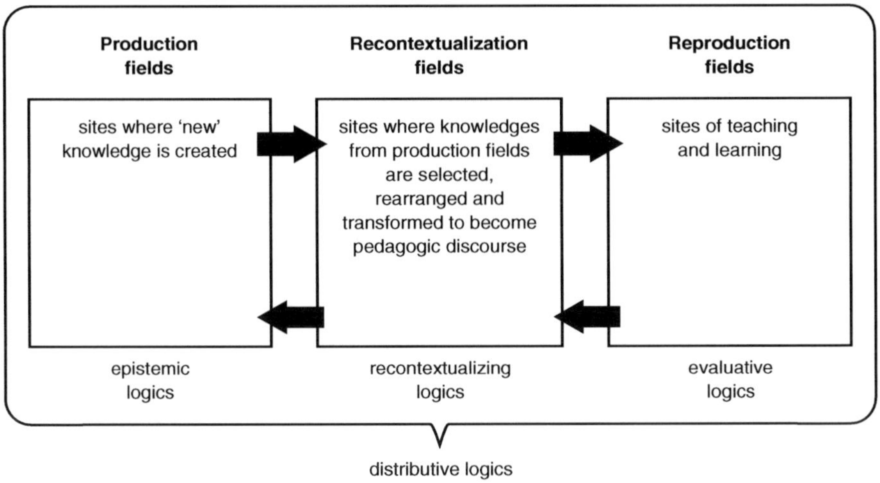

Figure 3.2 Arena created by the epistemic–pedagogic device

directions. First, 'rules' are redescribed as 'logics', avoiding mistaken claims that they posit practices as deterministically rule-governed (e.g. Harker and May 1993) and potential confusion between their referents in both models. Second, the arrows emphasize that recontextualization between fields occurs in both directions, though not evenly. While reverse flows are not precluded in the inherited model, its focus on the pedagogizing of knowledge foregrounds flows from left to right. However, knowledge circulates around the arena in multiple directions. The arrows from left to right highlight how knowledge is: ***curricularized*** from production to recontextualization fields; and ***pedagogized*** from recontextualization to reproduction fields. Those from right to left highlight that curricular products from recontextualization fields may be ***intellectualized*** or absorbed into production fields as part of the antecedent knowledge that serves as raw material for creating 'new' knowledge. Similarly, educational knowledge enacted in pedagogic practice (reproduction fields) may be ***recurricularized***: delocated, refocused and relocated within the curricular products of recontextualization fields. (I have resisted adding more arrows to Figure 3.2, but one could also highlight how educational knowledge may also be intellectualized into production fields.) These four processes of transformation of knowledge re-emphasize the fallacy of 'reading off' the practices of one field from another, such as learning from research.

Third, 'distributive logics' now encompass activities across the entire arena rather than underpinning fields of production, and the notion of 'epistemic logics' is introduced to describe the basis of practices in those fields.[3] The intrinsic grammar of the EPD is thus constituted by four logics (Figure 3.2):

- *epistemic logics* regulate the delocation, refocusing and relocation of antecedent knowledge to become 'new' knowledge in production fields;
- *recontextualizing logics* regulate the delocation, pedagogizing and relocation of knowledges in recontextualization fields to become pedagogic discourse;
- *evaluative logics* regulate the teaching and learning of pedagogic discourse in the pedagogic practice of reproduction fields; and
- *distributive logics* regulate access to transcendental meanings (esoteric or non-everyday knowledge whose creation, circulation and change is the domain of all three fields) and *within* this realm to the 'unthinkable' (or means of creating new knowledge) and the 'thinkable' and, within the latter, to various thinkable worlds.

By embracing all three fields, the notion of 'distributive logics' highlights that a precondition to playing the game is entering the arena. They regulate access not only to the means of thinking the 'unthinkable' offered by production fields but also to the means of constructing 'thinkables' in recontextualization fields and to an array of different 'thinkables' offered in reproduction fields. Distributive logics thereby specialize forms of knowledge, consciousness and practice to social groups through regulating access to the entire arena and then, within this arena, to fields of production, recontextualization and reproduction, and to different positions and trajectories within these fields. One can, therefore, distinguish levels of distributive logics: arena, inter-field, and intra-field. Thus, distributive logics mark and distribute who may claim what to whom and under what conditions, and attempt to set the outer limits of legitimate discourse (cf. Bernstein 2000: 31). Put simply, if a key question for research is 'Who gets to claim/know/learn/do what?', then epistemic, recontextualizing and evaluative logics regulate the various 'whats', and distributive logics regulate 'who' enjoys access to which 'whats'.

Struggles over the EPD

These three fields and four logics theorize the arena created by the EPD. Actors struggle over control of the arena as a whole, relations between fields, and relations within fields. As Bourdieu would argue, these struggles are for the power to decree which measures of achievement are effective and 'conversion rates' among them. Having built on Bernstein's model, however, we can now go further than Bourdieu to conceptualize the basis of these struggles. Through their practices actors are struggling for control of the EPD, for whoever controls the device determines the ruler of legitimacy in the social field (or arena) and so maximizes their own position within its status hierarchies. Actors in positions of power are able to control the device such that dominant measures of achievement reflect the characteristics of their own practices; that is, higher status specialization codes in the field match their own. Thus, where Bourdieu described the field as the object, means and stakes of struggles, we can now distinguish the EPD as the object of struggles, specialization codes as the means of struggles, and the structure of the field as the stakes of struggles.

To control the EPD is to control the comparative values of specialization codes and thereby the structuring of a social field.

A dominant code is thus both privileged in the sense of having priority in a social field and privileging by conferring power upon its protagonists (cf. Bernstein 1990: 88). However, the code dominating as the (typically unwritten) 'rules of the game' may not be transparent, universal or uncontested. Actors whose dispositions are characterized by different codes may experience difficulty in recognizing and realizing stances deemed valuable. Actors' status positions are thereby shaped by relations between the codes characterizing their practices and those dominating the field; and their strategies are shaped by relations between the coding orientations of their dispositions and those dominant codes. For example, actors whose coding orientations clash with the code dominating a social field risk being deemed failures and may choose to avoid or leave that field (Chen *et al.* 2011). In the arena created by the EPD, these relations shape the positions and practices of intellectuals, recontextualizers, teachers and students, as well as shaping actors' dispositions through their experiences of trajectories within its fields.

Echoing Bernstein (1990: 180), the EPD can thereby be described as generating a symbolic ruler of consciousness, in both senses of having power over consciousness and measuring the legitimacy of its realizations – it interrelates power, knowledge and consciousness. Understanding the EPD is thus crucial to exploring symbolic domination and control in society, for it translates power relations into discursive practices and translates discursive practices into power relations (cf. Bernstein 1990: 205). This reaches beyond education. Struggles over the EPD include actors from beyond the arena attempting to ensure their social dominance through the creation and maintenance of particular specialization codes. The EPD is thus the focus of domination and resistance, struggle and negotiation, both within education and across wider society. The question posited by Bernstein as crucial to research, 'Whose ruler, what consciousness?' (1990: 180), now becomes: who controls the EPD and what specialization codes are they attempting to impose as dominant measures of legitimacy? Put simply: whose EPD, what specialization codes?

Principles: Coding realizations of the device

As the above discussion highlights, specialization codes represent a crucial mediator between the EPD and empirical realizations. The device itself is not available empirically – to seek a physical apparatus, complete with dials set to specific codes, would be empiricist folly. Similarly, the intrinsic grammar of four logics highlights what needs to be analysed but not the organizing principles of expressions of these logics – they identify the principal specific foci of practices, not the nature of those practices. Nonetheless, to postulate a generative principle whose realizations cannot be analysed in substantive research would be intellectual gymnastics – hypothesizing a 'device' without code concepts is idle speculation. As I illustrate in this and later chapters, the EPD is known through its *effects* in shaping practices, and the organizing principles underlying practices can be conceptualized using specialization codes. Put another way, 'devices' operate at a relatively high level of abstraction and become enacted in research through such mediating concepts as 'codes'.

From pedagogic codes to specialization codes

In Bernstein's model of the pedagogic device, the organizing principles of actors' dispositions and practices are analysed as 'pedagogic codes', centred on 'classification' and 'framing'. In the EPD model, dispositions and practices are analysed as specialization codes. This returns us to the question of whether these new concepts represent a break with existing ideas. As Chapter 10 will discuss, the LCT dimension of Specialization extends and integrates Bernstein's conceptual landmarks of 'classification'/'framing', 'the pedagogic device' and 'knowledge structures' within *specialization codes* (Chapter 2), the *epistemic–pedagogic device* (this chapter) and *knowledge–knower structures* (Chapter 4), respectively. Rather than break with past ideas, these LCT concepts add a second dimension to classical code theory.

The notion of specialization code highlights that for every reading of classification and framing offered by the inherited framework, one can use the same concepts to generate another, often different, reading. Strength of 'classification' (+/–C) refers to the strength of boundaries between contexts or categories; strength of 'framing' (+/–F) refers to the locus of control within contexts or categories. There is now a considerable body of empirical research using these concepts (Moore 2013b). However, to echo Bernstein's classic exposition (1977), I will illustrate how two readings of classification and framing can be generated using conventional descriptions of 'traditional' and 'progressivist'/ 'constructivist' pedagogies. I begin with the classic reading.

In 'traditional' pedagogy, the academic subject being taught is clearly demarcated from other knowledge: strong boundaries are maintained between academic knowledge and common sense, and between different subjects (such as teaching in a dedicated space, like a science classroom). There is also strong control from above 'over the selection, organization, pacing and timing of the knowledge transmitted and received' (Bernstein 1977: 89). These characteristics exhibit relatively *strong classification* and *strong framing* (+C, +F). In contrast, 'constructivist' pedagogies are typically described as blurring boundaries around academic subjects, such as through their subordination to cross-curricular themes, and encouraging connections to students' everyday experiences. The teacher is portrayed as a 'facilitator' for students who enjoy greater freedom over what they learn, when, and in what order. Such characteristics exhibit relatively *weak classification* and *weak framing* (–C, –F).

These are, albeit to simplified examples, the classic applications of these concepts. However, they can also be applied to a second dimension. Crudely put, classic applications conceptualize knowledge, while specialization codes conceptualize both knowledge and knowers. (Notably, Bernstein originally described modalities of classification and framing as 'educational knowledge codes'; 1977.) More precisely, classic readings describe boundaries around and control over realizations of what LCT terms *epistemic relations*; the same concepts can be used to describe boundaries around and control over realizations of *social relations;* and together these generate *specialization codes.*[4]

Returning to the examples but now focusing on social relations, 'traditional' pedagogy is typically described as 'one-size-fits-all' teaching that takes little account of the dispositions of individual learners, their existing experiences, or nurturing the learner's 'inner': relatively *weak classification* and *weak framing* (of social relations). In contrast, constructivist pedagogies are often described as valorizing the experiences of distinctively individual learners, building on their dispositions, and tailoring learning to individual needs: relatively *strong classification* and *strong framing* (of social relations). As LCT studies show (Chen *et al.* 2011), constructivism is premised on a particular kind of knower whose dispositions include a willingness to reveal the 'inner' by relating one's personal experiences and feelings. (This makes visible what is, ironically, less than fully visible in Bernstein's notion of 'invisible pedagogy', where the focus is not on the explicit transmission and acquisition of knowledge.) In short, the examples of 'traditional' and constructivist pedagogies exhibit opposing readings (both +C, +F and –C, –F), depending on whether one is addressing realizations of epistemic relations (ER) or of social relations (SR). In these examples, 'traditional' pedagogy exhibits ER(+C, +F) and SR(–C, –F); and constructivist pedagogy exhibits ER(–C, –F) and SR(+C, +F). These specialization codes are condensed as ER+, SR– (knowledge codes) and ER–, SR+ (knower codes), respectively.

This extension and integration of pedagogic codes within specialization codes is thus not a fundamental break with inherited code theory. Indeed, not only the original concepts but also studies using those concepts remain active within the extended framework. Classic research can be integrated with LCT studies or re-analysed using specialization codes to bring knowers more fully into the picture (see Chapter 10). Conversely, not all new studies need to use classification and framing – the choice of concepts should depend on the problem-situation. Accordingly, though chapters in this book begin from Bernstein's concepts so as to make explicit the foundations of new concepts, studies using specialization codes typically begin from the concepts of epistemic relations and social relations.

Embracing the arena

Returning to the EPD, the model highlights three features required by a theoretical framework for analysing practice. First, concepts must be capable of capturing diverse practices across the three fields of the arena. For example, to trace transformations of knowledge between intellectual production, curriculum construction, and teaching and learning, requires moving beyond empirical descriptions to analyse their organizing principles in ways not locked into any specific context or practice. Specialization codes offer a means of doing so. To paraphrase Bernstein (2000: 133), they allow a set of practices to be conceptualized as 'X', a description of its internal structure as one of a range of possibilities, such as 'W, X, Y, Z'. This overcomes the gravity well of the concrete specificities of particular cases to enable the systematic analysis of similarity, variation and change. As a growing number of studies demonstrate (Chapter 10), the concepts can be used to analyse a wide variety of practices (including research, curriculum and pedagogy), at different levels of analysis (from whole education system to close textual reading), using both qualitative and quantitative methods.

Moreover, LCT goes further than the typologizing suggested by 'W, X, Y, Z' and by classic descriptions of codes as bounded categories of 'strong' and 'weak' (classification and framing).[5] All LCT dimensions operate with *both* boundaries *and* continua; all legitimation codes describe *both* typologies *and* topologies. This combination is embodied by the Cartesian planes on which legitimation codes are plotted, a pictorial shift of significance in developing code theory into LCT. Specialization codes, for example, are mapped by the *specialization plane* of Figure 2.1 (see page 30). The plane combines:

(i) a typology of four principal code modalities (knowledge, knower, élite and relativist codes) – the quadrants generated by modalities of epistemic relations and social relations (ER+/−, SR+/−); and
(ii) a relational topological space – the plane as a coordinate system of potentially infinite positions given by the continua – in which the strengths of relations are relative to those of other practices.

LCT thus embodies a shift to describing continua of relative strengths ('*stronger*' and '*weaker*' epistemic and social relations). One can thus foreground processes of *strengthening* and *weakening* relations through time, supplementing the notation '+/−' (inherited from Bernstein) with '↑/↓'. In addition, not only changes *between* but also changes *within* code modalities (movement across a quadrant of the plane) can be explored. Changes in the strengths of relations may not involve a code shift; for example, relatively strong epistemic relations may be weakened over time but remain relatively strong (ER+↓+): a shift downwards within the top half of Figure 2.1. Specialization thereby combines the strengths of both typologies and topologies.

Second, the model highlights that concepts must capture the 'play of ideology' in the creation, recontextualization and reproduction of knowledge. Against the false dichotomy of positivist absolutism and constructivist relativism dominating educational research (Chapter 1) in which practices are either purely non-arbitrary or merely arbitrary, specialization codes brings together *epistemic relations* to objects of study and *social relations* to subjects (Chapter 2). These concepts do not provide demarcation criteria for what is arbitrary or non-arbitrary – they are, to reiterate, for analysing practices not ontologies. Rather, they conceptualize how actors articulate these relations within their practices. In effect, specialization codes represent different answers to the question of whether legitimacy should be viewed as ontologically or logically necessary (epistemic relations), contingent upon socially and historically contextualized actors or ways of acting (social relations), or configurations of both. They thus explore the degree to which greater or lesser space for the 'play of ideology' is enabled by the nature of knowledge practices themselves.

Last, the model emphasizes the need for concepts capable of analysing not only practices across the three fields but also the dispositions or habituses actors bring to the arena by virtue of past and ongoing experience. Practice is, as Bourdieu argued, the meeting of two evolving histories (1993b: 46), those of the social field and an actor's habitus (or 'coding orientation' in code theory). The organizing principles of fields, actors' practices, and dispositions can all be conceptualized using specialization codes. As well as providing conceptual economy, they thereby enable Bourdieu's 'thinking tools' to be realized as operative relational concepts (Chapter 1) for understanding the practices of actors as strategies in struggles for control of the EPD.

Breaks and continuities in intellectual fields

Exploring fully the implications of the EPD model is beyond the scope of this chapter or, indeed, this book. Here I shall briefly illustrate a key issue raised earlier as necessitating thinking in terms of an epistemic–pedagogic device. I argued that intellectual fields are concerned with not only access to the 'unthinkable' but also how this 'new' knowledge is created, positioned and evaluated. In other words, production fields are concerned with *epistemic logics* which, *inter alia*, articulate the arbitrary and non-arbitrary in providing resources for specialization codes. To illustrate these logics and the effects of differing code settings of the EPD on knowledge-building, I return to the chapter's opening focus to explore breaks and continuities in intellectual fields, specifically: humanities and social sciences; and mathematics.

Talkin' bout a revolution

From the early 1960s notices of births and deaths became widespread across the humanities and social sciences (Maton 2005b). For example, traditional philosophy was said to be 'finished off' and 'over' (Gellner 1964: 66) and economists proclaimed 'Political economy is dead; long live economics!' (Sargent 1964: 144). Revolutions proliferated in, among others, anthropology, psychiatry, history and teaching (Maton 2005b: 213). These were not singular events; philosophy and the arts, for example, were described as undergoing 'permanent revolution' (Gellner 1964), with 'leaps from vanguard to vanguard' soon becoming a 'tradition of the new' (Rosenberg 1962: 23). This 'age of the neophiliacs' (Booker 1969) continued beyond the 1960s. Kuhn (1962) had described 'normal science' as steady intellectual development within an accepted framework and 'revolutionary science' as a sudden leap to a new paradigm of thinking. Within a decade Kuhn's history of natural science had become widely used to characterize change in social science. This is where the chapter began: by the 1970s, revolution was normalized.

In terms of the EPD model, these practices are concerned not simply with distributive logics of social access but also with epistemic logics of how ideas should be selected, recontextualized and evaluated to create new knowledge.[6] Proclaimed 'breaks' have ontological and epistemological implications. First, they often project an *apocalyptic ontology* whereby a fundamental break in the world is proclaimed. Beniger (1986), for example, lists 75 distinct names used to describe new kinds of society between 1950 and 1985, since when many more have appeared. Second, such claims often project an *apocalyptic epistemology*, whereby a fundamental break in understanding the world is proclaimed. In the early 1960s, for example, proponents of revolution typically portrayed their predecessors as epitomizing delusion and error and claimed that, as Gellner (1964: 48) summarized, past thinkers 'have left behind a heritage of theory so confused, yet so ingrained, that it is almost beyond sorting out. Better by far to turn to new areas.' In philosophy, for example, Winch's influential *The Idea of a Social Science* (1958) described all past philosophy as not merely offering wrong answers but asking the wrong questions.

Such expressions of epistemic logics serve as resources for constructing, maintaining and changing code modalities. However, determining which code(s) is a matter for substantive research – the same expression may become resources for different codes in different contexts. In this example, proclaimed 'breaks' aimed at revitalizing knower codes within the field of higher education (see Maton 2005b). By the 1960s the high status of the humanities was perceived by protagonists as under threat from natural science; the resulting 'two cultures' debate can be understood as a struggle between proponents of knower codes and knowledge codes, respectively (see Chapter 4). Claims of revolution formed part of attempts to retain control of the EPD by reasserting knower codes as the basis of legitimacy. Typically, belief in a fundamental break was less a conjecture to be tested than a starting point for legitimate participation in debate. Winch (1958), for example, declared a coup that was *fait accompli*; and as Rosenberg stated, the 'tradition of the new' quickly became 'the accepted tradition, taken for granted and no longer the object of thought' (1970: 15). Rather than the new world/view specializing knowledge claims, knowers required the capacity to see the new world/view at all; the proclaimed change represented the *doxa* of new legitimate knowers. Knowledge practices thereby downplayed epistemic relations and emphasized social relations as the basis of legitimacy, regenerating knower codes.

The EPD model suggests such claims are likely to be contested by actors whose practices are characterized by other codes. However, where they do come to dominate, one effect is to set the present adrift from the past. The form expressing their epistemic logics pronounces: existing ideas are no longer legitimate, new times require new thinking, and revolution not evolution. For this fresh page of intellectual history, the field's past is redundant and only nostradami whose works are proclaimed to foreshadow the change may survive. For actors, to question the break is to be assigned to the other side of the divide and have no access to legitimate knowledge of the post-apocalyptic world/view. Claims of fundamental change thus specialized legitimate understanding to a location in time or social space: temporal schisms specialized the present by legitimating knowers whose gaze was fashioned by the revolutionary break; and contemporaneous standpoints specialized a social category by legitimating knowers whose gaze were shaped by a specific social position. Both forms of knower code thereby problematized communication among members of production fields, resulting in a series of restricted epistemic communities based on segmented approaches or voices (Moore and Maton 2001).[7]

Timeless melody

By way of contrast to proclamations of breaks, consider the following summary of the history of Fermat's Last Theorem (from Hoffman 1998: 183–201). In 1637 in France, Pierre de Fermat was reading *Arithmetica* by Diophantus, a thinker who lived in Alexandria, possibly during the third century AD. In this treatise, Diophantus discussed at length the 'Pythagorean theorem', observing 'there are an infinite number of Pythagorean triplets, whole numbers *x, y* and *z* that solved the equation $x^2 + y^2 = z^2$' (ibid.: 187). Pythagoras lived in the sixth century BC. The Babylonians had known about these triplets a thousand years earlier. Returning to seventeenth-century France, Fermat formulated his famous 'Last Theorem' in response to a problem he derived from Diophantus and declared he had 'a truly marvellous demonstration' that was too big to write in the margin of the *Arithmetica*. Fermat died in 1665 and his marginalia was published by his eldest son, but the 'demonstration' was never found. Over subsequent centuries numerous attempts to solve the theorem were undertaken by scores of mathematicians from countries across the globe, until in 1993 Andrew Wiles, concluding a series of lectures at Cambridge University, 'wrote one last statement on the blackboard and said, softly, "This proves Fermat's Last Theorem. I think I'll stop here."' (ibid.: 198). By the end of the year Wiles admitted to an inconsistency in his proof, but in September 1994, with the help of a colleague, 'the hole was patched' (ibid.: 199) and Fermat's Last Theorem was considered officially resolved.

As above, these practices are primarily concerned with epistemic logics concerning the selection, recontextualization and evaluation of ideas in the creation of new knowledge. However, the form taken by the expressions of these logics differ. Here, the field's past, present and future co-exist: the past as an intellectual resource for the present; the present as potential for the future. What is striking about this story is its sheer scale across time and space: a mathematician in late-twentieth-century England is communicating with a lawyer in seventeenth-century France, and through him with Babylonians from three millennia past. That, unusually for mathematics, Wiles worked on the problem in isolation (Hoffman 1998: 183–184) makes the example more pertinent: despite working alone, he participated in what Collins (2000: 7) described as 'coalitions in the mind'. The example thereby represents an epistemic community extended across time and space, where living members interact with the dead to produce contributions which, when they have died, will be in turn the living concern of future members.

Such expressions of epistemic logics may serve as resources for a number of specialization codes (such as cultivated knower codes; see Chapter 5). In this case they served as resources for the construction of knowledge codes. In similar fashion to claims of new kinds of society, mathematicians can create imaginary worlds; as Ronald Graham explains:

> In so many areas of mathematics it seems natural or appropriate to create your own mathematical world. You have a lot of choices. I want to consider structures that have thus-and-such properties. I want this structure and not that one.
>
> (quoted, Hoffman 1998: 265)

However, mathematicians cannot explore these worlds just as they please. Once a problem is established, its parameters and the criteria of its solution remain relatively constant – epistemic relations are relatively strongly bounded and controlled. These explicit criteria are said to transcend differences in the social and temporal coordinates of actors – social relations are relatively weakly bounded and controlled. In a field dominated by such a code problem-situations may persist over centuries and span the globe, previous work may be built on regardless of context, and answers may be adjudicated and progress judged by anyone sufficiently trained in the specialized procedures. Indeed, trust in their application by specialists enables other mathematicians to declare Fermat's Last Theorem to be solved despite very few understanding the proof (Hoffman 1998: 198). Though mathematics may be segmented according to specialisms and mathematical worlds, this knowledge code thereby enables its epistemic community to extend both temporally and across its range of languages.

Conclusion

The EPD model addresses the chapter's originating questions by: mapping the ground over which actors struggle as an arena comprising at least three fields of specialized activities; accounting for what actors struggle over in terms of the epistemic–pedagogic device; and relating struggles to social fields and actors' practices and dispositions in terms of specialization codes. To illustrate one element of the model, I showed how the practices of intellectual fields are concerned with, *inter alia*, epistemic logics whose form, conceptualized as specialization codes, helps shape their morphologies and capacities for cumulative progress. I also described how the model extends and integrates existing ideas rather than breaking with the past. However, evolutionary intellectual development does not equate to limited progress or lack of ambition. The reason that exploring the implications of the EPD is beyond the scope of this book is that the model offers an organizing framework, an analytic framework, and a generative framework for relating, integrating and suggesting studies of education. As such, it sketches the outlines of an ambitious and progressive research agenda.

First, the EPD model provides an *organizing framework* capable of *relating* diverse studies of education. The model highlights differences between the logics underlying production, recontextualization and reproduction, practices often conflated by existing approaches. However, to use the model does not require researching all three fields: a study of practice within one field can be situated within the arena, relating its focus to other studies, delimiting its findings, and raising questions for further research. Taking the preceding discussion of breaks and continuities as an example, the model can be used to: (i) locate the analysis as exploring practices in production fields, enabling this focus to be compared and contrasted with those of other studies; (ii) delimit its conclusions as not necessarily reflected within the disciplines' recontextualization and reproduction fields; and (iii) raise questions of how these breaks and continuities might be reflected within the curricular and teaching artefacts generated by practices in those fields.

Though I have focused on education, the EPD model is also applicable to other social fields of practice. For example, in a series of innovative papers, J.R. Martin and colleagues analyse specialization codes active in 'youth justice conferences' – meetings between young offenders, victims, legal officials and police officers – to reveal the nature of the ideal offender (a legal analogue of the ideal knower; Chapter 5) and its relations to different strategies of young people (Martin 2009; Martin *et al.* 2012). Drawing on the model, these studies can be described as exploring practices in a reproduction field of the legal arena, raising questions of the creation of ideas of 'restorative justice' and their recontextualization into this policy in its production and recontextualization fields.

Second, the EPD model provides an *analytic framework* capable of *integrating* diverse studies of education. By theorizing practices as struggles over the device that take different forms according to the logics of the arena's fields, the model neither homogenizes the array of activities within education nor fragments its varied contexts. Moreover, specialization codes can be used to conceptualize practices from all fields, as shown by empirical studies of research (Hood 2010, 2011), curriculum and educational policy (Maton 2004; Howard and Maton 2011; Shay 2011), and teaching and learning (Doherty 2008; Martin *et al.* 2010; Chen *et al.* 2011). Such flexibility thereby allows studies of different topics, issues and practices to speak to one another. Moreover, this is not confined to education: studies using specialization codes are exploring museums (Carvalho 2010), freemasonry (Poulet 2010), legal practices (Martin 2009; Martin *et al.* 2012) and other fields. By providing a basis for analyses of different social fields of practice, the model thereby enables the possibility of an integrated account of social domination. Analysing the codes required to succeed in different social fields (the legal system, education, etc.) can reveal how seemingly different practices (youth justice conferencing, pedagogy, etc.) represent the same organizing principles refracted into the specific activities of those fields, and the degrees to which these match the dispositions of different social groups.

Third, the EPD model offers a *generative framework* capable of *suggesting* diverse studies of education. The model of the arena raises questions of the basis of knowledge practices in intellectual fields, of how that knowledge is selected, rearranged and pedagogized in recontextualization fields, and how the resulting educational knowledge is recontextualized into reproduction fields. This highlights issues requiring further study, such as suggesting research into how breaks and continuities in social science and mathematics are recontextualized in curriculum and reproduced in pedagogic practice. Further, the model is theoretically generative. A defining feature of LCT is foreseeing its own repeated reformulation – the theory is designed to evolve. Accordingly, the EPD is itself part of a hypothesized generative principle, the *Legitimation Device*, whose dimensions are yet to be fully explored. To adapt a passage from Bernstein (1990: 190), any sociology of education and knowledge should have a theory of the Legitimation Device. Indeed, such a theory provides its necessary foundation and fundamental theoretical object. However, this is not to identify an end to enquiry: the Device may be analytically inexhaustible. Bernstein conceptualized 'the pedagogic device'; that model has been extended by the 'epistemic–pedagogic device'; and Chapter 7 will describe an 'epistemic–semantic–pedagogic device'. Other existing dimensions (Autonomy, Density, and Temporality) delineate further aspects of the Device, as will future dimensions of LCT, where each provides code concepts for analysing its aspect of the Device in empirical research. In turn, substantive studies using these codes and devices reveal the yet-to-be-theorized, requiring further conceptual development.

Last, the EPD model offers the basis for a genuinely critical research agenda. By theorizing how actors struggle to control the device to ensure their coding orientations are reflected in high-status practices, it provides a means for revealing and contesting the mechanisms by which social groups exert symbolic control through education. Lacking such a theorization of devices, 'critical' theories of education too often blame shadowy forces operating through vague processes. Though watchwords of 'domination', 'resistance' and 'struggle' feature in such accounts, the means of symbolic control lies beyond their analytical reach: how these practices come to be realized within education and how they relate to wider relations of power remain unclear. More damagingly, lacking concepts for analysing the organizing principles of practices and dispositions, such approaches may unwittingly proclaim the virtues of practices that underpin social domination. Student-centred learning, for example, has been widely portrayed as intrinsically progressive (see Chapter 8). However, for several decades empirical studies by code sociologists and systemic functional linguists have been revealing that these pedagogies match the dispositions of cultural-middle-class students and clash with those of working-class students (e.g. Holland 1981; Williams 2001; Hasan 2009). Additionally, pedagogic interventions have been attempting to redistribute this cultural capital by enabling students from a wider range of social backgrounds to recognize and realize what is required to succeed (e.g. Morais and Neves 2001; Rose and Martin 2012). These endeavours to reveal and contest control of the EPD by the cultural middle class have been subjected to vehement opposition (Martin 2012a), often by actors wishing to defend the interests of dominated social groups but whose stances not only unintentionally underpin their domination but also mask that complicity. For example, constructivism obscures relations between its stances and cultural-middle-class dispositions by individualizing and psychologizing educational practices across the three fields of the arena. Such ironies highlight how wishful thinking and commitment are not enough for genuinely critical practice – one also needs analytic tools and consequence. In short, a theory critical in reality and not only rhetoric requires a theorization of the Legitimation Device.

The theorization of the Device begun here is enabled by its foundation frameworks, and above all by Bernstein's pioneering model of the 'pedagogic device'. It does not propose a revolutionary break but rather works *within* code theory to modestly extend and refine a key element of the framework; it is not possible without Bernstein's approach, to which it offers a small but steady advance. It thus works in an 'essential tension' (Kuhn 1968) with established ideas. This way of working is not particularly fashionable. In sociology 'revolution' has become associated with notions of 'great leaps forward', critical intent and radical credentials. In reality, however, claims of 'revolution' may be conservative and lead to fragmentation, stagnation and uncritical acceptance of the status quo. However, as the EPD model demonstrates, sociology is not doomed to an eternal return of proclaimed 'breaks'. The EPD not only offers an organizing, analytic and generative framework, it also embodies a form of theorizing that moves beyond normalizing pseudo-revolution and points towards the possibility of a revolutionary period of normal and critical social science.

Notes

1 To avoid confusion between the uses of 'field' by Bourdieu and Bernstein I shall denote which 'field' I am referring to and denote Bourdieu's notion (which is analogous to Bernstein's 'arena') by 'social field'.

2 The paper first calling for theorization of what we initially called an 'epistemic device' was titled 'Founding the sociology of knowledge' (Moore and Maton 2001). However, as Scott (2010) illustrates by criticizing the paper for offering little to ontology, even clearly labelled sociology can be subjected to ontological reductionism.

3 For philosophers alert to the 'epistemic fallacy', I should emphasize that 'epistemic–pedagogic device' and 'epistemic logics' are *technical concepts* from *sociology* and not philosophical claims concerning ontology and epistemology or being and knowing. For sociologists who believe 'epistemic logics' suggests intellectual production is devoid of sociological issues, I suggest reading lessons.

4 Chapter 9 distinguishes two sub-dimensions of epistemic relations, enabling classic readings to be more precisely described as exploring 'discursive relations'.

5 Bernstein was aware of degrees of difference within codes. However, awareness is one thing and concepts enacting that awareness are another. Because they conceptualize organizing principles, 'classification' and 'framing' can be re-presented as describing continua of strengths. Other concepts (e.g. knowledge structures, singulars/regions, etc.) cannot be redescribed in this way

because their organizing principles first require elucidation (cf. Bernstein 2000: 124).

6 The terms 'recontextualization' and 'evaluation' can be used to describe practices within any field; it is as part of compound nouns with 'logics' or 'fields' that their meanings become more specific.

7 This is not portraying knower codes as always detrimental to progress – Chapters 5, 6 and 9 explore how knower codes underpin cumulative knowledge-building and Chapter 9 explores how knowledge codes may limit such development. This is also not suggesting claims to 'breaks' are accurate: new knowledge is created from antecedent knowledge, but the way that relationship is construed has effects.

4 Knowledge–knower structures

What's at stake in the 'two cultures' debate, why school Music is unpopular, and what unites such diverse issues

For every knowledge structure there is also a knower structure.

Introduction

Why bother reading this chapter? On what grounds do the ideas presented here offer insight? On what basis am I proclaiming myself a 'sociologist'? To such questions different approaches yield different kinds of answers. As discussed in Chapter 1, most educational research suffers from knowledge-blindness and sociological studies typically explore 'relations to' rather than 'relations within' knowledge. Their answer to such questions would be that claims to epistemic power mask claims to social power. Of these kinds of accounts, Bourdieu's 'field theory' avoids crude social reductionism by revealing the effects of the relatively autonomous social fields of practice that mediate relations between practices and wider social structures. Nonetheless, field theory remains focused on 'relations to' practices, viewing them as the epiphenomena of struggles over status and resources within fields, such that claims to knowledge are understood as misrecognized social power. In contrast, Bhaskar's critical realism and Popper's critical rationalism emphasize that knowledge claims possess differing degrees of explanatory power. Moreover, Bernstein's 'code theory' highlights the role played by the structuring of knowledge itself in shaping both that explanatory power and the play of positions within fields. Taken together, these approaches indicate that both epistemic and social forms of power are important to achievement, status and identity. Chapters 2 and 3 outlined the beginnings of an explanatory framework for integrating these ideas around the notion of 'legitimation'. This chapter continues that process by building on Bernstein's analysis of intellectual fields as 'knowledge structures' (2000: 155–174).

The concept of 'knowledge structures' is a landmark in Bernstein's code theory. A trajectory that Bernstein (2000: 155) highlighted through his work begins from the analysis of pedagogic practices in educational fields in terms of 'classification' and 'framing' (1977), through an account of the construction of educational knowledge in terms of the 'pedagogic device' (1990), to the study of intellectual fields from which this knowledge is selected and pedagogized in terms of 'knowledge structures' (2000). These concepts show how the forms taken by knowledge have significance for everything from societal structure, through institutional organization, to individual identity and consciousness. Chapters 2 and 3 can be understood as mirroring the conceptual development resulting from this trajectory, with the aim of extending its concepts to embrace more phenomena with greater fidelity and economy. Chapter 2 shows that 'classification' and 'framing' can be applied not only to knowledge (*epistemic relations*) but also to knowers (*social relations*), and how these can be integrated as *specialization codes*. Chapter 3 reveals the 'pedagogic device' to be part of a more complex generative mechanism underlying social fields – the *Legitimation Device* – of which one aspect, the *epistemic–pedagogic device*, was explored. This chapter focuses on the third conceptual landmark in code theory identified by Bernstein: 'knowledge structures'.

Specifically, the chapter addresses two questions raised by Bernstein's concepts. First, the concepts of 'knowledge structures' provide dichotomous types for describing differences between intellectual fields but leave open the question of what principles underlie fields with different knowledge structures. Bernstein (2000: 123–124) emphasized the need to conceptualize the organizing principles underlying practices to overcome the generative weakness of such dichotomous types. He also insisted that code theory was an evolving framework: 'a paper is often not terminal but a beginning, an opening to an enlarged problematic and an initial development of the language of its articulation and research' (Bernstein 1990: 6). The concepts of 'knowledge structures' were just such an opening; the language of their articulation and research requires development.

Second, the inherited framework offered different concepts for analysing intellectual fields of production ('knowledge structures') and educational fields of recontextualization and reproduction ('classification' and 'framing') without systematically explicating their relations. This raises the question of how these fields can be analysed within the same conceptual framework. An integrated account of education requires concepts applicable to the whole arena created by the epistemic–pedagogic device (Chapter 3). For example, exploring the degrees to which curriculum, pedagogy and evaluation in a subject area are arbitrary reflections of social power or based on non-arbitrary ontological and epistemological principles requires analysing knowledge practices across three fields, from intellectual creation in production fields through pedagogization in recontextualization fields to pedagogic enactment in reproduction fields. This, in turn, requires concepts applicable across these different contexts.

To address these questions I shall propose that social fields of practice comprise not just 'knowledge structures' but also 'knower structures', and that conceiving fields as *knowledge–knower structures* provides greater understanding of how practices specialize identity, consciousness and relations. I elaborate this argument in two main stages. I begin by considering intellectual fields, focusing on the example of the famous 'two cultures' debate. The characterizations of science and the humanities by participants in the debate are analysed in terms of not only knowledge structures but also knower structures, enabling a fuller, less binary typological account of fields. The organizing principles of these knowledge–knower structures are then conceptualized using specialization codes to offer a topological account that overcomes the limitations of typologies. Second, I briefly illustrate how these concepts are not confined to intellectual fields but, rather, can also be used to examine educational fields, drawing on substantive studies addressing the marginalized position of Music in the English school curriculum. I conclude by considering how knower structures and specialization codes reveal the organizing principles of fields, bring together analyses of intellectual and educational practices, and thereby contribute towards a fuller and more integrated approach to education.

Knowledge–knower structures in intellectual fields

The notion of knowledge–knower structures can be approached by considering the well-known 'two cultures' debate. This was sparked by C.P. Snow's famous lecture of 1959 in which he claimed the intellectual life of Western society was being split into 'two polar groups' that 'had almost ceased to communicate at all', with 'between the two a gulf of mutual incomprehension – sometimes … hostility and dislike, but most of all lack of understanding.' (1959: 3, 2, 4). Snow's concern lay beyond the academy, with the influence on society of technology and modernist writers. However, his description of 'two cultures' quickly became associated in public debate with science and the humanities and their antinomy constructed as a struggle within higher education. The resulting 'two cultures' debate was ferocious, bitter, spread widely, and remains a source of contention. Why Snow's lecture sparked such depth of feeling becomes clearer when one considers the contrasting fortunes science and the humanities were said to be enjoying.

On the one hand, what Snow termed 'scientific culture' was commonly portrayed as enjoying a meteoric rise in stature. As one commentator tartly expressed: 'You cannot open a newspaper, let alone the 'quality' journals, without the importance of science and technology being trumpeted at you from the headlines' (Morris 1959: 374). Feted by and enjoying massive funding from industry and the state, revered by the media and worshipped by the public, by the late 1950s scientists were said to be enjoying unprecedented prestige. In contrast, the humanities were portrayed by proponents as embattled, insecure and in decline. For example, an influential (though now largely forgotten) collection of essays entitled *Crisis in the Humanities* (Plumb 1964a) included accounts of proclaimed crises within Classics, history, philosophy, Divinity, literary education, sociology, the fine arts, and economics, as well as the humanities in schools. All these subjects were described as unwanted by higher ability students, considered irrelevant to a modern economy by industrialists, increasingly excluded from the corridors of power by politicians, no longer considered the repository of culture, and publicly ridiculed as offering little genuine knowledge. One historian, for example, claimed that 90 per cent of his colleagues believed their subject to be 'meaningless in any ultimate sense' (Plumb 1964b: 25).

According to participants, the disciplinary map was thereby undergoing a seismic shift of power between humanist and scientific cultures in their long-standing struggles for status and resources. Two questions this raises are: what was the basis of their differences, and why was this shift of power occurring? A common contemporary description of their differences held that scientists and humanist intellectuals 'speak different languages' (Editorial, *The Listener*, September 3, 1959: 344). A code theory approach suggests focusing instead on the *organizing principles* underlying their languages. I shall begin by describing the two cultures in terms of knowledge structures and knower structures, before bringing these together to show how the notion of 'knowledge–knower structures' can be analysed using 'specialization codes' to shed light on the bases of intellectual fields.

Knowledge structures

Analysing the form taken by knowledge in intellectual fields, Bernstein (1996, 2000) distinguished, first, between 'horizontal discourse' (everyday or common-sense knowledge) and 'vertical discourse' (scholarly or professional knowledge), and, second, within 'vertical discourse' between 'horizontal knowledge structures' and 'hierarchical knowledge structures'. These concepts of 'knowledge structures' can capture one aspect of the way the 'two cultures' were portrayed in the debate. Humanist culture was described by proponents as riven by competing claims for status between strongly bounded disciplines. Commentators argued that while Classics had previously served as the basis of a 'common culture' or 'unifying force' (Lee 1955), its decline had fragmented a single, organic culture into a series of rival subcultures, with little dialogue among these disciplines and no means of adjudicating between their competing claims to offer a new unifying centre. Humanist culture thereby resembled what Bernstein defined as a 'horizontal knowledge structure':

> a series of specialised languages each with its own specialised modes of interrogation and specialised criteria ... with non-comparable principles of description based on different, often opposed, assumptions.
>
> (Bernstein 1996: 172–173)

This knowledge structure comprises a series of segmented, strongly bounded languages which, developing Bernstein (2000: 161), can be visually represented as:

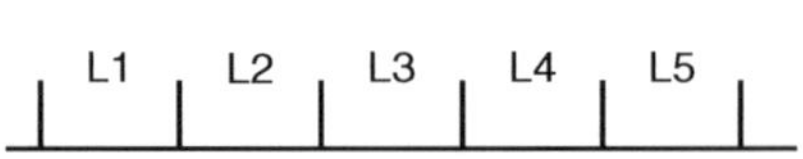

Bernstein further distinguished between horizontal knowledge structures with 'strong grammars', 'whose languages have an explicit conceptual syntax capable of *relatively* precise empirical descriptions and/or of generating formal modelling of empirical relations' (2000: 163; original emphasis), such as Mathematics, Linguistics and Economics, and those where these powers are weaker, such as Anthropology, Cultural Studies and Sociology. Humanist culture, as characterized by proponents, possessed a 'weak grammar': its objects of and procedures for study were defined in ethereal, nebulous, even mystical terms, most famously and widely expressed, following Matthew Arnold (1869), as immersion in the best that has been known and thought in the world.

In contrast to humanist culture, proponents claimed scientific culture comprised an organic community; scientists were said to share 'common attitudes, common standards and patterns of behaviour, common approaches and assumptions' (Snow 1959: 9). Unlike the pluralized humanities, science was often referred to in the singular and portrayed as integrated and whole. Though scientists were proliferating new knowledge and creating sub-disciplinary specialisms at a prolific rate, they were said to be able to integrate this fast-growing knowledge. Scientific culture thereby resembled what Bernstein described as a 'hierarchical knowledge structure': 'an explicit, coherent, systematically principled and hierarchical organisation of knowledge' which develops through the integration of knowledge at lower levels and across an expanding range of phenomena (1996: 172–173). This he visualized as a triangle where the tip represents the number of axioms or propositions and the base represents the range of empirical phenomena covered by the theories based on those axioms:

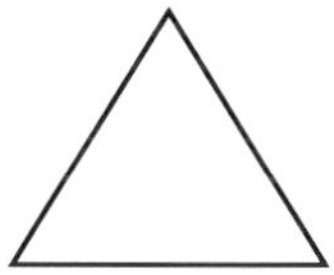

Knower structures

Bernstein's concepts enable the form taken by the knowledge structures characterizing the 'two cultures' to be described. However, this is only part of the picture. To reach an understanding of their underlying principles, first we need to also consider their *knower structures*. Doing so offers a different perspective on the 'two cultures'.

I described above how the humanities were portrayed by practitioners as having previously comprised a 'common culture' centred on the Classics. However, it was not Classics as principles or procedures that was said to have integrated the humanities into a culture but rather the dispositions or (adopting Bourdieu) 'habitus' that a classical education was thought to guarantee. The ideal humanist intellectual was a gentleman amateur who pursued (usually) his studies 'for the love of it', viewing them as secondary to a clerisy role of cultivating the cultured sensibility of the 'English gentleman' among students selected to fit into the established character of the university (Maton

2004, 2005b). The humanities were said to humanize; underpinning such claims was an image of what it meant to be human and humane – the sensibilities, character and personal attributes of an ideal knower. The basis of specialization in humanist culture was thus not explicit knowledge (indeed, disciplinary specialization was strongly devalorized in favour of the all-round 'generalist') but the dispositions of an ideal knower, for which a classical education served as shorthand. This cultural focus was, moreover, underpinned by a social trajectory. To be educated in the Classics was (in the main) to have enjoyed a particular social and educational background, typically male, higher social class, private school and 'Oxbridge'.

In other words, humanist culture can be described as exhibiting what I shall term a ***hierarchical knower structure***: a systematically principled and hierarchical organization of knowers based on the construction of an ideal knower and which develops through the integration of new knowers at lower levels and across an expanding range of different dispositions. As illustrated by Table 4.1, this can be portrayed as a triangle of knowers with, in the case of humanist culture, the ideal of the 'English gentleman' at its pinnacle. (There may be more than one idealized knower and triangle of knowers; see Chapter 5.) The basis of the principles of selection, recontextualization and evaluation of humanist culture and thus its ruler (in both senses of measuring legitimacy and dominating the field) was an idealized knower.

Analogously to Bernstein's strong and weak 'grammars', we can here further distinguish between hierarchical knower structures with stronger 'knower-grammars', where the (biological and/or social) categories of ideal knowers are articulated relatively explicitly (such as standpoint theories), and those with weaker 'knower-grammars', where the basis of being the right kind of knower is less strongly defined, such as an emphasis on enjoying a particular education. (I return to elaborate this notion in Chapter 5.)

Table 4.1 The 'two cultures' as knowledge structures and knower structures

	Humanist culture	*Scientific culture*
Knowledge structures	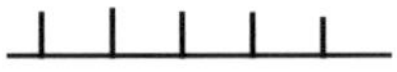 horizontal	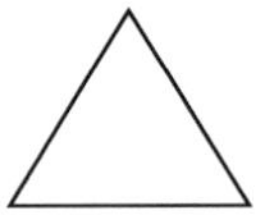 hierarchical
Knower structures	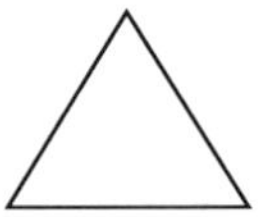 hierarchical	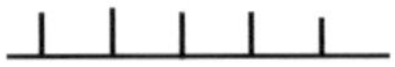 horizontal

In terms of knowers, scientific culture was portrayed differently. Where the humanist intellectual's 'ability is a personal matter, which on the whole he does not owe to his advanced training', scientific knowledge was widely said to be 'fairly independent of the personal merits of its possessor' (Gellner 1964: 75–76). Snow, for example, compared the class-bound basis of humanist culture to the democratic and meritocratic nature of scientific culture. He claimed science was blind to colour, race, creed; it cut 'across other mental patterns, such as those of religion or politics or class' (Snow 1959: 9). In short, the basis of specialization in science was knowledge of scientific principles and procedures, regardless of the biological or social backgrounds of knowers. Science was thus portrayed as possessing what I shall term a *horizontal knower structure*: a series of strongly bounded knowers, each with specialized modes of being, thinking, feeling and acting, with non-comparable habituses (or embodied dispositions) based on different trajectories and experiences. In terms of their dispositions, scientists were portrayed as a series of segmented knowers (Table 4.1), each strongly bounded from one another in terms of their (non-scientific) 'gaze' and capable of being based on very different, even opposed, assumptions. In short, science was portrayed in the 'two cultures' debate as possessing not only a hierarchical knowledge structure but also a horizontal knower structure, and the humanities were characterized as both a horizontal knowledge structure and a hierarchical knower structure.

Knowledge–knower structures

By conceptualizing 'knowledge structures', Bernstein enables us to overcome knowledge-blindness. However, focusing only on 'knowledge structures' would leave us blinded to anything but knowledge, offering only a partial view. It would also leave the approach vulnerable to accusations of idealizing intellectual fields with hierarchical knowledge structures and projecting a deficit model of those with horizontal knowledge structures. The notion of 'knower structures' overcomes these issues, through cumulatively developing the framework rather than horizontally accumulating another approach. Crucially, it also highlights something that is unclear from exploring knowledge structures alone: as Table 4.1 illustrates, it is not only knowledge structures that may embody a hierarchy. The location of the 'hierarchical' in a social field of practice is the basis of its recontextualizing principles. Fields with hierarchical *knower structures* thereby also possess systematic principles for selecting and arranging actors and discourses into a hierarchy. Thus, even where fields have a horizontal knowledge structure, they may have a hierarchical knower structure. That is to say, in social fields of practice actors and discourses are judged on the basis of principles that may emanate from the knowledge structure, the knower structure or, as I shall discuss, both or neither. In the case of the 'two cultures', the portraits of proponents located these principles in the knowledge structure for science and in the knower structure for humanities. Thus, differences among fields are less about *whether* they are hierarchical or not and more about *where* their hierarchizing principle lies.

For every knowledge structure there is also a knower structure, so to focus solely on knowledge structures is to see only one dimension of fields. The analysis thus far provides the basis for a fuller typology of intellectual fields: we can identify combinations of these knowledge structures and knower structures (see Figure 5.1 on page 93). Viewing the knowledge practices of intellectual fields as comprising ***knowledge–knower structures*** that specialize actors and discourses in different ways thereby provides a means of conceptualizing differences among intellectual fields. However, the resultant typology, though more refined than the inherited binary model of knowledge structures, is still only a first step. It remains necessary to analyse the principles underlying these fields. This can be achieved by using *specialization codes of legitimation* (Chapters 2–3).

Actors and discourses are not only positioned in both a structure of knowledge and a structure of knowers but also establish different forms of relations to these two structures. One can thereby analytically distinguish between *epistemic relations* (ER) to knowledge structures and *social relations* (SR) to knower structures. Each of these relations can exhibit relatively stronger (+) or weaker (–) classification and framing. As elaborated in Chapters 2 and 3, varying their strengths for each relation independently generates four principal *specialization codes*: ER+/–, SR+/–. In other words, practices may emphasize the knowledge structure, the knower structure, both or neither as the basis of distinctiveness, authority and status. These specialization codes represent different readings of the epistemic–pedagogic device, the means whereby intellectual and educational fields are maintained, reproduced, transformed and changed (Chapter 3). Whoever controls the epistemic–pedagogic device possesses the means to set the shape of the field in their favour, making the legitimation codes (including specialization codes) that characterize their own practices the basis of status and achievement in the field. This brief and somewhat formal definition can be fleshed out by considering the different ways in which the 'two cultures' established relations to their knowledge–knower structures.

Specialization codes

Perhaps the most controversial claim Snow made in his lecture was that science was the basis of a true 'common culture': 'the scientific culture really is a culture ... Without thinking about it, they respond alike. That is what a culture means' (1959: 9, 10). According to participants in the debate, the basis of this culture was scientists' 'sense of loyalty to an abstraction called "knowledge"' (Mackerness 1960: 15), commitment to 'truth' and allegiance to their discipline, which specialized their identity and claims to insight, regardless of their social backgrounds or personal attributes (Maton 2005b). In other words, epistemic relations to its knowledge structure were relatively strongly classified and framed (ER+), and social relations to its knower structure were relatively weakly classified and framed (SR–): a ***knowledge code***.

In portrayals of humanist culture, the 'abstraction called "knowledge"' mattered a lot less. Possession of specialized principles and procedures for providing knowledge into determinate objects of study was viewed as relatively unimportant in defining identity and achievement. Epistemic relations to the knowledge structure of the humanities were thus relatively weakly classified and framed (ER–). Instead, the basis of specialization was possessing the right kind of dispositions or character – one had to be the right kind of knower. In other words, the humanities were said to strongly classify and frame legitimate knowers (SR+). For the humanities, stronger social relations to its knower structure were the key to legitimacy within the field: a ***knower code***. Comparing the 'two cultures' reveals it is that which is hierarchical (triangles in Table 4.1) that strongly classifies and frames actors and discourses within each intellectual field (in italics in Table 4.2): epistemic relations to the knowledge structure for scientific culture; and social relations to the knower structure for humanist culture.

Having described the 'two cultures' in terms of their knowledge structures and knower structures and analysed the role they play in specializing legitimacy and identity in terms of specialization codes, we can now return to the questions of differences between the 'two cultures' and of reasons for the shift of power between them. First, the debate can be redescribed as a struggle for control of the epistemic–pedagogic device between intellectual fields characterized by contrasting specialization codes. These different codes shape the kinds of resources actors bring to the struggle. This is clearly illustrated by its founding and most prominent protagonists, C.P. Snow and F.R. Leavis. Snow repeatedly emphasized:

> On these issues our personalities mean nothing: but the issues themselves mean a great deal ... The important thing is to take the personalities, so far as we are able, out of the discussion.
>
> (Snow 1964: 56, 59)

In contrast, Leavis was concerned with Snow as a legitimate knower: 'It is not any challenge he thinks of himself as uttering, but the challenge he *is*, that demands our attention' (1962: 10–11; original emphasis).

For humanists, as Leavis put it, a 'judgement is personal or it is nothing; you cannot take over someone else's' (1962: 28). This represents a struggle between 'what is known about and how' (knowledge code) and 'who you are' (knower code) as the basis of status and identity – a *code clash* between different measures of achievement or 'rules of the game'.

Table 4.2 Specialization codes in the 'two cultures' debate

	Humanist culture	*Scientific culture*
Epistemic relations	–C, –F	*+C, +F*
Social relations	*+C, +F*	–C, –F
Specialization code	knower code (ER–, SR+)	knowledge code (ER+, SR–)

Given this code clash it is little wonder that between the 'two cultures' was said to lie, as Snow (1959: 3) put it, 'a gulf of mutual incomprehension'. Leavis could be speaking for both sides of the debate when he exclaimed: 'He doesn't know what he means, and doesn't know he doesn't know' (1962: 10). Moreover, the rise of science and proclaimed crisis in the humanities were intimately interrelated: rising status for science threatened to change the basis of the distribution of resources and status within the field and relegate humanists to second-class citizens. If scientists controlled the epistemic–pedagogic device, then the field would tilt in their favour by making a knowledge code the basis of achievement.

Second, the difference in codes also suggests why this shift in power seemed imminent. One reason lies in the different relationships these codes establish between their knowledge formations and everyday knowledge or what Bernstein termed 'horizontal discourse'. As discussed above, science was portrayed as specialized by its knowledge rather than its knowers: what they were talking about and how was said to be important, while who was speaking was deemed less significant. The mathematization of science from the seventeenth century onwards meant this knowledge had become progressively different to commonsense understanding, making ***discursive distinction*** from the contents and form of everyday knowledge the basis of the specialization of science. The scientist B.C. Brookes, for example, claimed 'it will never be possible' to translate between the two and that 'the learning of science is the learning of a *first*, not a foreign, language' that needed 'lengthy and ruthless indoctrination' (1959a: 502–521, 1959b: 783–784; original emphasis). Measured in terms of its knowledge code, science was thereby becoming evermore specialized in relation to everyday knowledge or 'horizontal discourse'.

In contrast, the knower code of the humanities made ***dispositional distinction*** the basis of status; that is, distinction between the dispositions of humanist knowers and the laity. In these terms the status of academic humanists was being undermined on two fronts. First, expansion was threatening to bring a wider range of knowers into higher education, presenting challenges to its hierarchical knower structure under social conditions where belief in the integrating knower was waning. By the 1960s the idea of an 'English gentleman' was viewed as outdated in what was portrayed as an increasingly 'meritocratic' society (Maton 2005b). In other words, dispositional distinction was under threat. Second, when judged by the discursive distinction of science's knowledge code, the humanities were becoming less special. The extension of literacy under educational expansion was giving birth to 'the articulate society' where everyone felt entitled to speak and in which the 'clerk is a nobody not merely because he is not a scientist, but also because in the developed societies *everyone* is now a clerk' (Gellner 1964: 78; original emphasis). According to proponents, the humanities did not involve learning specialized principles or procedures, there 'is no enormous discontinuity, a yawning gap, bridgeable only by prolonged training', instead one could pick up a discipline 'simply by soaking in the ambience' (Gellner 1964: 70). Humanists were thereby vulnerable to being viewed as speaking little more than a jargon-ridden form of everyday language. In short, the double threat facing humanist culture was the entry of new knowers into a field of higher education in which knowledge codes were on the ascendancy.

To recap, thus far I have been addressing the first question raised at the outset of this chapter: how to conceptualize principles underlying intellectual fields. Alongside Bernstein's 'knowledge structures' I introduced the notion of 'knower structures' to more fully typologize fields. I argued that analysing these knowledge–knower structures in terms of *specialization codes* provides a means of moving beyond dichotomous types by conceptualizing their underlying principles. I also illustrated the kinds of insights these concepts provide into the forms taken by intellectual fields, introducing the notions of 'code clash', 'discursive distinction' and 'dispositional distinction' to help explain features of the 'two cultures' debate. The second question asked how analyses of fields of production, recontextualization and reproduction can be integrated. The framework inherited from Bernstein conceptualized curricular and pedagogic practices in terms of 'classification' and 'framing' and intellectual fields in terms of 'knowledge structures'. I shall now argue that both sets of concepts are extended and integrated within specialization codes, enabling analyses of the three fields underpinned by the epistemic–pedagogic device to be brought within a unified framework. To do so I now turn to consider educational fields of recontextualization and reproduction.

Knowledge–knower structures in educational fields

Analysing curriculum, pedagogy and evaluation, Bernstein (1977) outlined two 'educational knowledge codes': a 'collection code' of stronger classification and framing (+C, +F); and an 'integrated code' of weaker classification and framing (–C, –F). These codes, he argued, shape educational identity and consciousness in different ways. A collection code emphasizes educational knowledge, producing what he called a 'clear-cut and bounded' educational identity based on one's academic subject (ibid.: 95). Specialization is thus based on the possession of knowledge: it 'makes of educational knowledge something not ordinary or mundane, but something esoteric, which gives a special significance to those who possess it' (ibid.: 99). In contrast, under an integrated code the role of educational knowledge is weakened and one's educational identity is less certain. Where the concepts of 'knowledge structures' explored intellectual fields, these concepts of 'educational knowledge codes' addressed educational fields. However, in both cases Bernstein focused exclusively on how formations of knowledge specialize actors and practices.

As discussed in Chapter 3, the classic use of 'classification' and 'framing' (which give rise to collection and integrated codes) can be understood as conceptualizing *epistemic relations* to educational knowledge structures. In other words, collection codes (+C, +F) can be redescribed (and condensed) as expressing ER+ and integrated codes (–C, –F) as expressing ER–. To reprise the argument of this chapter: for every educational knowledge structure there is also an educational knower structure. Put another way, practices comprise not only the epistemic relations highlighted by classic applications of code theory but also social relations. Thus, in addition to the above, we can also code the role in specialization of *social relations* to *educational knower structures.*

The strength of social relations depends on the particular empirical case being examined, but, for simplicity of illustration, one can say it is likely (and studies using code theory suggest) that under collection codes the dispositions of knowers play a lesser role (–C, –F). When emphasizing the possession and transmission of their subject knowledge as the basis of professional identity and practice, teachers may also downplay the significance of their (and their students') dispositions. In contrast, under integrated codes there is more space for knowers' dispositions to play a greater role in identity and consciousness (+C, +F); for example, more emphasis may be given to the capacity to develop the dispositions of the 'whole child'. These classification and framing strengths, which invert those usually associated with Bernstein's concepts of collection and integrated codes, refer to *social relations* to educational knower structures (in these cases, SR– and SR+). Bringing the above together to consider *educational knowledge–knower structures*, the two main modalities identified by Bernstein, collection and integrated codes, can now be more fully described as knowledge codes (ER+, SR–) and knower codes (ER–, SR+), respectively.

In other words, the concepts developed by Bernstein to analyse educational fields can be extended to embrace relations to educational knower structures, and then redescribed in a way that enables their integration with analyses of intellectual fields. Put simply, both intellectual and educational fields can be analysed using specialization codes. This enables a more integrated framework. It also brings into the light forms of knowledge practices not visible using the inherited framework. Thus far I have focused on examples where the strengths of epistemic relations and social relations are inverted. However, as outlined in Chapter 2, the strengths of these two relations may vary independently of each other, generating four principal specialization codes within a topological space, as represented by Figure 2.1 in Chapter 2 (p.30). Of these, I have discussed examples of:

- *knowledge codes* (ER+, SR–), where possession of specialist knowledge of specific objects of study is emphasized as the basis of achievement; and
- *knower codes* (ER–, SR+), where attributes of knowers are emphasized, whether described as innate or natural (such as notions of genius), inculcated (such as an artistic or literary sensibility cultivated through prolonged immersion in great works) or resulting from the knower's social position (such as standpoint theory).

In addition one can also highlight two further specialization codes that conceptualize phenomena obscured by the inherited framework:

- *élite codes* (ER+, SR+), where legitimacy is based not only on possessing specialist knowledge but also being the right kind of knower; and
- *relativist codes* (ER–, SR–), where legitimacy is ostensibly determined by neither specialist knowledge nor knower attributes.

I shall return to discuss relativist codes in Chapter 5. Elite codes in intellectual fields are exemplified by science during the early Enlightenment period; as feminist historical scholarship shows, it was not enough to follow 'scientific' procedures to be considered a legitimate scientist, one also had to be a 'gentleman'. I discuss an élite code in educational fields, below.

These codes describes the 'rules of the game'; in the four codes what matters is 'what you know about and how' (knowledge codes), 'the kind of knower you are' (knower codes), both (élite codes) or neither (relativist codes). As outlined in Chapter 3, dominant codes may not be transparent, universal or uncontested: not everyone may recognize and/or be able to realize what is required and there may be more than one code present, with struggles over which is dominant. Using specialization codes one can thus describe degrees of ***code clash*** and ***code match***, such as between: protagonists in debates (such as between the 'two cultures', above); learners' dispositions and educational contexts (Chen *et al.* 2011); different approaches within an intellectual field (Carvalho *et al.* 2009); or the aims of educational policies and ways of working of subject areas (Howard and Maton 2011). The dominant code may also change, such as between subject areas, classrooms and stages of a curriculum. These ***code shifts*** effectively change the 'rules of the game'.

Having used these concepts to analyse intellectual fields, the question remains of their capacity for examining educational fields and thereby enabling a fuller analysis of the arena created by the epistemic–pedagogic device. To illustrate their usefulness I shall briefly discuss substantive research addressing the position of Music in the English school curriculum.

School Music: An élite code qualification

At the time of the research I shall discuss (the early-mid 2000s), the English school system comprises a number of Key Stages (henceforth 'KS') at which children are tested:

- KS1: school years 1–2 (ages 5–7)
- KS2: years 3–6 (ages 7–11)
- KS3: years 7–9 (ages 11–14)
- KS4: years 10–11 (ages 14–16)

Students study a compulsory curriculum of ten academic subjects for KS1–3. At this point they can choose, from a wider range of available subjects, which ones they wish to study for GCSE qualifications (comprising a combination of coursework and examination) which are completed by the end of year 11. Music is popular among students up to the end of KS3 (Lamont *et al.* 2003), but there is very low uptake for GCSE qualifications: during the early 2000s approximately 8 per cent of students chose to take GCSE Music, compared to 20 per cent for physical education, 36 per cent for art, and higher for traditional subjects such as History. Though often noted by commentators and policymakers, the reasons for this unpopularity are unclear (see Lamont and Maton 2008, 2010). Differences of value in the occupational marketplace, for example, cannot by itself account for the uptake rate for Music being roughly one fifth that of art.

Most studies of music focus on learning and playing musical instruments outside school and music in the curriculum is simply said to be 'out of touch' or viewed as irrelevant by most children. Studies of school Music itself, including the few studies addressing low uptake, typically offer speculation or *ad hoc*, piecemeal and largely descriptive accounts of best practice in teaching. The question of why Music is so comparatively unpopular thus remains unanswered.

A series of inter-disciplinary studies are using the concepts of specialization codes to investigate how achievement and educational identities in Music are constructed (Lamont and Maton 2008, 2010). The developing hypothesis of this research is that GCSE Music represents an élite code and that this code plays a role in its low take-up rate. To illustrate how these concepts can be used to analyse educational fields I shall selectively and very briefly summarize early stages of this research, focusing on three pilot studies that address: definitions of achievement in National Curriculum documents and syllabi; students' perceptions of self-ability in, the significance of, and the basis of achievement in a range of subjects; and perceptions of university students of the significance of and basis of success in various school subjects.

1. Curriculum documents

The first study I shall touch upon explores the levels of achievement expected of students at different Key Stages expressed in National Curriculum attainment targets and programmes of study (for KS1–3), and in the GCSE syllabi of major examination boards. These documents were analysed in terms of their degrees of emphasis on: knowledge, skills and procedures; and dispositions of the learner, such as aptitude, attitude and personal expression. The analysis suggests the official requirements for Music embody different specialization codes for different stages of the curriculum. In KS1–2 the National Curriculum defines achievement in terms of students' capacities to express themselves rather than demonstrate musical knowledge or skills. At the end of KS2, for example, students are expected to be able to 'develop their own compositions ... with increasing personal involvement, independence and creativity. They explore their thoughts and feelings through responding physically, intellectually and emotionally to a variety of music' (DfES/QCA 1999: 18): a ***knower code***. At KS3 (ages 11–14) attainment targets downplay aptitude, attitude and personal engagement in favour of the demonstration of musical skills and knowledge; students should show an 'increasing ability to discriminate, think critically and make connections between different areas of knowledge' (DfES/QCA 1999: 20): a ***knowledge code***.

This ***code shift***, I suggest, is echoed across the curriculum and reflects the codes more broadly associated with primary and secondary schooling. However, at GCSE level there is a second code shift in Music. Examination syllabi for GCSE Music require students to demonstrate ***both*** their capacity for personal expression ***and*** their ability with technical skills. The QCA Subject Criteria for GCSE states 'each scheme of assessment must define how musical expression and technique' will be assessed (QCA 2005). Accordingly, the syllabus of one examination board includes a solo musical performance assessed for being both 'accurate and fluent' and 'an expressive performance that is generally stylish', with equal emphasis given to 'Accuracy' and 'Interpretation' (Edexcel 2002: 21, 22): an *élite code.* This suggests one possible reason for low uptake may be a shift in specialization code underlying prescribed definitions of achievement in Music: from knowledge code at KS3 to élite code at GCSE.

2. Perceptions of students

Having analysed the National Curriculum, the next pilot study focused on whether these definitions of achievement are reflected in the perceptions of students. A questionnaire was completed by 912 students aged 8–14 years at four comprehensive schools of average size and achievement rating. The survey included three main questions about: Music, the core curriculum subjects of English, Mathematics and Science (compulsory in KS4), and History (for comparison). For each subject students were asked to rate the importance of being good at the subject, rate their self-ability, and describe the basis of success at the subject. I shall focus on the third question here: 'What do you think makes someone good at [the subject]?' Respondents were offered a forced choice of one of four options, representing a first attempt at capturing relativist, knowledge, knower and élite codes, respectively:

[A] Anyone can do it, nothing special is needed.
[B] You need to learn special skills or knowledge.
[C] You need to have 'natural ability' or a 'feel' for it.
[D] Only people with 'natural ability' can learn the special skills needed.

From analysis of the data for all students across all years, modal responses were knowledge option B for Science, Mathematics and Music, and relativist option A for English (marginally, over B) and History. (As I discuss below, the last two may result from our wording of options C and D.) However, this global picture conceals significant differences in results for different subjects and different student ages. One such result is that among students who have chosen their GCSE subjects in year 9, Music was far more often characterized as embodying an élite code than other subjects: 19 per cent chose élite option D for Music, compared to a maximum of 3.6 per cent for the other subjects. This figure almost doubles to 35 per cent among those students who choosing to study Music at GCSE. I return to consider the implications of these results shortly.

3. Perceptions of university entrants on school subjects

A third pilot study explored, through surveys and focus groups, the perceptions of students who have already made a number of subject choices and are starting their university studies. The survey comprised 93 new entrant, first-year students at a middle-ranking English university. This included similar questions about significance, self-ability and success for the same five subjects as well as Psychology (in which all students were taking at least a module). For this study we redesigned the question of the basis of success in subjects for three main reasons. First, the dispositional option C offered only ‘natural ability’ or ‘feel’, neglecting the notion of cultivated sensibilities or refined judgement, such as often emphasized in humanities and arts subjects (see Chapter 5). This, we believe, contributed to previous low response rates for options including ‘natural ability’. Second, the phrasing of élite option D made ‘natural ability’ the precursor to access to ‘special skills’ rather than bringing together dispositions and knowledge, potentially inhibiting the choice of this option. Third, the forced-choice design incorrectly began from the four code modalities rather than from the relative strengths of epistemic relations and social relations that underlie codes. Such a categorical scale design suits typological groupings whereas the theory emphasizes the *relative* strengths of the two relations and so requires a more continuous scaling approach.

To address these issues we developed the instrument by: (i) including the issue of ‘taste’ or ‘gaze’ and as a separate option to ‘natural talent’ because they are often opposed in well-known debates over, for example, ‘nature versus nurture’; (ii) removing the possibility of sequencing between factors; and (iii) replacing a forced-choice with a rating scale approach to allow independent ratings of each relation. Figure 4.1 shows this iteration of the instrument.[1] For brevity I shall refer to its three lines as ‘skills’, ‘talent’ and ‘taste’. This design asked respondents to rate the significance of epistemic relations to the knowledge structure (‘skills’) and of social relations to the knower structure (‘talent’ and ‘taste’) for each academic subject.[2]

In your opinion, how important are these things for being good at [the subject]?

	Not at all	Not very	Quite	Very
Skills, techniques and specialist knowledge	☐	☐	☐	☐
Natural-born talent	☐	☐	☐	☐
Taste, judgement or a developed ‘feel’ for it	☐	☐	☐	☐

Figure 4.1 University students survey – basis of achievement item

The theory’s emphasis on relative strengths was also reflected by the analysis. The ratings were coded numerically as 1–4 and mean scores calculated across all subjects for the ‘skills’ scale and for the ‘talent’ and ‘taste’ scales taken together, to give baseline scores for the epistemic relations and social relations, respectively. The scores of each subject for these two relations were then compared to these two overall mean scores. As shown by Figure 4.2, Science (and, to a lesser extent, Psychology) scored higher for ‘skills’ and lower for ‘talent’/‘taste’; these results were reversed for English; Mathematics was average for both; History scored lower for both ‘skills’ and ‘talent/taste’; and Music scored higher for both. Figure 4.3 maps these results onto the specialization plane (Chapter 2) to reveal their codes more clearly. For these participants Science and Psychology are knowledge codes, English is a knower code, History is a relativist code, and Music is an élite code.[3]

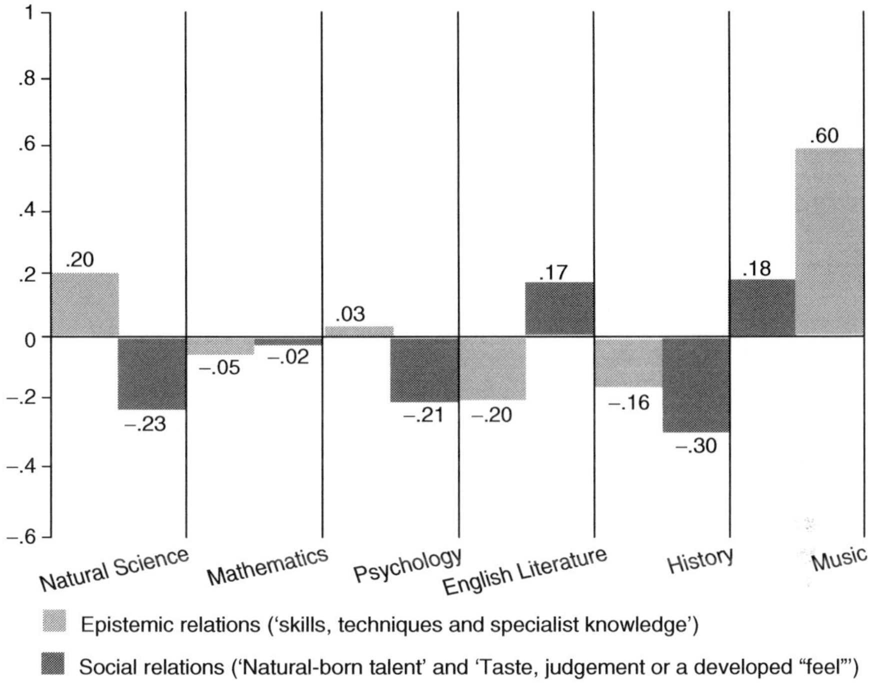

Figure 4.2 University students' perceptions of bases of achievement

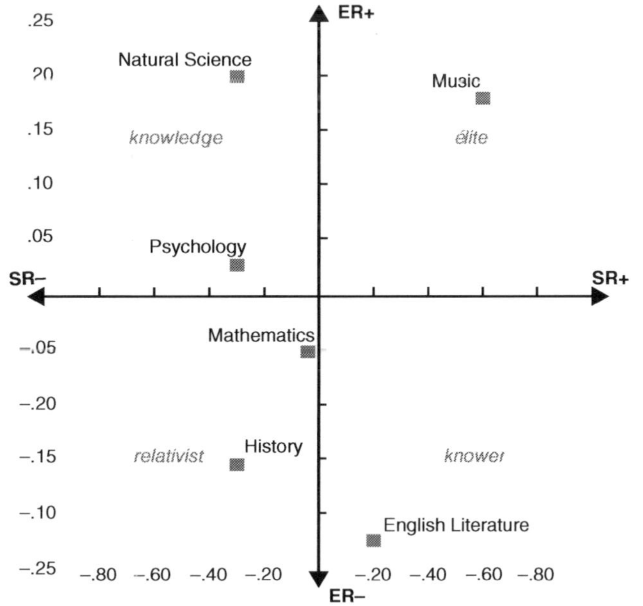

Figure 4.3 University students' perceptions as specialization codes

In a series of focus groups with members of the same population, these codes were reflected in how participants discussed achievement. Group discussions of Science and English, for example, illustrated their knowledge code and knower code, respectively. Participants typically stated that for English the knower is the source of a legitimate gaze which underpins achievement, whereas in Science it is educational knowledge that forms the basis of success; for example:

Moderator: What does it take to be good at English?
Participant 1: I learnt to have my own opinion and back it up with my own evidence but then use evidence from other people that have the same opinion as me, so you're still using other opinions but you're finding them after you've made your own.
Moderator: Is that different from Science or Maths?
Participant 2: Yeah, definitely. You can't really say 'Well, my theory of evolution is …'. It's not like you can make up your own theory.
Participant 1: You're given theories and you choose one, rather than having your own opinion and then finding someone who agrees with you.

The élite code of Music was reflected by the way participants would often alternate between or iteratively add knowledge-based and knower-based issues as essential to success; for example:

Participant 3: It's more talent-based, you have to have a natural ability.
Participant 4: You can't just throw anyone in there and teach them, they have to have that ability before they start. Everyone can learn the basics but to get to the top ….
Participant 3: Music takes a lot of practice. You have to practice every day to get better at it.
Participant 5: You can never say you've done all the work for it. You can always do a bit better. Whereas in Science if you learn it there is a point where you've learned everything that you need to know.
Participant 3: Even someone with natural talent that's very good at Music still has to practice.
Participant 5: It's talent and skills and hard work.
Participant 3: You need to be able to portray emotion too.

Implications of Music's élite code

If Music represents an élite code in curriculum documents and the perceptions of school students and university entrants, the question is how this code relates to its low uptake at GCSE level. The above, necessarily brief, discussion summarizes only part of the data, which includes age differences, social variables such as gender and ratings of self-ability. Further studies are required for a fuller picture, including analyses of: the social distribution of specialization codes among students; constructions of achievement within the field of music education research; the formulation of curriculum in the recontextualization field; and the ways school Music is taught at different Key Stages. However, the discussed results are themselves suggestive in several ways. First, the shift to élite code at GCSE level is not simply another code shift (as happens between KS2 and KS3, from knower code to knowledge code) but to one that is doubly demanding: students must *both* demonstrate possession of musical knowledge and skills ***and*** express musical dispositions. In other words, not only do the rules of the game change, it becomes harder to succeed – élite codes have two hierarchies. Second, this may make Music unenticing, particularly in relation to its perceived significance. When asked to rate the importance of being good at a subject, Music was the least important subject for both school students and university entrants. Its élite code, therefore, does not seem to be reflected by an elite status; as one focus group described it:

Participant 6: I don't think if you were going to apply to be a doctor they'd say 'Have you got your grade 9 piano' or whatever.
Participant 7: I think if I told people I was doing a Music degree everyone would be like 'What's the point? Waste of time!' kind of thing.
Participant 8: Yeah, everyone thinks doing Music at university is learning to play 'Three Blind Mice' on the recorder.

Last, if Music's élite code is not widely distributed socially and the keys to the code not made visible in pedagogic practices, then school qualifications are likely to remain unpopular.

Conclusion

Why bother reading this chapter? It has extended and integrated existing ideas within conceptual tools that offer greater explanatory power by embracing a wider range of phenomena within a more integrated and economic framework. The concept of 'knower structures' extends Bernstein's conceptualization of intellectual fields as 'knowledge structures' to embrace a hitherto obscured dimension. Bringing these together to view social fields of practice as knowledge–knower structures ensures that overcoming the knowledge-blindness of most studies of education does not come at the cost of being blind to everything but knowledge. It thereby extends the potential of analysis by highlighting new issues of interest. For example, analysing the 'two cultures' debate reveals that while portrayed as a horizontal knowledge structure the humanities were also described as a hierarchical knower structure. This helps explain features not visible from the viewpoint of 'knowledge structures' alone, such as the significance for the humanities of an ideal knower (the 'English gentleman') and the role played in the 'crisis in the humanities' by educational expansion bringing a wider range of knowers into the field and thereby reducing the 'dispositional distinction' of humanist intellectuals. Moreover, it represents a new way of seeing intellectual fields that recasts theoretical questions.

Rather than asking *whether* intellectual fields possess a hierarchy, the question becomes *where* a hierarchy resides: in their knowledge structure, knower structure, both or neither. In other words, the principles of hierarchization, as Bourdieu would put it, of a social field of practice may be discursively and/or dispositionally based (knowledge and/or knowers), with implications for the strategies adopted by actors within the field.

Adding knower structures provides a fuller typological account of intellectual fields. Analysing the resulting knowledge–knower structures in terms of specialization codes of legitimation moves beyond typologies to explore the principles underlying intellectual fields. This also enables further insights. For example, analysing the 'two cultures' reveals a code clash between contrasting measures of legitimacy: the knowledge codes of science and the knower codes of the humanities. This helps explain the ferocity and longevity of the debate – they embody different 'rules of the game'. What was at stake in the debate was thus the definition of success; in struggles for status and resources, nothing is more important than control of this epistemic–pedagogic device.

These concepts also enable a more integrated account of the arena created by the device. The framework inherited from Bernstein offers different concepts for intellectual fields ('knowledge structures') and educational fields ('educational knowledge codes'). The notion of specialization codes extends and integrates these concepts in a way that can be used to analyse both kinds of fields. This was illustrated here by research into the comparative unpopularity of qualifications in school Music. Preliminary results from these studies suggest this unpopularity may be related to a code shift as students approach GCSE qualifications, from a knowledge code to an élite code. The double hierarchy this code entails, where legitimacy depends on both demonstrating musical knowledge and skills and expressing musical dispositions, is not balanced by a belief among students in the significance of the subject area.

To recall the title of this chapter: at stake in the 'two cultures' debate was which specialization code would dominate; school Music qualifications are unpopular at least partly because they demand an élite coding orientation from students; and what can unite such diverse issues are concepts such as ***knowledge–knower structures*** and ***specialization codes***. By bringing together phenomena separated by gulfs of time, context, discipline, and level of education within an integrated framework, these concepts provide a further step towards building knowledge about knowledge-building. That, the analysis suggests, is why the chapter is worth reading.

Notes

1 The instrument has subsequently evolved during large-scale studies of schooling; see Howard and Maton (2014) for a detailed account of its evolution and more recent iterations.

2 Chapter 9 provides the theoretical basis for exploring 'natural-born talent' and 'taste, judgement or a developed "feel"' – they reflect sub-dimensions of social relations: subjective relations and interactional relations.

3 Mathematics requires further investigation; studies using more recent iterations of the quantitative instrument suggest it represents a knowledge code in secondary schooling (Howard and Maton 2011).

5 Gazes

Canons, knowers and progress in the arts and humanities

If no one can be eyeless in this Gaza, we need to see 'gaze' itself.

Introduction

Over recent decades few academic debates have been as intense as the 'culture wars' over the rationale, role and form of the arts and humanities. These battles have reached far beyond the academy. Books such as *The Closing of the American Mind* (Bloom 1987), *Cultural Literacy* (Hirsch 1987), *The Western Canon* (Bloom 1996), *The Great Books* (Denby 1996) and *What Good are the Arts?* (Carey 2005) have become international best-sellers. Central to this controversy has been a 'canon brawl' (Morrissey 2005) over not simply what should be considered great cultural works but also whether canons should exist at all (e.g. von Hallberg 1984). The ongoing debate has raised questions of the possibility of progress in these fields, the basis of claims to artistic or humanist 'knowledge', and who can be said to 'know'.

The same questions are broached from a different angle by Basil Bernstein's theorization of 'knowledge structures' (2000). One key feature by which Bernstein distinguished knowledge structures is their mode of development. 'Hierarchical knowledge structures', exemplified by the natural sciences, are explicit, coherent, systematically principled and hierarchical organizations of knowledge which develop through extending and integrating existing knowledge to embrace more phenomena. They thus exhibit a high capacity for cumulative knowledge-building or 'verticality' (Muller 2007). In contrast, 'horizontal knowledge structures', such as the arts, humanities and social sciences, comprise a series of segmented, strongly bounded approaches that develop by adding another approach alongside existing ones. Here, any knowledge of new phenomena remains strongly bounded from existing knowledge. A second key distinguishing feature is the strength of what Bernstein termed their 'grammars' or capacity for generating unambiguous referents. For Bernstein the arts and humanities are characterized by 'weak grammars', where the ability to define the referents of knowledge claims is lacking. This, he suggested, removes a crucial resource for cumulative knowledge-building: the ability to compare competing explanations with consensually agreed-upon evidence.

Bernstein's model offers a fresh perspective on debates over the arts and humanities. These concepts also help overcome the knowledge-blindness endemic to educational research and social science (Chapter 1). However, the model itself raises questions. First, like other typologies, such as 'hard/soft' and 'pure/applied' (Biglan 1973a, b), its strongly bounded categories are difficult to relate to actually existing subject areas (see Chapter 7). Empirical examples do not easily fit the model's dichotomous knowledge structures and grammars. Second, focusing on how the arts and humanities develop over time, the model raises questions of whether these fields are equally ill-disposed towards knowledge-building. Do the arts and humanities display no verticality, as some social realists state (e.g. Muller 2009: 223n5), or are some able to cumulatively build on past knowledge? Third, if they do possess different capacities for knowledge-building, what is the basis of these differences? The existing model portrays these fields as characterized only by weakness: they are said to possess weak (if not no) verticality and weak grammar. However, might such fields possess a different 'strength', one unseen by Bernstein's model, that enables cumulative progress and shapes knowledge-building? Specifically, given that the inherited framework focused on knowledge (see Chapters 3 and 4), what further insights can be discovered through also seeing how practices legitimate knowers?

This chapter addresses these questions, theoretically and substantively. Theoretically, I argue that cumulative progress is possible in fields with horizontal knowledge structures and weak grammars (as Bernstein characterizes the arts and humanities). However, to grasp the particular form taken by this progress requires a different way of viewing fields. Specifically, one must see not only their knowledge structures but also what Chapter 4 defined as their ***knower structures*** and what this chapter will define as their different ***gazes***. Bernstein (2000) highlighted the significance of 'gaze' but left it relatively undefined. We need, I argue, a fresh look at 'gaze'. I begin by arguing that radical critiques of canons and working critically within a canonic tradition both represent horizontal knowledge structures but possess differing capacities for cumulative knowledge-building. To understand their differences, I then explore their knower structures and elaborate on the different kinds of gazes that underpin them. Doing so builds cumulatively on previous chapters: I extend and deepen the notion of ***knower structures*** (Chapter 4) by dynamizing the analysis to explore how they develop, conceptualizing different kinds of ***gazes***, clarifying their relations with ***specialization codes*** (Chapters 2 and 3), and showing how these concepts extend and integrate concepts from Bernstein's framework to not only overcome knowledge-blindness but also avoid knower-blindness.

Substantively, I continue to explore what enables and constrains cumulative knowledge-building, and especially the nature of knower codes and their effects on social fields of practice. Returning to the example of British cultural studies explored in Chapter 2, I examine the role played by different gazes in the fragmentation of the field, analysing the effects of moves during the 1970s from a ***cultivated gaze*** to ***social gazes***. This deepens and refines the analysis of Chapter 2 to more fully conceptualize the basis of changes within the field. I conclude by considering how the concepts introduced in this chapter cumulatively develop our understanding of the arts and humanities, and the implications of different gazes for cumulative and democratic progress within them.

Canons and critiques

The 'culture wars' have conventionally been portrayed as a struggle between two positions: conservative defences of an essentialist canon; and radical critiques of the possibility of canons (Graff 1992). Critiques typically portray the traditional belief in Western cultural understanding, following Kant, as maintaining that if someone judges something as, for example, beautiful 'he [sic] supposes in others the same satisfaction, he judges not merely for himself, but for everyone, and speaks of beauty as if it were a property of things' (1790/1951: 46–47). This position views the canonical status of a cultural work as immutable, universal and transhistorical, and 'insists on an orthodoxy that ought to be discernible at any time whatever, because of its essential perpetuity' (Kermode 1983: 21). The reader or viewer is then said to enjoy an unmediated, immediate relationship with the essential aesthetic value of these great cultural works.

Challenges to this view have been made by a variety of 'radical', 'critical' and 'post-' approaches. Despite their differences, one argument they share is that the essentialist vision is asocial and ahistorical. Highlighting the variety of meanings of the same work generated by different readers or viewers, such critiques argue there is no universal yardstick of 'Beauty' (or 'Truth' in epistemology or 'the Good' in ethics) but rather a series of different beauties dependent on the eye of the beholder. Rather than a single 'literature', for example, this argument posits a fluid plurality of different literatures (Kernan 1990). Particularly vocal in the 'culture wars' have been standpoint theories which take this point further to argue against not only specific canons but also the possibility of canons *per se*. They emphasize the subjective and arbitrary nature of cultural valuations and view canonical status as reflecting the interests of dominant social groups, so that a 'canon is commonly seen as what other people, once powerful, have made and what should now be opened up, demystified, or eliminated altogether' (von Hallberg 1984: 1). For example, feminist critiques have portrayed 'Western culture' as

> a grand ancestral property that educated men had inherited from their intellectual forefathers, while their female relatives, like characters in a Jane Austen novel, were relegated to modest dower houses on the edge of the estate.
> (Gilbert 1985: 33)

Standpoint critiques proclaim that not only the contents but also the basis of choice of a canon is, for example, Western, bourgeois or patriarchal and that 'the Master's tools will never dismantle the Master's house' (Lorde 1984: 112). In other words, different knowers are said to necessarily possess different tools – each social group lives alone, with its own ways of seeing. Thus, a canon is viewed as one of many of equal cultural value but enjoying different levels of social sponsorship. This move toward relativism reaches its zenith in a highly individualistic position that proclaims the value of art 'is a statement of personal taste' (Carey 2005: 9). From this perspective one cannot say a cultural work is better or worse than others except in terms of one's personal preferences: the meanings of cultural works are restricted to an individual's experiences which cannot be compared because we cannot access the minds of others (see Moore 2010). To differentially value art is thus to differentially value personal experiences and so there is no basis for a *cultural* hierarchy.

Two kinds of canonic critique

This choice between essentialism and relativism has often been described as defining the terrain of the 'culture wars'. Yet, this represents a false dichotomy, an *aesthetic dilemma*, analogous to the 'epistemological dilemma' of Chapter 1 that presents a limited set of choices that reduce the space of possibles. For, despite being portrayed as oppositional, both essentialism and relativism share a denial of the recontextualization of knowledge and thus the possibility of knowledge-building. Knowledge is either complete, for the value of a work is self-evident and resides within the work itself (essentialism), or it is exhausted by the values of the social context it reflects (reductionist relativism). One can, therefore, either add a new transhistorical work into the canon horizontally alongside existing works or one cannot have a canon for any length of time. Using Bernstein's model, these positions share a portrayal of the arts and humanities as flat and segmented: horizontal knowledge structures. Moreover, as Moore (2010) argues, this false choice between essentialism and relativism obscures a third position: working critically *within* a canonic tradition.

This third position can be illustrated by a depiction in 1756 of the poet Christopher Smart in the frontispiece of his periodical *The Universal Visitor, and Memorialist* (Ross 2000: 34). The author is shown working at a desk, looking up at a mantle supporting busts of five famous writers, each with a verse inscribed on its base that are reprinted below the frontispiece:

> TO CHAUCER! who the English Tounge design'd:
> TO SPENCER! who improv'd and refin'd:
> TO Muse-fir'd SHAKESPEAR! who increas'd its Praise:
> Rich in bold Compunds, & strong-painted Phrase,
> TO WALLER! Sweetner of its manly Sound:
> TO DRYDEN! who is full Perfection found.

Behind the busts are bookshelves including works by a host of English authors and above which a Latin inscription declares this to be Apollo's Temple of the English. This image illustrates a number of typical characteristics of a literary canon: a focus on authors; a story of writers enriching language and understanding; intertwining literature with a national culture; the dominating but inspiring shadow cast on the modern author by the past; and veneration of the sacred.

Crucially, it represents a canonic progression ('improved and refined', 'increased', 'sweetener of') and suggests knowledge-building. Such portrayals are not uncommon; Kundera espouses a widely held stance when describing the 'novel's spirit' as 'the spirit of continuity: each work is an answer to preceding ones, each work contains all the previous experience of the novel' (2000: 18–19); for example, it is oft-noted 'that Dante understood more than Virgil, but Virgil was a great part of that which he understood' (Kermode 1983: 25).

From this perspective, cultural works are considered context-laden rather than either context-free (essentialism) or context-determined (reductionism), allowing for the possibility of recontextualization and thus building knowledge over time. Moreover, as shown more fully further below by the example of British cultural studies, this process involves critique rather than merely consensus. As an introduction to a collection of papers debating the literary canon puts it:

> Indeed, traditions are made up of debates, diachronically (as past addresses present, and present the past), anachronically (as something ancient seems to matter for the present, and vice versa), and pluralistically (as an extraordinary range of voices make up a tradition, and the readings of that tradition).
>
> (Morrissey 2005: 1)

Nonetheless, using Bernstein's model, English literature represents a horizontal knowledge structure: different approaches to literary analyses remain strongly segmented (Christie and Macken-Horarik 2007).

In terms of their potential for building on the past, the two forms of critique outlined here present different profiles. Reductionist relativism denies its possibility, while critical canonic engagement is based on the wager that progress is possible. Yet, both embody horizontal knowledge structures, with weak verticality and weak grammars. This raises the questions of wherein their differences lie and the basis of their differing capacities for knowledge-building. To address these questions, we need to consider not only their knowledge structures but also their knower structures.

Knower structures and gazes

In conceptualizing 'knowledge structures', Bernstein focused on one dimension of social fields: their discursive or ideational formations. This reflects the wider tendency of his approach to focus on knowledge. For example, as discussed in Chapter 4, Bernstein's analysis of curriculum and pedagogy (1977) addressed the classification and framing of educational knowledge. Similarly, fields of intellectual production were conceptualized in terms of their structurings of knowledge (Bernstein 2000). This focus on the knowledge formation of social fields enables us to see knowledge as an object, overcoming the knowledge-blindness typical of studies of education (Chapter 1).

However, an exclusive attention to knowledge makes it difficult to understand fields where knowledge is not strongly structured and explicit. For example, in Bernstein's analysis of educational knowledge codes (1977), the identities of actors are said either to reside in the possession of subject knowledge (collection codes, where boundaries between academic subjects are stronger) or to be less certain and requiring some kind of 'ideological consensus' (integrated codes, where boundaries are weaker). Similarly, markers enabling actors to know they are operating within a hierarchical knowledge structure are explicit: 'the acquirer does not have the problem of knowing whether she/he is speaking Physics or writing Physics, only the problem of correct usage. The strong grammar visibly announces what it is' (Bernstein 2000: 163). However, in horizontal knowledge structures with weak grammars, where knowledge-based markers are less visible, the recognition and construction of legitimate texts is said to be more problematic.

Wherever knowledge is explicit (collection codes, hierarchical knowledge structures), Bernstein's analysis is explicit: the insight and identity of actors flow from this knowledge formation. Wherever knowledge is less explicit (integrated codes, horizontal knowledge structures), Bernstein's analysis also becomes less explicit. For fields like the arts and humanities, the basis of hierarchization remains unclear. The question becomes: if they are not based on explicit structures of knowledge specialized to objects of study, then what are they based on?

To answer this question requires a change of focus: one needs to see there are two analytically distinct structures that *together* shape educational and intellectual fields. In other words, social fields comprise more than formations of knowledge, they also comprise formations of knowers. This represents a shift of perspective because the inherited framework explores knowers only indirectly, as epiphenomena of analyses of knowledge, making the basis of fields where knowledge is less explicit harder to see. I am arguing that for such fields this basis resides in a *knower structure* that has its own structuring significance.

Fields as knowledge–knower structures

As outlined in Chapter 4, for every knowledge structure there is also a knower structure; that is, social fields are *knowledge–knower structures*. These structures are empirically inseparable as a social field of practice but analytically distinguishable. Crucially, each may be independently arranged hierarchically or horizontally. For example, science can be characterized as possessing not only a hierarchical knowledge structure but also a *horizontal knower structure*: a series of strongly bounded knowers, each with specialized modes of being and acting, with non-comparable dispositions based on different trajectories and experiences. The social profile of scientists is often held to be irrelevant for scientific insight – anyone can ostensibly claim legitimate knowledge so long as they follow scientific principles and procedures. So, in terms of their non-scientific dispositions, scientists can represent a segmented series of strongly bounded knowers. This can be visually represented as follows, where each segment represents a different set of dispositions or what Bourdieu terms 'habitus' (Kr1, Kr2, etc.):

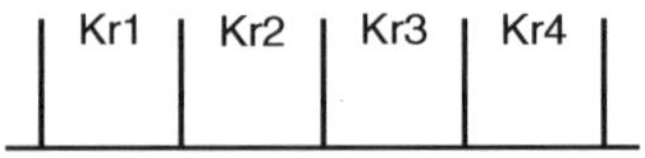

In contrast, the humanities can be characterized as possessing not only a horizontal knowledge structure but also a ***hierarchical knower structure***: a systematically principled and hierarchical organization of knowers based on an ideal knower and which develops through the integration of new knowers at lower levels and across an expanding range of different dispositions. The position and trajectory of knowers within the field's hierarchies are arranged in relation to the ideal knower. This can be represented as a triangle of knowers (though a field may have more than one ideal knower and triangle of knowers):

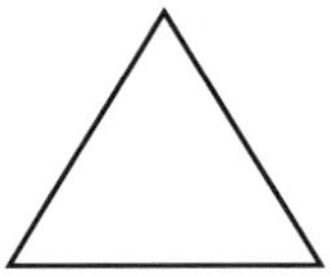

Varying knowledge and knower structures independently gives four modalities of knowledge–knower structures, describing the form taken by intellectual and educational fields. The principles underlying these forms are analysed in terms of ***specialization codes of legitimation***. Figure 5.1 brings these typological and topological accounts together in the ***specialization plane***, here adapted from Figure 2.1 (page 30) to make explicit knowledge–knower structures. The specialization code is given by epistemic relations to the knowledge structure (ER) and social relations to the knower structure (SR). Each may be more strongly or weakly classified and framed or, briefly, more or less emphasized (+/–) as the basis of claims to legitimacy. Varying the strengths of these relations independently generates four principal code modalities (ER+/–, SR+/–). Typically, a stronger relation ('+') reflects the presence of a hierarchical structure; for example, stronger epistemic relations (ER+) are associated with hierarchical knowledge structures. So, if the sciences exhibit hierarchical knowledge structures and horizontal knower structures, these are underpinned by emphasizing knowledge, skills and procedures and downplaying the dispositions of knowers: ***knowledge codes*** (ER+, SR–). Conversely, if the humanities embody horizontal knowledge structures and hierarchical knower structures, these are underpinned by placing less emphasis on principles or procedures and more on aptitudes, attitudes and dispositions: ***knower codes*** (ER–, SR+). In addition, one can describe ***élite codes***, where both possessing specialist knowledge and being the right kind of knower are emphasized (both structures are hierarchical; ER+, SR+), and ***relativist codes***, where neither is significant (both structures are horizontal; ER–, SR–).

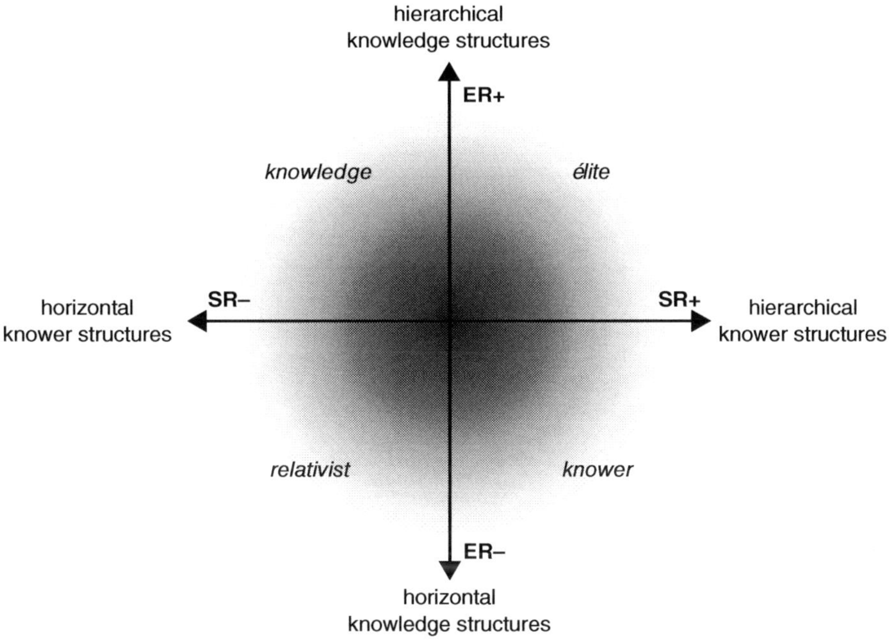

Figure 5.1 Knowledge–knower structures and specialization codes

This approach enables fields to be seen along two dimensions, revealing issues that were previously obscured. As Chapter 4 highlights, it shows that a field's hierarchy may reside in its knower structure rather than its knowledge structure. Put another way, it shows us what is 'vertical' in horizontal knowledge structures. Bernstein described educational or official knowledge as 'vertical discourse', where meanings are hierarchically linked to other meanings (see Chapter 6). However, his model of horizontal knowledge structures, one form taken by vertical discourse, appears to have no verticality. By conceptualizing fields as knowledge–knower structures we can now see that *in vertical discourse there is always a hierarchy somewhere* – something serves as the principle of hierarchization. Instead of *whether* fields are hierarchical, we should ask *where* the hierarchy resides (Chapter 4). In distinguishing among fields the question becomes: where is the 'vertical' in different forms of vertical discourse? Or, where is the '+' in the specialization code (ER+/–, SR+/–): the knowledge structure (knowledge codes), knower structure (knower codes) or both (élite codes)? (If neither, relativist codes, the field is not characterized by vertical discourse.)

A second issue the approach reveals returns us to the issue of progress in the arts and humanities. Having introduced knower structures, we now need to explore how they develop over time by dynamizing their conceptualization. Bernstein states that fields with hierarchical knowledge structures develop through the integration of knowledge: 'verticality'. We can now add that fields with hierarchical ***knower*** structures develop through the integration of knowers or what I shall term ***sociality***. In other words, where one kind of field progresses through knowledge-building, another kind does so through knower-building. Knower structures can thus be distinguished by the degree to which they integrate new knowers, their sociality, highlighting whether they develop through integration or accumulation of knowers' dispositions. So, while the knowledge structure of the arts and humanities may exhibit weaker verticality, their knower structures may exhibit stronger sociality. This is not to argue that such fields must ***necessarily*** develop in this way or cannot build cumulative knowledge but rather to provide a way of seeing how actually existing progress may be occurring within them.

Gazes and 'knower-grammars' (or social relations)

The issues brought into view – that the principle of hierarchization and locus of growth of fields may be related to their knower structures – in turn raise two further questions. First, what is the basis of this principle of selection, recontextualization and evaluation in these fields? As mentioned earlier, for hierarchical knowledge structures this resides in their 'strong grammars'; for example, truth claims can be judged against available evidence using shared criteria. In contrast, Bernstein argued that for horizontal knowledge structures, 'especially those with weak grammars, "truth" is a matter of acquired "gaze"; no one can be eyeless in this Gaza' (2000: 165). He described a 'gaze' as 'a particular mode of recognising and realising what counts as an "authentic" ... reality' (ibid.: 164) but did not conceptualize different modes or ***kinds*** of gaze. If no one can be eyeless, then we need to see 'gaze' itself.

I defined knower structures as based on legitimate knowers; each ideal knower possesses a privileged gaze and the form taken by this gaze shapes the knower structure.[1] A simple way of conceptualizing different gazes is offered by the concepts of Specialization outlined in previous chapters. I shall outline it shortly. However, for the purpose of making the cumulative knowledge-building embodied here explicit, I need to bring together Bernstein's disparate concepts and explicate how they are extended and integrated within Specialization. This requires several steps. First, if knowledge structures possess 'grammars', which I shall rename 'knowledge-grammars' for now, then knower structures possess 'knower-grammars' (Chapter 4). That is, just as knowledge structures have different strengths of relations to their referents, so do knower structures. Second, where knowledge-grammars can be said to refer to the strength of classification and framing of objects of study and their specialized knowledges, knower-grammars refer to the strength of classification and framing of subjects of study and their dispositions. The strengths of these two kinds of 'grammars' may vary independently (so that, for example, fields with weaker knowledge-grammars may also have stronger knower-grammars). Thus far, we have described social fields as knowledge–knower structures with stronger and weaker knowledge-grammars and knower-grammars. This consolidates and extends the inherited model. However, we can now achieve greater conceptual integration and economy, for these concepts have already been articulated in previous chapters: 'knowledge-grammars' are ***epistemic relations***, 'knower-grammars' are ***social relations***, and they come together in ***specialization codes***.

In other words, specialization codes extends and integrates Bernstein's concept of 'grammars'. Specialization conceptualizes what Bernstein termed 'grammars' more systematically as epistemic relations (see Chapter 9); additionally highlights what I temporarily described as 'knower-grammars', which are conceptualized as social relations; and brings them together as codes to reveal previously obscured modalities. Bernstein's notion of 'grammars' and the new notion of 'knower-grammars' can now both be dispensed with: they represent temporary bridging concepts for enabling the extension and integration of this part of the inherited framework. Having elaborated the steps, the shortcut is simple: different kinds of gaze can be conceptualized in terms of their strengths of social relations.[2]

As shown in Figure 5.2, I shall here define four gazes: born, social, cultivated and trained. I refer to 'gaze', but one could just as well talk of 'ear', 'taste', 'touch', 'feel', and so forth, depending on the knowledge practices being discussed. Such language underscores my argument that the hierarchizing principle is portrayed as embodied by knowers or their actions. (As Muller [2012] highlights, hierarchical knower structures may involve an emphasis on procedural rather than propositional knowledge, or 'knowing how' rather than 'knowing that'.) The relatively strongest social relations are illustrated by notions of 'natural talent' and 'genius' in debates over artistic ability and by biological and genetic explanations of practice, where the legitimate knower is held to possess a ***born gaze***. Less fixed but still relatively strong is where legitimate knowers possess a ***social gaze*** determined by their social category, such as standpoint theories based on social class or on race, gender and sexuality when these are constructed as social categories. Weaker is the ***cultivated gaze***, where legitimacy arises from dispositions of the knower that can be inculcated; for example, in literary or art criticism legitimate understanding has often been held to result from prolonged exposure to a range of great cultural works. Relatively weakest is the ***trained gaze***, gained through training in specialized principles or procedures. For example, in the sciences the source of the privileged gaze is less the knower than

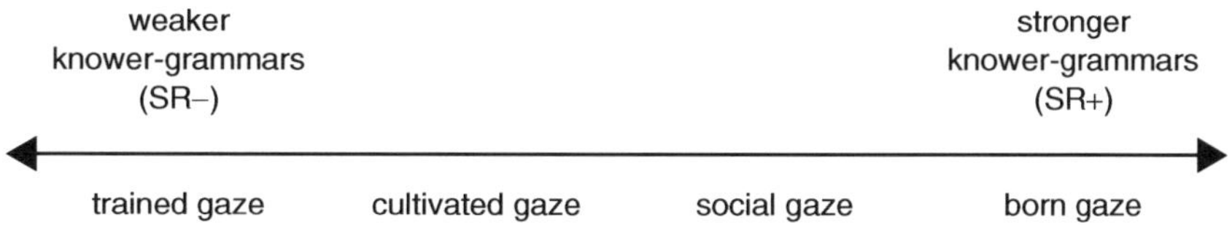

Figure 5.2 Gazes and knower-grammars

the knowledge they possess, and in principal anyone can be trained into the legitimate gaze.

It should be emphasized that there are always knowledges and always knowers – social fields are ***knowledge–knower*** structures. So, all fields include gazes: knowledge-code fields involve trained gazes; knower-code fields involve born, social or cultivated gazes (see Chapter 9). Scientists, for example, do not merely follow scientific procedures; they also gain, as Bernstein (2000: 164) put it, 'a developed sense of the potential of a phenomenon arising out of practice'. Conversely, the arts and humanities have theories, methodologies, and so on. A key distinction is how knowledge and knowers are articulated. For knowledge-code fields the principal basis for legitimacy is developing knowledge, and training specialized knowers is a means to this end. For knower-code fields the principal basis for legitimacy is developing knowers, and creating specialist knowledge is a means for doing so. It is also important to note that, whatever the gaze attributed to the legitimate knower, actors within a field will recognize and/or realize that gaze to varying degrees. Ascertaining which potential knowers do so depends always on empirical research.

This conceptualization brings us to a second question: why might some kinds of fields have greater capacity for progress than others? The answer relates to the kind of gaze underlying a field's knower structure. The gazes outlined above trace a continuum of progressively weaker social relations and so increasing openness to potential knowers. These different strengths help shape the conditions for entry, position and trajectory within a field's hierarchies. The stronger the social relations, the more tightly restrictions are placed on membership of and ascension through the hierarchy of a knower structure. The born gaze is the most difficult to attain for those not already a member of the privileged knower group because, if knowers are born not made, there is little the unlucky can do to become one; the social gaze restricts legitimacy to social categories that may be difficult to join; the cultivated gaze offers the possibility of attaining legitimacy through prolonged immersion in a way of being, seeing or acting; and the trained gaze proclaims openness to anyone willing to be trained in specialized principles or procedures. The kind of gaze underlying the knower structure of a field may thus be crucial to the extension of its epistemic community through time and space (Chapter 3): gaze may shape sociality and capacity for growth of the knower structure. Moreover, sociality may in turn affect verticality, the capacity for knowledge-building in a field; that is, knower structures may affect knowledge structures. It is to exploring these effects on sociality and verticality that I now turn.

Cultivated and social gazes

Earlier I outlined two kinds of critique of canons that offer different pictures of the arts and humanities: reductionist relativism and working critically within a canonic tradition. They can now be redescribed as representing a social gaze and a cultivated gaze, respectively. To illustrate the effects these gazes have for the progress of fields, I shall now explore an example of each from within the history of an intellectual field. To build on Chapter 2 and illustrate what this conceptual advance can add to our understanding, I focus on the history of British cultural studies.

A cultivated gaze

Faced with the rise of new commercial forms of mass media, many educators argued in the early 1960s for teaching young people how to 'look critically and discriminate between what is good and bad in what they see' (Newsom Report 1963: 156). The founding figures of British cultural studies – Richard Hoggart, Raymond Williams, E.P. Thompson and Stuart Hall – argued that such calls for teaching discrimination were often accompanied by a devaluing of the 'popular arts' (Hall and Whannel 1964: 23–37). They agreed with the need to cultivate a critical gaze and retained a conviction that much 'high' culture was of value, but highlighted that existing canons excluded the experiences of the working class and the basis of choosing such canons could be extended to include new forms of culture. Through their work in adult education and the first New Left movement, they aimed to enable working-class learners to critically appreciate both 'high' culture and new media and so bring them into a cultural conversation from which they had been excluded. This 'attempt at a majority democratic education' (Williams 1989: 154) strove to democratize access to a cultivated gaze based on Leavisite literary criticism. In his Inaugural Lecture at the Centre of Contemporary Cultural Studies at Birmingham University (CCCS), Hoggart described this as:

> an increased ability to appreciate the many ways in which the literary imagination explores human experience ... by creating the 'felt sense of life' in its complicated fullness – of sense and feeling and thought, of time and place and persons.
>
> (Hoggart 1963: 75–76)

The founders of cultural studies argued that to inculcate this gaze in new kinds of learners required new forms of pedagogy. In particular, they emphasized the need to build on the experiences of students; as Williams stated: 'I believe that communication cannot be effective if it is thought of as simply transmission. It depends, if it is to be real ... on real community of experience... sharing real experience' (Hoggart and Williams 1960: 30). This pedagogy should begin but, they argued, not end with learners' experiences. The 'community of experience' was thus not pre-existent but one created by teachers in the classroom through shared engagement with cultural works. Williams (1968), for example, argued that 'the teacher who pretends he [sic] is not a teacher ... is a pathetic and irrelevant figure'. It thus aimed to integrate the interests and experiences of (mainly) working-class learners without slipping into 'that sloppy relativism which doesn't stretch *any* student because "they are all, in their own ways, doing wonderfully"' (Hoggart 1969, in 1982: 12; original emphasis). In short, the cultivation of a 'literary imagination' required an explicit and 'thoroughly-planned syllabus' to help 'fill out the sense of a coherent journey' towards the appreciation of a canon of cultural works in which neither

> the tutor nor the student should be in doubt about the overall aims of the course and its larger pattern of working over the session; nor about the place of each week in that pattern; nor about the shape of any one week in itself. The syllabus should be as clear a guide as we can make it, and so should its partner – the reading list.
>
> (Hoggart 1982: 9)

In terms of 'the reading list', as the field developed its own corpus of studies, this emphasis on directed cultivation of a gaze through engagement with exemplary works became focused on a canon of cultural studies texts. During the early 1970s, the CCCS engaged on a major project of trying to 'distil the field in terms of a basic set of core-texts' along with critical commentaries, with the goal of producing *A Reader in Cultural Studies* to 'prevent succeeding generations of students having to start again at first base' (Hall 1971: 5). This canon aimed to provide a basis for cumulative knowledge-building through cultivating cultural studies knowers.

Progress with cultivated gazes

Using the concepts outlined above, we can describe the kind of canonic critique exemplified by early cultural studies as representing a hierarchical knower structure, one which works to integrate new habituses into the field through the cultivation of actors into legitimate dispositions. This is illustrated by Figure 5.3, where the tip of the triangle is the ideal knower's gaze and the base represents the range of habituses integrated through education. The development of this hierarchical knower structure can then be understood along two dimensions: the spread of the base of the triangle represents an expansion of the range of habituses embraced by the field; and the vertical arrow indicates the ascension of knowers towards the legitimate gaze through the cultivation of their dispositions. New knowers are thus brought within the field and then rise to greater legitimacy through prolonged immersion in exemplars and models within master–apprentice relations. Bernstein stated that hierarchical *knowledge* structures appear by their users to be motivated towards integrating the greatest number of empirical phenomena into the smallest number of axioms (2000: 161). One can describe hierarchical *knower* structures as appearing, by their users, to be motivated towards integrating the greatest number of habituses into the smallest number of gazes. They are, therefore, characterized by relatively strong sociality.

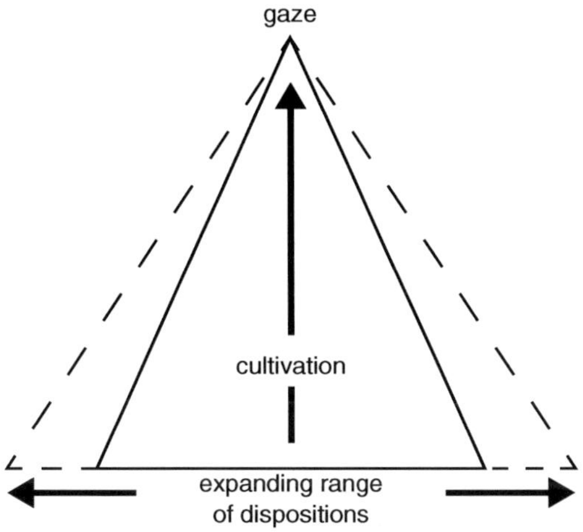

Figure 5.3 Growth of hierarchical knower structure with a cultivated gaze

Whether this relatively strong sociality enables the building of cumulative knowledge depends on the degree to which the legitimate gaze inculcates a shared tribunal or library among its practitioners. The cultivated gaze is based on the belief that knowers are not born but made through the re-formation of their dispositions. The principles of hierarchization are thus embodied in the knower – the cultivated gaze resides in the mind's eye (or cultivated 'feel' in the sense of touch, and so on). A gaze is a canon introjected. One form this takes is what the cultural critic Robert Hughes described as 'an invisible tribunal':

> Every writer carries in his or her mind an invisible tribunal of dead writers, whose appointment is an imaginative act and not merely a browbeaten response to some notion of authority. This tribunal sits in judgement on our own work. We intuit standards from it. ... If the tribunal weren't there, every first draft would be a final manuscript.
>
> (Hughes 1993: 111)

The works of this tribunal may also represent a kind of mental library that enables allusions, references, intertextual play and the myriad effects of what Bloom (1973) called the 'anxiety of influence' – the desire to go beyond what has come before – to be assumed and left tacit.

This invisible tribunal or mental library represents a gateway to the public sphere of such fields. The more they are shared, the greater the possibility of building knowledge, for the principles of hierarchization of 'art' or 'literature' introjected from canonic models are in turn projected by the artistic or literary gaze onto new cultural works. The resultant evolving canon provides an Archimedean point for debate. Thus, canons and cultivated gazes may represent for the arts and humanities the knower-based equivalents of the objects of study and specialized principles and procedures of the sciences: a focus and basis for intersubjective debate across an extended epistemic community. Because the cultivated gaze is based on a canon, immersion in which helps develop a 'community of experience', it both enables the possibility of debate over something (a canon) and a shared means of conducting that debate (the shared sensibilities or dispositions of knowers).

Social gazes

The reductionist form of critique begins from a similar position to early cultural studies. It too highlights that dominated social groups have been denied access to the means of creation and circulation of cultural products and their experiences often excluded from canons. However, it differs in being based on a social gaze. Such a form came to dominate cultural studies during the 1970s. At this time, having previously attempted to include working-class learners among its range of knowers, cultural studies increasingly focused on including women. As Stuart Hall, Director of the CCCS during the 1970s, later recounted: 'we tried to buy it in, to import it, to attract good feminist scholars' (1992: 282). However, 'many of the women in cultural studies weren't terribly interested in this benign project' and, rather than 'good, transformed men', scholars such as Hall were portrayed as 'fully installed patriarchal power, which believed it had disavowed itself' (ibid.). The practices and beliefs of male practitioners were redefined by feminist critics as gendered and rooted in unequal relations of power. This became particularly salient when deciding canonic exemplars:

> There are no leaders here, we used to say; we are all graduate students and members of staff together, learning how to practice cultural studies. You can decide whatever you want to decide, etc. And yet, when it came to the question of the reading list ... Now that's where I really discovered about the gendered nature of power.
>
> (Hall 1992: 282–283)

The influence of standpoint theory saw feminist critiques of the emerging canon of cultural studies proclaim that not only its contents but also its basis of choice was patriarchal, denying the legitimacy of the gaze and those who possessed it. The personalized nature of struggles at this time echo in Hall's proclamation that: 'Talking about giving up power is a radically different experience from being silenced' (1992: 283). Similarly, Michael Green, who taught at the CCCS during most of its lifespan, described encounters around feminism and race as 'very serious and unpleasant and difficult' (interview with the author, February 1999).

The cultivated gaze was thus redefined as socially based: a male gaze. From this perspective, integrating women into the field was attempting to inculcate them into social ways of knowing other than their own – symbolic violence. One response was thus to call for 'a literature of our own' and 'a criticism of our own' or 'gynocriticism', a female framework for analysing literature written by women (Showalter 1977, 1989). As a result, the attempt of the early 1970s to develop a canon or shared reading list for cultural studies, as a means of inculcating new members into the field, faltered. Instead, the redefining of its cultivated gaze as a social gaze set in train similar debates over the imperialist, Western, racialized and sexualized nature of knowledge in the field, with new, previously excluded, groups often proclaiming their own social gazes (see Chapter 2).

Progress with social gazes

Critiques based on social gazes correct the essentialist temptation to misrecognize a canon as asocial and ahistorical. However, as early cultural studies illustrates, this can be achieved without eschewing belief in the value of canons and cultivated gazes; the move to a social gaze is thus not necessarily integral to such critique. Such a move has consequences for intellectual and educational fields. Where critiques based on cultivated gazes aim to integrate previously excluded knowers by broadening the base of a field's knower structure (see Figure 5.3), those based on social gazes create their own, new knower structure within the field. The former aim to inculcate more potential knowers into an established conversation; the latter aim to carve out a new space for already legitimate knowers to create a conversation of their own. When a field moves from a cultivated gaze to social gazes, as cultural studies did during the 1970s, it thereby remains based on a knower code but the social relations underpinning that code are strengthened, affecting the ways in which the field develops over time. Specifically, it can lead to the kind of fragmentation into segmented 'voices' that affected British cultural studies.

Figure 5.4 illustrates the form of development that social gazes can engender in fields. (As emphasized in Chapter 2, these tendencies may be unexercised because enabling conditions are absent or exercized unrealized because countervailing pressures are present.) Social gazes may restrict the sociality of fields along the two dimensions discussed above for cultivated gazes. First, the range of potential knowers may diminish. If the knower structure begins as a single triangle (Figure 5.4, no. 1), then instead of extending the base of the triangle, a social gaze may add a second, separate triangle (no. 2). Where a cultivated gaze may be shared by knowers originating from a range of different social backgrounds, a social gaze is shared only by those who possess it already, unless others can successfully change gender, social class background, ethnicity, etc. With such a broad social category as 'women', this may at first appear to dramatically expand the field as a whole: a new space is carved out for a previously excluded social group. However, the new knower structure can be maintained as a singular and integrating triangle only so long as its social category remains unified. As Chapter 2 shows, the tendency is for the social category to be fragmented as more adjectives are added based on other social categories, especially under conditions of educational expansion. With each successive adjective

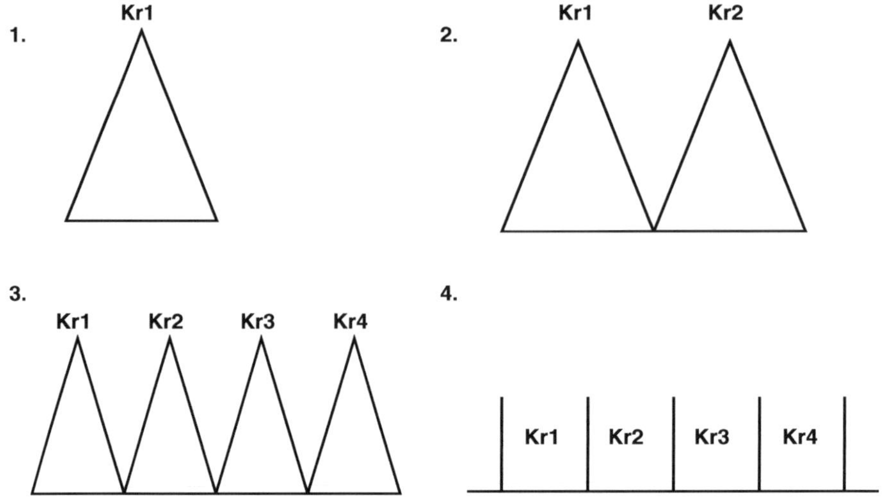

Figure 5.4 Impact of social gazes on a hierarchical knower structure

(e.g. white-female-heterosexual-Western-etc.) more separate knower structures emerge within the field, one for each new social gaze. This adds more triangles with successively smaller bases (as shown by no. 3). Though embracing more kinds of knowers, each new group has its own knower structure, fragmenting the field as a whole. The result is a move towards a horizontal knower structure (no. 4).

If the field already has a horizontal ***knowledge*** structure, this process further diminishes the capacity of members to engage in intersubjective debate and build knowledge over time – there are no shared principles of hierarchization. Different social groups are then said to have their own gazes and so their own objects, their own canons – each a literature or culture or art of their own. There is thus no Archimedean point, no shared object of study over which debate between segments can be engaged and no shared means of doing so.

A second dimension concerns the height of the knower structure or distance between the dispositions of learners upon entry as novices and those characterizing the legitimate gaze. This distance may diminish, progressively reducing the height of the triangles in Figure 5.4. Pedagogy is less likely to focus on a prolonged apprenticeship for inculcating sensibilities and more on removing ideological obstacles (including prior cultivation) to enable the authentic social self to shine forth and so raise to consciousness one's pre-existing social gaze. The gaze is still a gateway to a public sphere but that sphere is now more restricted; one cannot enter or ascend the knower structure unless one is already an ideal knower. This also fragments the educational experience. In British cultural studies, for example, Richard Johnson (CCCS Director 1979–1988) described the early 1980s as witnessing 'the apparent splitting up of the field of cultural theory by the often separated and even antagonistic claims of different political movements', illustrated by a Masters degree course being 'organised around the political sequence of class, gender, and "race" rather than some more synthesizing account of tensions and best options in the field' (1997: 65). Thus, instead of a coherent journey towards a cultivated gaze, students may experience segmented learning as they move between the approaches associated with segmented social gazes; indeed, a common criticism of the Masters course was its lack of 'coherence' (ibid.).

The endpoint of this process of horizontalization is subjectivist relativism, the notion that there is nothing beyond the different subjective knowing of a potentially endless range of different knowers. The social category underpinning the gaze is thus broken down and replaced by individual gazes, as illustrated by arguments such as:

> The art-world has lost its credibility. The electorate has extended, has, indeed, become universal. My answer to the question 'What is a work of art?' is 'A work of art is anything that anyone has ever considered a work of art, though it may be a work of art only for that one person.' Further, the reasons for considering anything a work of art will be as various as the variety of human beings.
>
> (Carey 2005: 30)

From this perspective critical discrimination is only misrecognized social power. There is no hierarchy of achievements and nothing to be taught or learned; there is only the horizontal addition of new lists of personal preferences (cf. Moore 2010). Instead of a cultural conversation to join, there can be only turn-taking. Any 'invisible tribunal' would be a result of individual biography: 'we assemble our own literary canon, held together by personal preferences' (Carey 2005: 242). Though critics such as Carey believe this is democratic as it overthrows the rule of 'the art-world', it does so by emptying 'art' of meaning. Moreover, he misleads in arguing the electorate has become universal, for there is now no election. From this position, anything goes:

> If this seems to plunge us into the abyss of relativism, then I can only say that the abyss of relativism is where we have always been in reality – if it is an abyss.
>
> (Carey 2005: 30)

Returning to the question of finding the 'vertical' in vertical discourse, its principles of hierarchization, this is to now move from a social knower code towards a relativist code (ER–, SR–), where the field comprises a segment of knowledge for each segmented knower. Both knowledge and knower structures have now become horizontal, diminishing any hope of verticality or sociality. In this situation of a multitude of personal gazes, Nietzsche's aphorism would hold: 'There are many kinds of eyes. Even the Sphinx has eyes – and consequently there are many kinds of "truths", and consequently there is no truth' (1968: §540).

Conclusion

Both the 'culture wars' and Bernstein's concepts of 'knowledge structures' raise questions of the basis of knowledge and possibility of progress in the arts and the humanities. Both also present only part of the picture. Bernstein's model would describe these fields as horizontal knowledge structures with weak verticality and weak grammars – weakness abounds. It would also point to the crucial significance of gaze in such fields but the forms this takes and their effects on fields had yet to be theorized. This partial picture, I suggested, reflects the focus of the framework on knowledge formations. To extend this outlook, I outlined a second dimension of social fields: knower structures based on the gazes of legitimate knowers. I argued that where knowledge structures are characterized by verticality and knowledge-grammars (or epistemic relations), knower structures are characterized by sociality and knower-grammars (or social relations). 'Sociality' describes whether knower structures develop through accumulation or integration of dispositions; and 'knower-grammars' refer to the ways in which legitimate knowers are defined. We can now move beyond Bernstein's concept of 'grammar' and leave behind the temporary scaffolding concept of 'knower-grammar' in favour of epistemic relations and social relations. Thus, fields can be more fully understood as ***knowledge–knower structures*** and their forms analysed as ***specialization codes***. This extends and integrates the inherited model within a broader and more systematic model that enables different kinds of gaze underpinning knower structures to begin to be conceptualized.

Exploring the effects of the move from cultivated to social knower codes in British cultural studies during the 1970s showed how different gazes shape the sociality and verticality of a field in different ways. The cultivated gaze affords greater opportunities for cumulative knowledge-building because more habituses can be integrated. Fields with horizontal knowledge structures can, therefore, develop through integration, if they have hierarchical knower structures. Such fields display 'verticality' as a product of their principal mode of progress, sociality. Here integration occurs through the dispositions of knowers rather than explicit formations of knowledge. It is integration of ***knowing*** embodied in knowers as gazes. This form of cumulative development is limited to ***within*** the knower-defined field, to those sufficiently cultivated into the legitimate gaze to judge the merits of cultural works, but defining this gaze as teachable and learnable enables this field to be potentially more inclusive, allowing the possibility for (though not guaranteeing) cumulative knowledge-building. In contrast, social gazes restrict sociality and verticality because access into and ascension through the field's hierarchy of knowers is restricted to particular social groups. Moreover, this may fragment the field into separate knower structures, moving towards subjectivist relativism. The underlying rule of cultivated gazes is thus 'dispositions must be brought together' and that of social gazes is 'dispositions must be kept apart'.

More broadly, one can say that the trained gaze (of science, for example) reflects a hierarchy of knowledge; the cultivated gaze reflects a hierarchy of knowing; and the social gaze reflects a hierarchy of socialized being (although these positions typically deny such hierarchies of being and so move towards horizontalism).

The capacity for cumulative development within fields like the arts and humanities thereby depends at least partly on their underlying gaze – knower structures can shape knowledge structures. This is also the key to understanding differences among fields with horizontal knowledge structures – they are neither all the same nor confined to horizontal development. Rather, fields with horizontal knowledge structures may progress 'vertically' through their knower structures (if operating a knower code); their 'strength' lies within these structures (stronger sociality and stronger social relations); their principles of hierarchization reside in a gaze; and some fields are more capable of sociality and verticality than others, depending on the nature of this gaze.

The conceptual developments offered in this chapter also bring into view a position obscured by the 'aesthetic dilemma' constructed by conventional accounts of the 'culture wars': critical engagement with a canonic tradition based on a cultivated gaze. Against essentialism, this position holds that definitions of culture are related to actors located in socio-historical contexts rather than universal and transcendent. Against relativism, it also highlights that there can be intersubjective bases for judgement that may be taught and learned. In a passage quoted earlier, Robert Hughes described invisible tribunals as imaginative acts rather than simply the result of browbeaten responses to social power. Such acts are not made outside society by decontextualized knowers but rather result from articulating the personal 'inner' with the social 'outer' via cultural authority; that is, a cultivated gaze. The key to avoiding the Scylla and Charybdis of symbolic violence and relativism is thus to discover a gaze and a means of cultivating that gaze capable of embracing knowers from a multitude of social backgrounds. This is an urgent task facing the arts and humanities (as well as education and society) if we are to forge a culture peace, one characterized not by unchanging, socially imposed canons, factional trench warfare or relativism, but by a growing cultural sphere in which everyone joins a visible tribunal. We cannot afford to be blind to gaze.

Notes

1 'Gaze' refers to the knower not to the discourse to be known, and to the outcome of the principles underlying fields not to the principles themselves (cf. Bernstein 2000: 172–173). For example, the 'cultivated gaze' shapes and is shaped by canons, rather than representing the gaze of a canon itself, and is the result of a knower code with a particular modality of social relations (see Chapter 9). The necessity of these distinctions becomes clear when considering 'social gazes', which reduce knowledge to knowers and conflate outcomes of principles of hierarchization with the principles themselves.

2 Gazes are more fully conceptualized in Chapter 9 as modalities of two subdimensions of social relations: subjective relations and interactional relations.

6 Semantic gravity

Cumulative learning in professional education and school English

Mastering semantic gravity is a key to cumulative learning.

Introduction

A spectre is haunting education – the spectre of segmentalism. This affliction occurs when knowledge or knowing is so strongly tied to its context that it is only meaningful within that context. In intellectual fields, segmentalism arises with the accumulation of new ideas or approaches that fail to integrate existing knowledge. Such segmented knowledge-building constrains explanatory power and cumulative progress in research. In educational fields, segmentalism is reflected in curricula or teaching and learning practices that comprise a series of discrete ideas or skills rather than cumulatively building on previously encountered knowledge. Such segmented learning can constrain students' capacities to extend and integrate their past experiences and apply their understandings to new contexts, such as later studies, everyday lives or future work. Having primarily explored the nature of knowledge-building in intellectual fields in previous chapters, here I shift focus to explore conditions of segmented and cumulative learning in educational fields.

Enabling cumulative learning is central to education. As Bransford and Schwartz put it:

> A belief in transfer lies at the heart of our educational system. Most educators want learning activities to have positive effects that extend beyond the exact conditions of initial learning.
>
> (Bransford and Schwartz 1999: 61)

This belief has become increasingly salient for economic and education policies in advanced industrialized societies. Contemporary debates suggest that education must prepare the young for 'lifelong learning' to meet the fast-changing demands of working in 'knowledge economies' (Field 2006). Policy rhetoric emphasizes the need for workers to continually build their knowledge, learn new skills and give new meanings to their existing abilities (Sennett 2006). At the same time, segmented learning remains a pressing concern in debates across the institutional and disciplinary maps of education, from school to university, arts to sciences, education to training (e.g. Christie and Macken-Horarik 2007; Wheelahan 2010). As these scholars argue, one issue often missing from these debates is the role played by educational knowledge itself, reflecting the knowledge-blindness of much educational research (Chapter 1). For example, research on 'transfer' focuses on forms of knowing ('knowing that', 'knowing how', etc.) rather than forms of knowledge (e.g. Bransford and Schwartz 1999). Thus the question remains of how educational knowledge enables and constrains cumulative learning.

As shown throughout this book, Basil Bernstein's code theory offers a valuable starting point for addressing this kind of question. Previous chapters have extended key concepts from this framework within the LCT dimension of Specialization, exploring principles underlying practices in terms of *specialization codes* (Chapter 2), the *epistemic–pedagogic device* (Chapter 3), *knowledge–knower structures* (Chapter 4) and *gazes* (Chapter 5). This chapter will continue to draw on this Specialization dimension but its principal theoretical focus lies in a new direction. It serves as a simple introduction to *semantic gravity*, a concept from another dimension to languages of legitimation, that of Semantics, which subsequent chapters (and Maton 2013) will develop more fully.

To begin exploring the bases for cumulative and segmented learning I draw on Bernstein's suggestive model of 'discourses' and 'knowledge structures' (2000).[1] These concepts highlight, *inter alia*, the significance of relations between meanings and contexts for the forms taken by knowledge but require development to address curriculum and learning, to be enacted in empirical research, and to reveal the generative principles underlying their dichotomous types. This chapter addresses these issues. First, I extend the model to describe hierarchical and horizontal educational knowledge structures and cumulative and segmented learning. Second, an organizing principle underlying these types is conceptualized as *semantic gravity*, or degrees of context-dependence of meaning. To illustrate the role of knowledge practices in cumulative learning I then use this concept to explore two examples of educational practices from contrasting disciplines and levels of education: an 'authentic learning' environment in professional education at university; and a thematic 'area of study' in English at secondary school. Both aim to enable cumulative learning, yet both often result in students' understandings remaining locked within their contexts. I argue that one basis for this segmented learning lies in a mismatch between their aims of enabling students to acquire a cultivated gaze and their means of minimal guidance and modelling that leaves many students unable to recognize or enact what is required for achievement and reliant on common sense. Analysing student work products in terms of their profiles of semantic gravity, I show how this mismatch can result in students' knowledge being characterized by consistently stronger semantic gravity that problematizes transferring knowledge across contexts and over time. I conclude by arguing that mastery of semantic gravity – the capacity to both strengthen and weaken the context-dependence of knowledge practices – is one key to cumulative learning and, more widely, to inclusion within a progressive society.

Conceptualizing cumulative and segmented practices

In his later work Bernstein outlined a model of knowledge practices in terms of 'discourses' and 'knowledge structures' (2000: 155–174). He distinguished first between 'horizontal' and 'vertical' forms of 'discourse'. 'Horizontal discourse' refers to everyday or 'commonsense' knowledge and 'entails a set of strategies which are local, segmentally organized, context specific and dependent' (ibid.: 157). The knowledges comprising this discourse are characterized by 'functional relations of segments or contexts to the everyday life' (ibid.: 158–159). In other words, meaning is dependent on its context, so knowledge acquired in one context does not necessarily have meaning or relevance in other contexts: 'Learning how to tie up one's shoes bears no relation to how to use the lavatory correctly. These competences are segmentally related' (ibid.: 159). In contrast, 'vertical discourse' refers to 'specialised symbolic structures of explicit knowledge' (ibid.: 160), or scholarly, professional and educational knowledge, and 'takes the form of a coherent, explicit, and systematically principled structure' (ibid.: 157). Here meaning is less dependent on its context and instead related to other meanings hierarchically.

Bernstein then distinguished within vertical discourse, between 'knowledge structures'. 'Hierarchical knowledge structures' are explicit, coherent, systematically principled and hierarchical organizations of knowledge which develop through new knowledge extending and integrating previous knowledge. In contrast, 'horizontal knowledge structures' comprise a series of strongly bounded approaches that develop through adding another segmented approach. A key difference is their mode of development: extension and integration of knowledges in one form, and accumulation and segmentation of knowledges in the other.

Bernstein's concepts thereby highlight how knowledge develops over time, a key issue for understanding segmentalism. However, to explore educational practices, the model needs to be developed in two principal directions. First, the concepts of knowledge structures are intended to describe only intellectual fields of production. An integrated approach to education requires concepts that embrace all fields of the arena created by the epistemic–pedagogic device: production, recontextualization and reproduction (Chapter 3). This is simple to resolve. One can extend the framework with concepts highlighting how the modes of development signified by Bernstein are realized within curriculum and pedagogy. Chapter 4 distinguished hierarchical and horizontal *educational knowledge structures* (or *curriculum structures*) according to whether a unit of study (lesson, module, year, etc.) builds upon knowledge imparted in previous units through extension and integration or through segmental aggregation.[2] Further, one can distinguish according to whether the knowledge students learn builds on their previously learned knowledge or remains strongly bounded from other knowledges. This is to describe what I have already been discussing as *cumulative learning*, where students are able to transfer knowledge across contexts and through time, and *segmented learning*, where such transfer is inhibited.[3]

The second direction for developing the inherited model is from its typological descriptions of features of practices towards a conceptualization of their organizing principles. The dichotomous types of discourses and knowledge structures raise questions of whether all horizontal discourse is the same and whether there are quantum leaps between the types. They obscure changes both within and between categories, problematizing the study of issues such as how to apprentice students from horizontal discourse into vertical discourse. As Chapter 3 argues, though Bernstein was aware of differences within his types, to enact that awareness in research requires concepts that capture those differences. Relatedly, the segmented types also problematize attempts to enact the model in substantive research studies. It is difficult to determine where in the array to assign particular disciplines, theories, curricula, and so on – few practices fit into the types, many combine their characteristics, and processes over time largely elude the concepts. Just as significantly, the model describes characteristic features of discourses and knowledge structures but not what makes a discourse 'horizontal' or 'vertical', or a knowledge structure 'hierarchical' or 'horizontal'.

While being good to think with and orienting our gaze to key issues, the concepts remain, as Muller states, 'locked into an early (lexical) metaphorical stage of discussion, where the terms are more suggestive than they are explanatory' (2007: 65). I shall elaborate on how this stage relates to their nature as dichotomous types in Chapter 7. Here I simply note that Bernstein (2000: 123–124) himself argued that such types represent a useful first step for theorizing practices but that their generative power remains relatively weak. The model thus needs development to capture the organizing principles underlying discourses and knowledge structures, as well as curriculum structures and forms of learning.

Previous chapters have outlined one means for exploring these organizing principles: Specialization. Put simply, specialization codes comprise *epistemic relations* between knowledge practices and their objects, and *social relations* between knowledge practices and their actors (Chapter 2). Each relation may be more strongly or weakly emphasized (+/–) as the basis of claims, generating four principal modalities, where legitimacy is determined by: the possession of explicit principles and procedures (knowledge codes); attitudes, aptitudes or dispositions (knower codes); both specialist knowledge and knower attributes (élite codes); or neither (relativist codes). Chapter 5 further distinguished strengths of social relations as giving rise to different *gazes* (from strongest to weakest): born, social, cultivated and trained. Specialization codes conceptualize one set of principles underlying practices and, as studies illustrate (Chapter 10), reveal the role they play in shaping social fields of practice. I shall draw on these concepts in this chapter. However, while shedding light on the bases of knowledge-building, they do not directly capture issues of context-dependence and condensation of meaning that, as I shall show (here and in Chapter 7), are central to the recontextualization of knowledge. To explore these issues another dimension underlying practices must be considered: Semantics, centred on the concepts of *semantic gravity* and *semantic density*. This dimension will be unfolded over coming chapters: this chapter will introduce *semantic gravity*; Chapter 7 additionally employs *semantic density* to conceptualize modalities of *semantic codes* and a topological *semantic plane*; and Chapter 8 builds on these concepts to explore different forms of *condensation* and *cosmologies*. (Further, Maton 2013 systematically dynamizes the concepts to describe *semantic profiles*.)

Semantic gravity

Bernstein's model highlighted relations between knowledge practices and their social and symbolic contexts: differences in context-dependence form part of the descriptions of discourses and knowledge structures. One can thus conceptualize practices in terms of the degree to which meaning relates to its context. This *semantic gravity* may be relatively stronger or weaker along a continuum. When semantic gravity is stronger, meaning is more closely related to its social or symbolic context of acquisition or use; when it is weaker, meaning is less dependent on its context. One can also describe processes of *strengthening* semantic gravity, such as moving from abstract or generalized ideas towards concrete and delimited cases, and *weakening* semantic gravity, such as moving from the concrete particulars of a specific case towards generalizations and abstractions whose meanings are less dependent on that context.

This conceptualization of semantic gravity begins to resolve issues raised above. First, as Figure 6.1 illustrates, discourses, knowledge structures, educational knowledge or curriculum structures, and forms of learning can be described not only as types but also as points on a continuum. Vertical discourse is characterized by weaker semantic gravity than horizontal discourse. Within vertical discourse, hierarchical (educational) knowledge structures exhibit weaker semantic gravity than horizontal (educational) knowledge structures, and cumulative learning represents weaker semantic gravity than segmented learning. I must emphasize that Figure 6.1 does not suggest that, for example, hierarchical knowledge structures are necessarily related to hierarchical curriculum structures or cumulative learning. The formations of knowledge in each field of the arena created by the epistemic–pedagogic device are always subject to empirical research; one cannot 'read off' practices of one field from practices of other fields (Chapter 3). Rather, Figure 6.1 shows that 'semantic gravity' can be applied to all three fields and so helps enable a more integrated account of education. Practices of production, recontextualization and reproduction can each be understood as realizations of different degrees of semantic gravity, enabling changes to be traced as knowledge is curricularized, pedagogized, intellectualized or recurricularized between fields. Second, the arrow of Figure 6.1 highlights that 'semantic gravity' augments the model's dichotomous types with a relational conception of difference with capacity for infinite gradations of strength and a processual account of change. As will become clear, tracing profiles over time is crucial for understanding enabling conditions for cumulative knowledge-building. Last, conceptualizing knowledge practices in terms of semantic gravity is suggestive: it highlights that one condition for cumulative knowledge-building and learning may be the capacity to master semantic gravity, in order for knowledge to be decontextualized, transferred and recontextualized into new contexts.

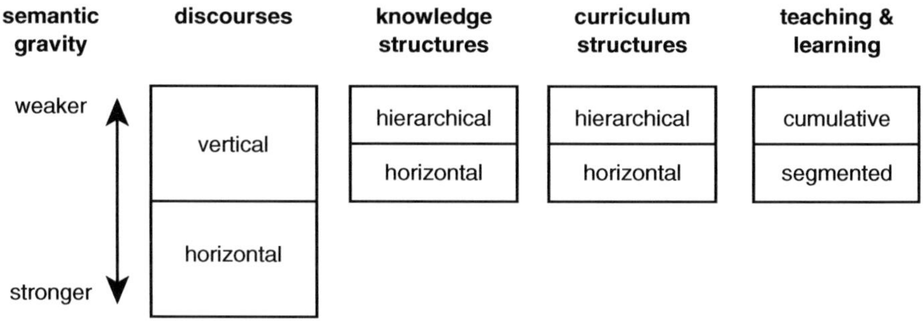

Figure 6.1 Semantic gravity and structurings of knowledge

I shall now use the concept to explore two examples of educational practices intended to enable students to experience cumulative learning but which often lead to segmented learning. This analysis itself illustrates the notion of mastering semantic gravity by using the same concepts to examine practices from contrasting institutional and disciplinary contexts: 'authentic learning' in professional education at university; and a thematic unit of study entitled 'The Journey' in secondary school English.

An 'authentic learning environment' in professional education

With the ascendancy of 'student-centred learning' approaches, professional education has been increasingly influenced in recent years by 'authentic' or 'situated' learning (Chapter 8). Proponents claim that for students to learn knowledge that will remain valuable beyond education they require tasks that reflect the realities of practices in those everyday contexts and which allow them access to the knowledge of experts with experience of real-world practice (e.g. Herrington and Oliver 2000). 'Authentic learning' is thus often associated with problem-based, case-based and project-based pedagogies that aim to provide students access to the working practices of, for example, designers or journalists (Bennett *et al.* 2002). Such 'authentic learning environments' are claimed to create cumulative learning experiences by building on students' prior experience and providing knowledge relevant to their future work (Herrington *et al.* 2004).

To analyse an example of this approach, I shall draw on data collected for a major study, Bennett (2002), of a Masters degree postgraduate course for training instructional designers (professionals who design learning resources). One aspect of this study explored a task designed according to 'authentic learning' principles that used 'case-based learning'. The unit of study required students to analyse two case studies of real-life instructional design projects, each case comprising approximately 15,000 words of unedited transcripts of interviews with three people who had worked on the project. The assessment task comprised a series of questions designed to encourage students to think beyond the context, as shown in Table 6.1 (Bennett 2002: 75–76, emphases added).

Three features of this task are salient for the current analysis. First, as Table 6.1 shows, the questions ask students to draw on knowledge from beyond the cases; question 2, for example, directs students to relate the experiences of designers in the case to 'other literature you have read' or 'your own experiences as a designer'. Second, the questions ask for progressively more generalization and abstraction: they begin by requiring students to describe key issues in the cases, and end by asking what general issues they have learned. These two features highlight the aim of weakening the semantic gravity of knowledge by encouraging students to make meanings that reach beyond the learning context.

Third, the task embodies a knower code by backgrounding specialized knowledge and emphasizing the dispositions of knowers as the basis of achievement. Though proponents of 'authentic learning' *espouse* the need for explicit reflection, articulation of tacit knowledge, and active scaffolding by teachers, *enacted* environments portrayed as 'authentic' typically downplay teacher activity and direct instruction (e.g. Herrington and Oliver 2000). In line with such enacted 'authentic learning environments', interaction between staff and students in this unit focused on explaining the nature of the task but did not involve explicitly teaching procedures of instructional design or principles for bringing such procedures to bear on the contexts being studied. Specialized knowledge was thus downplayed: weaker epistemic relations. Instead, students were expected to put themselves 'into the shoes' of the interviewed professionals, an empathy task focusing on their dispositions: stronger social relations. Further, as highlighted by italics in Table 6.1, the questions focused on eliciting from students 'your own experiences as a designer' rather than relating the cases to explicit principles of instructional design. The basis of achievement at the task was thus characterized

Table 6.1 Task questions

1 Describe the major stages and decision points in the process of developing the product. What are the major issues at each stage?

2 How do the experiences of the designers in this case relate to:
   a) other *literature you have read* about multimedia design and development or
   b) *your own experiences as a designer* (for example in your work or for EDGI913 [an earlier subject in the course])?

3 Choose a particular feature of the product which is discussed in the case.
   a) Describe *how you think* it relates to the original concept and goals of the project.
   b) From the information in the case *what do you think* were the major design issues in developing this feature?
   c) *Do you think* the feature is effective? Explain your reasoning.

4 What are the major project management issues in developing a multimedia CD-ROM that are highlighted by this case? (Use example situations from the case to support your ideas.)

5 What are the main things that *you think you learnt* from studying this case?

by a knower code based on immersion in exemplary models, including their own qualified experiences – a *cultivated gaze* (Chapter 5).

Analysing student responses

To explore students' understandings, their work products were analysed using what Bernstein (2000: 131–141) termed an 'external language of description' or means of translating between concepts and data (see Chapter 7). The external language developed for this specific object of study is shown in Figure 6.2. I should emphasize this is neither a definition of 'semantic gravity' nor the only way to enact the concept in empirical research. Each object of study requires its own translation device and other studies have developed different external languages or are adapting this example in the light of their own data (Chapter 10). It simply offers a way of translating between 'semantic gravity' and the data of *this specific research project*, one conducted

Semantic gravity	Coding of responses	Form taken by student responses	Example quote from student answers
weaker ↑	Abstraction	Presents a general principle or procedure that moves beyond the cases to address wider or future practice.	Legal and intellectual property issues are a major consideration when developing a product.
	Generalization	Presents a general observation or draws a generalizing conclusion about issues and events *in* the case.	Precious time would be wasted and deadlines not met when members did not have a full concept of the project.
	Judgement	Goes beyond re-presenting or interpreting information to offer a value judgement or claim.	While each metaphor provides a realistic learning environment ..., I felt that the *Nardoo* metaphor assists with navigation, while the *StageStruck* metaphor was a barrier to effective navigation.
	Interpretation	Seeks to explain a statement by interpreting information from the case or adding new information. May include use of other literature or personal experience.	While not alluded to in the interviews, this may have caused problems for the team, as there would have been a new software to work with, and transferral of information from *Hypercard* to *MediaPlant*.
	Summarizing description	Descriptive response that summarizes or synthesizes information presented in the case, including re-wording and re-structuring of a number of events into one statement. Does not present new information from beyond the case.	This involved creating the overall structure and content of the project, with design briefs and statements being forwarded to the client, with the final design statement being signed off by the client, giving a stable starting position for the project.
↓ stronger	Reproductive description	Reproduces information directly from the case with no elaboration (i.e. quotations).	The NSW Department of Land and Water Conservation (DLWC) approached the Interactive Multimedia Learning Laboratory (IMMLL) at the University of Wollongong to develop an educational multimedia package.

Figure 6.2 An external language of description for semantic gravity

prior to the concept's development and using a pre-existing approach. Bennett's original scheme (2002) built on Allen's (1995) use of several frameworks for classifying reflective writing; this scheme was then adapted in the light of the conceptualization of 'semantic gravity' and the results re-analysed. From left to right, the columns of Figure 6.2 outline: relative strengths of semantic gravity; the coding scheme used to analyse students' work products; a description of each coding; and examples of each coding drawn from student answers. Using this external language one can read from theory to data (left to right) and from data to theory (right to left). In terms of the coding scheme, 'reproductive description' (e.g. direct quotation from the cases) embodies the strongest semantic gravity because meanings remain locked into the context of the case from which the quote is taken, and 'abstraction' embodies the weakest semantic gravity, as meanings are decontextualized from the case to create abstract principles for use in a range of potential contexts.

Student answers to the task were broken down into individual 'units of meaning' (passages conveying a single coherent meaning) and each unit was coded using the scheme. The study comprised 12 students whose work products comprised 1,700 units of meaning in total. As shown by Figure 6.3, analysis reveals that relatively little of the students' work products (as a percentage of the whole) comprised 'reproductive description' or direct quotation. This is unsurprising because postgraduate students are (or should be) typically aware of the need for their submitted work to move beyond quotation, and the unedited interview transcripts did not lend themselves to extensive quotation. However, around one-third of the total units of meaning in

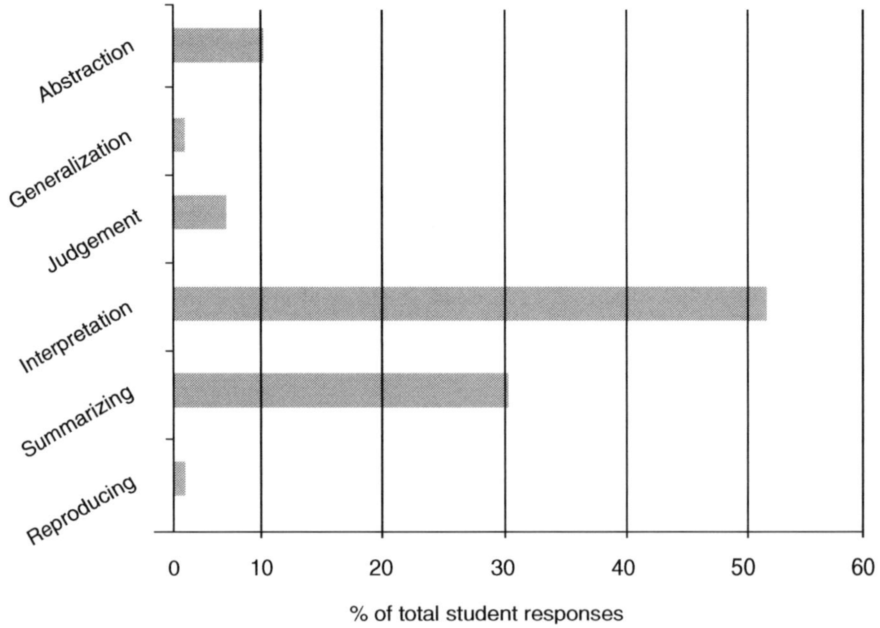

Figure 6.3 Total student responses by units of meaning

students' work comprised 'summarizing description' and just over half were 'interpretation'. Relatively less of the work products comprised 'judgement', 'generalization' or 'abstraction'. So, the majority of work produced by students in this group is characterized by relatively strong semantic gravity. Meanings are mostly strongly related to the context of the cases being studied, as shown by the comparatively low percentage of 'judgement' and 'generalization'. This, it should be emphasized, is despite the assessment task requiring students to reach beyond the specific cases.

Of course, one would not expect a very high percentage of students' responses to embody weaker semantic gravity or their work could become overly abstract and disconnected from the learning materials. However, comparing the responses of individual students shows that some were more capable than others of reaching beyond the cases. For example, Figure 6.4 compares the work of two students. Overall, the answers of student A exhibit weaker semantic gravity than those of student B; they are less weighed down in the context of the cases.

This difference is also shown by instances in which students' work moved beyond 'reproductive description' or 'summarizing description'. For example, when student C drew conclusions they remain grounded within the context of the cases; such as:

> Tasks and responsibilities often remain unclarified in this "design" phase (Phillips & Jenkins 1998). The reflections of Rob Wright ... seem to reflect on a type of "juggling act" between responsibilities with instructional design issues and scheduling a project of this magnitude.
>
> (quoted in Bennett 2002: 129)

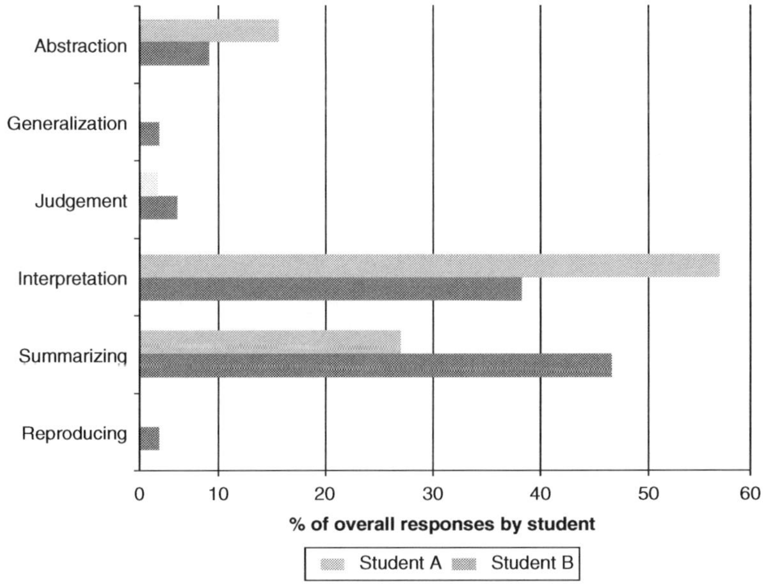

Figure 6.4 Responses of two students by unit of meaning

In this example the student used other literature ('Phillips & Jenkins 1998') to generalize about the design phase of the project, but the conclusions remain firmly located within the context of the cases (the experiences of 'Rob Wright', one of the interviewed designers) rather than developing principles for application to other possible projects. In contrast, student D's conclusions about the cases go further to offer more abstracted principles, including:

> ... a list of ideas that one might keep in mind when designing and producing a multimedia project. The issues examined in the two case studies sparked these ideas. Here are those ideas, listed in no particular order.
>
> Set priorities in your product development. Know what you must have and what aspects of the project are not vital.
>
> At some point, you must become precise in what features and content you want in your design. Working in generalities does not allow you to proceed effectively in the final stages of the project.
>
> Start small and build your project from there. By doing this you will not have to be cutting material all the time...
>
> (quoted in Bennett 2002: 147)

Student D thereby used the cases as a launch pad from which to offer knowledge that can be taken into other possible design contexts. This, however, was not the norm. While some students expressed understandings that included 'abstraction', most remain immersed in the pedagogic context.

An uncultivated gaze

While proponents of 'authentic learning environments' claim they enable students to learn knowledge transferrable beyond the learning context, this example and the larger study on which it builds suggest this is not necessarily the case. In the unit of study discussed here, many students' understandings exhibited stronger semantic gravity and so remained rooted within their contexts. This suggests that cumulative learning may be constrained by a lack of means offered by 'authentic learning' for overcoming semantic gravity. Drawing on constructivist ideas that emphasize the learner's role in constructing their own understandings of practice, 'authentic learning environments' typically expect students to make knowledge claims based on personal experiences and imagining themselves within the case being studied (stronger social relations), and downplay the role of direct instruction about procedures to be used or principles of knowledge to be learned (weaker epistemic relations). Thus, while proponents of 'authentic learning' claim it promotes 'higher-order thinking' (Herrington and Oliver 2000), the knowledge itself is not made explicit. Moreover, the task aimed at eliciting (and rewarded) responses that revealed the cultivated gaze of students as instructional designers ('your own experiences as a designer'; see Table 6.1) but the pedagogy offered a very limited number of exemplars (2 projects) and minimal immersion within them (transcripts of interviews with participants). It may thus set up many students to underachieve. Those students who do not already possess extensive experiences and/or the ability to generalize and abstract principles and procedures from those experiences, are at a disadvantage. Lacking the cultivated gaze required by the assessment, they remain rooted in the context of the cases. To explore this conjecture further I now turn to another unit of study aimed at enabling cumulative learning but located in a different disciplinary and institutional context: school English.

'The Journey' in secondary school English

School English has often been the focus of debates over fragmentation of the curriculum (Christie and Macken-Horarik 2007). A recent example of an English curriculum designed to enable cumulative learning is *The Journey*, a unit compulsory for all students taking the Higher School Certificate in New South Wales, Australia, during 2005–2008. (In 2009 the compulsory 'Area of Study' theme changed to 'Belonging', but the claims made for the unit and its form remained the same). The unit required students to explore the concept of 'the journey', with a choice of either 'physical', 'imaginative' or 'inner' journeys that are similarly structured. Focusing here on 'imaginative journeys', these are said to involve texts that 'take us into worlds of imagination, speculation and inspiration' (Board of Studies NSW [BoS] 2006a: 10). In 2005, students were set the question:

> To what extent has studying the concept of imaginative journeys expanded your understanding of yourself, of individuals and of the world?
>
> In your answer, refer to your prescribed text, ONE text from the prescribed stimulus booklet, *Journeys*, and at least ONE other related text of your own choosing.
>
> (BoS 2006b: 11)

The 'prescribed stimulus booklet' comprises two poems, short extracts from three books, and a book cover; the prescribed list of texts includes: a work of fiction (*Ender's Game* by Orson Scott Card), a selection of poems by Samuel Taylor Coleridge, Shakespeare's *The Tempest*, a popular history of science (*On Giants' Shoulders* by Melvyn Bragg), and the movie *Contact*.

The Journey syllabus is characterized by attempts to weaken the semantic gravity of students' understandings by reaching beyond a specific text to embrace principles of literary understanding applicable to a wide range of potential texts. For example, the syllabus claims that students will learn how to 'explore and examine *relationships* between language and text, and *interrelationships* among texts' and how to '*synthesise ideas* to clarify meaning and *develop new meanings*' (BoS 2006a: 9; emphases added). It thus expects students' understandings to exhibit a relatively high level of abstraction centred on the idea of 'The Journey', rather than on a particular text, literary genre or theory. The unit of study also includes texts from outside the traditional literary canon (such as a movie) and requires students to apply their knowledge beyond the curriculum by choosing at least one text of their own. It thereby aims to enable students to learn knowledge they can take into encounters with new texts: cumulative learning.

Though located in a different institutional setting and region of the disciplinary map to the first case study, *The Journey* shares similar features in the knower-code means employed to enable cumulative learning. The unit emphasizes social relations to knowers and eschews explicitly imparting specialized principles or procedures. For example, the assessment question asks for 'your understanding of yourself, of individuals and of the world' and expects students to empathize with texts (Christie and Humphrey 2008). There is little explicit guidance in curriculum documents as to how to select, recontextualize or evaluate texts in terms of the idea of 'The Journey', or indeed what this idea means. Instead, the syllabus incorporates modelling of best practice and guidance. It includes a book of *Student Answers* (BoS 2006b) comprising examples of essays rated as achieving medium and high grades, with examiners' comments included after each essay. These comments, though, are brief and often vague. For example, highly rated essays are typically described as a 'sophisticated discussion', 'insightful' and 'a very sophisticated and purposeful response' (BoS 2006b: 114), or 'complex' with a 'judicious selection of texts', and 'tightly written and strongly focused' (ibid: 101). Examiners' comments on medium-grade essays are typically a little longer but remain confined to stating, for example, that less description and more 'analysis and evaluation' are required (ibid.: 127), without explicating what the analysis and evaluation might comprise. Thus, modelling of exemplars of achievement is limited and guidance opaque.

Semantic gravity in student essays

To illustrate how *The Journey* relates to students' understandings I shall briefly explore two contrasting examples of student work. The first is an essay offered in official syllabus documents as exemplifying high achievement (BoS 2006b: 102–114).[4] The essay begins and ends by bringing its chosen texts together in relation to an overarching abstract idea; for example, its second sentence is:

> The journey, especially in the imaginative sense, is a process by which the traveller encounters a series of challenges, tangents and serendipitous discoveries to arrive finally, at a destination and/or transformation.
>
> (BoS 2006b: 102)

From this starting position of relatively weak semantic gravity, the essay moves down to the concrete particularity of each text that is discussed but then quickly upwards from that text towards more abstract ideas. After introducing and summarizing a text, specific aspects of that text are selected, recontextualized and evaluated in relation to the explicitly named and abstract notion of 'the journey'. For example, discussion of the first text, a history of science, begins:

> *On Giants' Shoulders* depicts the individual lives and achievements of 12 scientists as a collective imaginative journey over the last 2500 years. In portraying their separate profiles as one story in a chronological line up, Bragg delineates the concept of a cumulative and ongoing journey, reflected in his thesis that science is 'an extended kind of continuous investigation'.
>
> (BoS 2006b: 103)

This movement is repeated throughout the essay. As heuristically illustrated by Figure 6.5, the profile of this essay embodies a *gravity wave*, a recurrent weakening and strengthening of semantic gravity by moving between concrete examples and abstract ideas. Crucially, this high-achieving answer neither offers an abstract and decontextualized discussion – it includes specific examples and quotes from expert sources – nor remains rooted in its contexts. The key to its success is embodying a range of movement in semantic gravity, as well as beginning and ending with even weaker semantic gravity to connect with the abstract notion of 'imaginative journeys'.

Driving this gravity wave is a *cultivated knower code*. The essay exemplifies a knower code in that specialized principles and procedures are not explicitly the *basis* of claims made by the student. While the essay includes abstract ideas (such as 'the concept of the imaginative journey'), these are the *focus* of knowledge claims rather than their *basis* (Chapter 2). There are no explicit theoretical or methodological foundations to its principles of selection, recontextualization and evaluation of texts in relation to 'imaginative journeys'. Rather, the student as a knower is the basis of claims to legitimacy; it is her

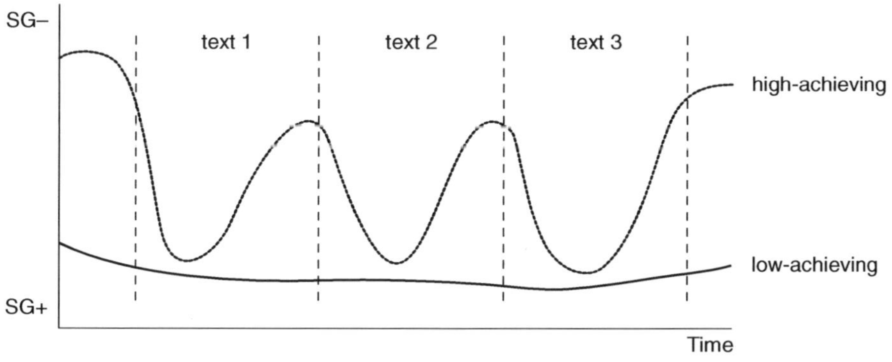

Figure 6.5 Profiles of semantic gravity for two essays in school English

gaze that provides these principles: a knower code (ER–, SR+). However, this gaze is based neither on a biological or social category nor simply on personal preferences. Instead, the student demonstrates their literary sensibilities and dispositions – a cultivated gaze. For example, even when discussing herself, the student relates her experiences in literary terms, with a corresponding degree of objectifying distance:

> I personally have learned the importance of individuals interlinking with others to achieve a greater end, and influencing or inspiring others, as inherent in the concept of scientists standing on 'giants' shoulders'.
>
> (BoS 2006b: 103)

In responding to the question, she recognizes the literary 'you' being addressed and provides a suitably cultivated knower, one transformed through engaging with texts:

> [T]he study of the concept of the imaginative journey has expanded my understanding significantly of myself as defined through challenges; of individuals as part of a great quest in the search for collective knowledge; and of the world as an experience not to be missed.
>
> (BoS 2006: 113)

This cultivated literary gaze becomes clearer in comparison to lower-achieving essays. The example chosen here is typical of a significant proportion of students' work at this level and represents a striking contrast.[5] The essay as a whole has a segmented form: discussion of each chosen text is strongly bounded. Even when bringing texts together, the student keeps them apart; the essay concludes: 'I took on three wonderful journeys' rather than one journey embracing three texts. Like the first essay, discussion of each text begins with relatively strong semantic gravity, however it remains firmly locked into the context of that specific text, with minimal attempts to move to broader themes. Moreover, not only are meanings strongly related to the context of each text, they are also strongly related to the context of the student's life. For example, when discussing the novel *Ender's Game*, the student writes:

> I found I could relate to Ender in many ways and I didn't stop to think that this story wasn't actually real, because when reading, I was so involved that I truly thought that what was happening around Ender and I was reality.

The essay is thus highly personal and subjective. It is replete with first-person pronouns that signal how the student's *personal* dispositions and experiences serve as the basis for selecting, recontextualizing and evaluating texts; for example:

> I felt very empathetic towards the character Ender. I found myself involved in the novel, travelling my Imaginative journey alongside Ender. I felt that Ender was a friend of my own.

Rather than the student being a knower whose dispositions have been cultivated by the experience of engaging with texts, the texts are given meaning by the life experiences of the student as an already-legitimate knower; for example: 'Anthony Browne's picture book "Willy the Wimp" is another text which I found myself in'. Moreover, segmented aspects of the texts are related to segmented contexts from everyday life; for example, writing of Ender's Game:

> It wasn't hard at all to imagine battle school as a real place because I was familiar with several scientific objects which surrounded us. For example, the 'Desk' sounds very familiar to a lap top computer.

In short, meanings are strongly related to contexts, not only the context of each text but also thence to everyday contexts, and based on a highly personalized and individualized knower code in which the gaze is untouched by education. This represents a personal gaze, close to subjectivist relativism, realized as the commonsense understandings of horizontal discourse.

As illustrated in Figure 6.5, this essay is characterized by a much lower range and at stronger levels of semantic gravity. Though both essays mostly discuss one text at a time, the differences in their profiles and knower codes are marked: the first integrates meanings around the idea of 'imaginative journeys' via the cultivated gaze of a literary knower; the second relates segmented meanings to segmented texts and experiences of everyday life. The first author recognizes and realizes the ideal knower to whom the question is addressed and responds as a student of literature; the second author either cannot recognize or realize that knower and responds instead with his or her everyday self. In terms of semantic gravity, it is as if the first student is able to leap up further from the concrete base of each text (and her own relations to each text) to reach more abstract ideas with which different texts can be related together before then returning downwards to a different concrete context, creating what I have termed a *gravity wave*. In contrast, meaning in the second essay is weighed down by the gravity of contexts: the student cannot see beyond each text and his/her own experiences, feelings and beliefs, creating a *gravity flatline*.

These brief examples highlight that, despite the espoused aims of the curriculum, many students may be unable to recognize or put into practice what they need to succeed at this compulsory unit of study. The syllabus claims to enable, and analysis of other high-grade essays confirms that achievement is measured in terms of integrating meanings from different texts. However, little guidance is offered in curriculum documents as to what the idea of 'imaginative journeys' means or how it should be used to analyse texts. Thus, unless students already possess an appropriately cultivated gaze, by virtue of their upbringing and/or previous education, they may respond with subjective descriptions of personal preferences, experience segmented learning, and fail to achieve higher grades.

Conclusion

The desire for students to experience cumulative learning is at the heart of education. However, without an understanding of the role played by knowledge, educational practices are unlikely to avoid or overcome segmented learning. Bernstein's model of 'discourses' and 'knowledge structures' provides a valuable starting point for engaging with knowledge, one he intended to be built on. This chapter has extended the model to embrace practices beyond intellectual fields and continued excavating the organizing principles underlying its forms of knowledge. Preceding chapters explored these principles in terms of the LCT dimension of Specialization. This chapter drew upon these concepts but also introduced a component of the dimension of Semantics, specifically *semantic gravity*. Conceptualizing discourses, knowledge structures, curriculum structures, and forms of learning as realizations of strengths of semantic gravity enables the existing dichotomous account of types to be supplemented by further exploration of the generative principles of practices across fields of production, recontextualization and reproduction. The concept thus offers another step towards a more integrated and ontologically deeper account of education.

Using these concepts to explore educational practices revealed ways in which the forms taken by knowledge practices may help to enable or constrain cumulative learning. Substantively, analyses of two units of study that aim to enable cumulative learning showed that their rhetoric does not necessarily match the reality. Though located in different disciplines and different levels of the education system, both units claimed students will learn higher-order principles of knowledge applicable to new contexts. However, both offer minimal explicit guidance as to the nature of this knowledge or the principles for their appropriate recontextualization. Instead, they emphasized students' dispositions as the basis of achievement, based on prior experience and case studies or models of practice. Both resulted in many students' understandings remaining rooted in their contexts, weighed down by relatively strong semantic gravity.

Focusing on specialization codes, these brief but illustrative analyses suggest that one feature constraining cumulative learning may be a mismatch between the *cultivated gaze* that students are expected to demonstrate in both these units and the lack of cultivation offered. A cultivated gaze results from the gradual re-shaping of dispositions, which requires prolonged and guided immersion in numerous and diverse context-situations (cf. Salomon and Perkins 1989). The minimal guidance and limited models offered in the two units meant that students not already capable of recognizing and realizing the requisite gaze – as a trainee designer or as a student of literature – were disadvantaged. For such students, assessment largely measured their pre-existing dispositions. Ironically, far from being authentic learning or representing a journey, these forms of pedagogy offered students limited opportunities for learning and left many where they began.

In terms of semantic gravity, the analyses suggest that cumulative learning requires mastering semantic gravity. Proponents of the approaches analysed in this chapter argue that the teaching and learning of decontextualized knowledge, such as abstract principles, necessarily leaves students incapable of enacting that knowledge in everyday contexts. This claim is not necessarily misplaced: teaching and learning entirely abstract, decontextualized and generalized knowledge would represent a flatline of weaker semantic gravity. Knowledge would thus be freely floating and never *re*contextualized. However, the analyses here suggest their proposed solutions, such as 'authentic' and 'situational' learning, merely replace one kind of flatline with another, at much stronger levels of semantic gravity. For, in eschewing explicit teaching of specialized knowledge, the units left the understandings of many students locked in their contexts. In the case of school English, this meant relying on the highly segmented meanings of everyday life (horizontal discourse).

I shall be exploring this issue further. Chapter 7 argues that this false dichotomy between two flatlines reflects the binary ways of thinking embodied by such static couplets as abstract/concrete and context-independent/context-dependent (Chapter 7). Chapter 8 describes how these are brought together as binary constellations of stances, such as 'teacher-centred' and 'student-centred', that are differentially valorized with little empirical basis. Nonetheless, we can already begin to overcome the polarized thinking that gives rise to this flatline dichotomy because the concept of semantic gravity describes a continuum of strengths that can be understood through time as tracing a profile. This conceptualization moves us beyond comparing static states to delineating a trajectory of change. As illustrated by Figure 6.5, a wave profile appears a key feature of achievement in the secondary school English unit analysed above. This chapter has, of course, been but introductory. However, a major study of secondary classroom practices in Biology and History reveals this profile – when brought together with a concomitant profile of semantic density to together create what are termed *semantic waves* (Maton 2013) – to be a key feature of cumulative knowledge-building (Macnaught *et al.* 2013; Martin 2013; Matruglio *et al.* 2013). This and a growing number of other studies (e.g. Shalem and Slonimsky 2010) are showing that the key to academic achievement in many subjects lies neither with stronger nor with weaker semantic gravity but with extending the range of movements between them, with *both* strengthening *and* weakening semantic gravity, a profile traced by this chapter's structure: theoretical framework – case study 1 – analysis – case study 2 – analysis – theoretical synthesis. These movements in semantic gravity provide a necessary (though not sufficient) condition for the decontextualization and recontextualization of knowledge and thus the possibility of cumulative knowledge-building and learning.

This issue is significant, for the spectre of segmentalism haunts not just education. Social realism holds that active engagement in the public sphere as a citizen requires the ability to engage with powerful knowledge. This ability depends on experience of what Richard Hoggart described as

> one of the best benefits I have been offered by this culture and this society … the introduction to the intellectual life, to generalization and its relations to particular things.
>
> (Hoggart 2005: 65)

This mastery over semantic gravity represents a gateway to joining 'society's conversation about what it should be like' (Wheelahan 2010: 163). However, such mastery is not equally available: students arrive at education with different semantic ranges. For example, studies drawing on Bernstein (e.g. Hasan 2009), as well as other theorists such as Bourdieu (1984), suggest that generalization, abstraction, objectifying distance, focus on form rather than function, and other orientations to meaning that weaken and enable greater range of semantic gravity are more associated with the socialization practices of cultural middle-class families than those of working-class families. Actors who feel 'the weight of the world' (Bourdieu *et al.* 1999) may also experience the weight of semantic gravity. Thus, discovering ways to maximize the semantic range of everyone may be key not only to cumulative learning but to enabling a more inclusive and far-sighted society.

Notes

1 Semantics can also be introduced via Bernstein's earlier concepts of 'elaborated code' and 'restricted code', which similarly highlight context-dependence and condensation of meaning without articulating their organizing principles. His later concepts are preferred as a launching pad because they have been discussed in previous chapters and represent more recent formulations.
2 Chapters 4 and 5 also introduced ***knower structures*** to describe intellectual and educational fields as ***knowledge–knower structures***. I restrict my discussion here to 'knowledge structures' for simplicity of exposition.
3 Bernstein described the process of acquisition of horizontal discourse as 'segmental pedagogy' and distinguished this from the 'institutional pedagogy' of vertical discourse (2000: 159). In contrast, cumulative and segmented learning may refer to acquisition of either form of discourse.
4 See Christie and Humphrey (2008) and Christie and Derewianka (2010: 80–83) for complementary analyses of this essay using systemic functional linguistics.
5 This essay was collected as part of a major study discussed in Christie and Derewianka (2010).

7 Semantic density

How to build cumulative knowledge in social science

$$\textit{Cumulative modality} = \frac{SG^i-, SD^i+; SG^e+, SD^e-}{ER+, SR-}$$

Introduction

In the early 1950s Talcott Parsons lamented the lack of cumulative sociological research and pointed to a failing of theory:

> *probably the most crucial factor* has been precisely this lack of an adequate theoretical *working* tradition which is bred into the 'bones' of empirical researchers themselves, so that 'instinctively' the problems they work on, the hypotheses they frame and test, are such that the results, positive or negative, will have *significance* for a sufficiently generalized and integrated body of knowledge so that the mutual implications of many empirical studies will *play directly into each other*.
>
> (Parsons 1954: 350, original emphases)

By 'adequate working theoretical tradition', Parsons meant not a specific theory but rather what Bernstein (2000) termed a 'hierarchical knowledge structure': a systematically principled and hierarchical formation that develops through extending and integrating past knowledge to embrace more phenomena within a coherent and economic framework. Parsons' lament holds true today: sociology and educational research suffer from segmentalism. They represent what Bernstein termed 'horizontal knowledge structures': strongly bounded series of knowledges that develop by adding another approach alongside or instead of existing approaches. Rather than integrating knowledge of more phenomena, they often refurbish existing ideas under the guise of a decisive 'break'. As Chapter 3 argued, in sociology what Kuhn called 'revolutionary science' is normal and a period of 'normal science' would be revolutionary. This raises the question of what enables cumulative knowledge-building: what characteristics would an 'adequate working theoretical tradition' possess?

To address this question I begin this chapter by considering attempts to describe different kinds of theoretical traditions. Focusing on Bernstein's exemplary typology of 'knowledge structures' (2000), I discuss how the model highlights but does not fully conceptualize what needs to be analysed. However, rather than representing a limitation of Bernstein's typology, I argue that it is the nature of such models that limits their capacity for grasping the bases of practices. In short, to understand the kind of theorizing that enables cumulative knowledge-building additionally requires a different kind of theorizing, one which augments typologies of characteristics with analyses of their organizing principles. Previous chapters have begun addressing this issue: Chapter 2–5 elaborated concepts from the dimension of Specialization; and Chapter 6 introduced *semantic gravity*, one component of a second dimension, Semantics. This chapter continues to unfold this dimension by introducing *semantic density*. Brought together *semantic gravity* and *semantic density* conceptualize organizing principles of practices in terms of *semantic codes* and *semantic profiles* through time. They also reveal a new aspect to the Legitimation Device, the generative mechanism underlying social fields (Chapter 3).

To substantively explore how different forms of theorizing enable and constrain knowledge-building, I focus on Bernstein's code theory and Bourdieu's field theory, arguably the most influential approaches in post-war sociology of education and foundational frameworks for LCT. I analyse the organizing principles of internal relations among their ideas and external relations to their referents in terms of semantic codes and specialization codes. Put simply, I highlight how code theory reaches higher levels of context-independence and condensation through stronger vertical relations among concepts, and involves explicit 'external languages' for their engagement with empirical data, while field theory comprises horizontally related concepts whose legitimate use is based on a less explicit, cultivated gaze. I then discuss how the code modalities of these internal and external relations enable and constrain cumulative knowledge-building. I conclude by relating this analysis to the different roles played by these two frameworks within the development of LCT, and discuss how extending and integrating these approaches provides the possibility of a more powerful and inclusive theoretical tradition.

From types towards principles

There are many ways of describing forms of academic knowledge. Durkheim (1938/1977) discussed the structuring of medieval universities into Trivium and Quadrivium. Kuhn (1962) divided sciences into 'pre-paradigmatic', 'normal', and 'revolutionary'. More recently, Biglan (1973a, b) typologized disciplines into hard/soft, pure/applied, and life/non-life; Kolb (1981) offered abstract/concrete and active/reflective; and Becher and Trowler (2001) drew on both to taxonomize disciplinary 'tribes'. To these examples can be added an ever-growing list: effective/ineffective, propositional/procedural, context-independent/context-dependent, singulars/regions, conceptual/contextual, and so forth. The creation of knowledge typologies is a thriving cottage industry.

These models valuably bring knowledge into view as an object of study, overcoming the knowledge-blindness endemic to educational research. However, they also possess an inbuilt limit to their explanatory power thanks to their segmental form. Whether expanding or contracting, overlapping or integrating the forms of knowledge delineated, they nonetheless offer a series of static types into which few empirical practices and processes fit. This problem is often mentioned when such models are proposed and debated. Proponents admit they 'cannot do justice to the complexity and variation of inquiry processes and knowledge structures in various disciplines' (Kolb 1981: 245). Critics focus on difficulties matching empirical data to types, identify missing types of knowledge, and argue for further categories. Such caveats and criticisms highlight the problem but typically misunderstand its nature. The problem is not whether typologies offer sufficient categories to capture the manifold diversity of knowledge practices but rather that *this kind of theorizing* cannot *by itself* embrace such diversity. This is not to argue that typologies are a misstep but rather that they are a valuable first step. The next step is to additionally conceptualize the organizing principles that generate these diverse types (and other types yet to be delineated). To illustrate this argument, I shall consider Bernstein's model of 'knowledge structures'. By foregrounding ways in which knowledge develops, it is the most relevant typology; as the most analytically suggestive, it reveals the limits of this kind of theorizing, limits Bernstein himself highlighted.

Bernstein's typology

Bernstein (2000) described two key differences between hierarchical and horizontal knowledge structures, which Muller (2007) has termed 'verticality' and 'grammaticality'. 'Verticality' describes the form taken by relations among ideas within hierarchical knowledge structures, specifically the creation of ever-greater integrating propositions at ever-greater levels of abstraction which 'integrate knowledge at lower levels, and in this way shows underlying uniformities across an expanding range of apparently different phenomena' (Bernstein 2000: 161). 'Grammaticality' describes relations between ideas and their referents, specifically how some knowledge structures generate relatively unambiguous referents ('strong grammar'), while others do not ('weak grammar'). These two features are said to shape the capacity of intellectual fields to build cumulative knowledge. They are echoed in Bernstein's model of individual theories as comprising internal (L1) and external (L2) 'languages of description'. L1 'refers to the syntax whereby a conceptual language is created' or how constituent concepts of a theory are interrelated; and L2 'refers to the syntax whereby the internal language can describe something other than itself' (ibid.: 132) or how a theory's concepts are related to referents. Bernstein describes the 'syntax' of each language as strong or weak: a strong L1 is where concepts are tightly interrelated; a strong L2 is where concepts and data are related in relatively unambiguous ways.

Both models highlight internal relations among ideas and external relations to referents as key features generating different forms of knowledge. This points to where their organizing principles may be found. However, the models raise several issues. First, as Muller (2007, 2009) states, Bernstein's model describes 'verticality' in terms of presence/absence: a field either has it or does not. The characterization of horizontal knowledge structures (exemplified by the humanities and social sciences) as possessing no verticality can be read as a deficit model. Yet, as Chapter 5 shows, such fields *are* capable of integrative development. Second, the framework is segmented into separate concepts for internal relations and external relations and for intellectual fields and theories. An integrated account of education requires concepts to embrace both relations and all levels of analysis. Third, and most importantly, it is not clear what the concepts of verticality, grammaticality, L1 and L2 refer to, how they can be used in substantive research, and how they work together to enable cumulative knowledge-building. The concepts are intuitively suggestive but nebulous; ironically, they exhibit 'weak grammar', a 'weak L2'.

Keep the ball rolling

Bernstein himself highlighted the limitations of these kinds of concepts. He stated that, at this stage of theorization, understanding of the principles organizing such dichotomies is 'very weak' in its generative power (Bernstein 2000: 124). As Muller (2006: 14) argues of the model of knowledge structures, 'for all its richness, this analysis merely starts the ball rolling'. However, contrary to the logic underpinning the relentless creation of typologies, the way forward is not to succumb to the empiricist desire of drawing a map as big as the country and develop evermore categories. Rather, this kind of theorizing must be built upon by a different kind of theorizing. Usefully, Bernstein's framework itself offers blueprints for how to keep the ball rolling. The problem, as he highlighted of other ideas (Bernstein 2000: 133), is that each concept is known by its outcomes and cannot be replaced by X, that is by a description of its internal structure as one of a range of possibilities (e.g. W, X, Y, Z). Put another way, the concepts redescribe empirical characteristics rather than conceptualize organizing principles; they highlight the presence or absence of cumulative knowledge-building but not its bases. The question remains as to what gives a knowledge structure 'verticality' or 'grammaticality' and what makes internal or external languages of description 'strong' or 'weak'. Thus, the way forward is to generatively conceptualize the organizing principles of practices and, to embrace diversity, provide a means for showing how these principles are realized within different empirical practices.

Previous chapters have conceptualized some of these principles. Chapters 2–5 began outlining the LCT dimension of Specialization, which describes social fields of practice as ***knowledge–knower structures*** whose organizing principles are conceptualized as ***specialization codes*** of ***epistemic relations*** and ***social relations***. I shall continue to draw on concepts from this dimension. However, my principal focus here is another dimension of LCT that Chapter 6 began to introduce: Semantics. This dimension views social fields as ***semantic structures*** whose organizing principles are conceptualized as *semantic codes* based on *semantic gravity* and *semantic density*.

The concepts of Semantics do not, of course, arise *ex nihilo*, nor do they herald a revolutionary 'break'. LCT foresees its own repeated refinement, deepening and extension through relations with empirical studies, foundational frameworks and complementary approaches (Chapter 10). Semantics has its genesis in all three of these relations. First, substantive studies using Specialization – including those of Chapter 6, this chapter and Maton (2013) – 'spoke back' to the framework, highlighting issues of context-dependence and condensation of meaning not explicitly captured by this dimension. Second, these issues are broached by Bernstein's model of discourses and knowledge structures (2000) and his earlier work on elaborated and restricted codes (1971), highlighting their significance. However, in both models they remain conflated within dichotomous types and their organizing principles remain untheorized. Third, inter-disciplinary collaborations with systemic functional linguists (e.g. Martin and Maton 2013) raised questions of how linguistic features such as 'grammatical metaphor' are expressed in knowledge practices. These three impulses helped highlight what needed to be conceptualized. The ways they are conceptualized in Semantics are similarly grounded: the form taken by the concepts builds on Bernstein's framework, specifically his key notions of 'codes' and 'devices'. To explain why they take this form, however, first requires the new concepts to be introduced and enacted, for, as I have discussed, new concepts are needed to show how this mode of theorizing enables cumulative knowledge-building.

Semantics

Semantic gravity (SG) refers to the degree to which meaning relates to its context. Semantic gravity may be relatively stronger (+) or weaker (–) along a continuum of strengths. The stronger the semantic gravity (SG+), the more meaning is dependent on its context; the weaker the semantic gravity (SG–), the less dependent meaning is on its context. One can thus describe processes of: *weakening* semantic gravity (SG↓), such as moving from the concrete particulars of a specific case towards generalizations and abstractions whose meanings are less dependent on that context; and *strengthening* semantic gravity (SG↑), such as moving from abstract or generalized ideas towards concrete and delimited cases.[1] Changes in the semantic gravity of an individual item can also be described as processes of *gravitation*, whereby its meanings become contextually located, and *levitation*, whereby they are shorn free of their contextual moorings.

Semantic density (SD) refers to the degree of condensation of meaning within socio-cultural practices (symbols, terms, concepts, phrases, expressions, gestures, actions, clothing, etc).[2] Semantic density may be relatively stronger (+) or weaker (–) along a continuum of strengths. The stronger the semantic density (SD+), the more meanings are condensed within practices; the weaker the semantic density (SD–), the less meanings are condensed. The strength of semantic density of a practice or symbol relates to the *semantic structure* in which it is located. For example, Martin (2013) shows how the term 'cilia' is situated by the academic discourse of biology within: compositional structures that describe the physical constituents of cilia and what cilia are constituents of; taxonomic structures that involve different ways of classifying parts of the body; and a range of biological processes and causal explanations in which cilia play a role. In short, by virtue of its positions within the relational systems of meanings comprising the semantic structure of the intellectual field of biology, 'cilia' possesses a semantic density of considerable strength. A term may thus represent a semantic TARDIS: more resides within than may at first appear. This strength is, though, not essential or intrinsic to the symbol itself. Within biology, the semantic density characterizing 'cilia' in research publications is likely to be stronger than that characterizing its use within school textbooks, which in turn may be stronger than use in classroom discourse or student work products, thanks to the differing semantic structures of the production, recontextualization and reproduction fields of biology. Furthermore, for terms also in everyday use (unlike 'cilia'), these pedagogic realizations are, in turn, likely to exhibit stronger semantic density than uses in horizontal discourse.[3]

Dynamizing the concepts, one can describe *strengthening* semantic density (SD↑), such as moving from a practice or symbol that denotes a small number of meanings towards one that implicates a greater range; for example, moving from discussion of places, time periods, customs, ideas, and beliefs to the term 'Mycenaean Greece' in History, or relating structures of cells, proteins, pigments, etc., within a leaf to describe 'photosynthesis' in biology. Strengthening semantic density is thus creating (or revealing) constellations of meanings. Conversely, one can describe *weakening* semantic density (SD↓), such as moving from a highly condensed practice or symbol to one that involves fewer meanings. For example, explaining a technical concept from an academic source in simpler terms typically enacts only a limited number of its meanings, weakening semantic density by delocating the term from its constellational relations with other terms in its semantic structure. Changes of semantic density at the level of an individual item thus involve processes of *condensation*, whereby meanings are packed into something (as this sentence is doing) and *rarefaction*, whereby they are unpacked or removed (such as describing what something no longer means).

The nature of the context (for semantic gravity) and the meanings being condensed (for semantic density) may take a variety of forms whose nature can be analysed using other concepts. Different dimensions of LCT may thus be used together to generate further distinctions. For example, Chapter 8 will use specialization codes to describe forms of semantic density that involve: *epistemological condensation* of formal definitions (such as concepts) and empirical descriptions; and *axiological condensation* of affective, aesthetic, ethical, political and moral stances. Throughout this chapter I shall focus on epistemological condensation when describing strengths of semantic density. (I return to axiological condensation in Chapter 8.)[4]

Semantic codes

The dimension of Semantics conceptualizes social fields of practice as semantic structures whose organizing principles are given by semantic gravity and semantic density.

In contrast to established models discussed above, 'semantic gravity' and 'semantic density' are not categories into which variegated and changing empirical practices are to be crammed. All practices are characterized by *both* semantic gravity *and* semantic density; the question for substantive research concerns their respective strengths. (How these strengths are realized empirically depends on the specific object of study; 'external languages of description' provide a means of translating between concepts and data, as I discuss below.)

The relative strengths of semantic gravity and semantic density may be varied independently to generate a range of *semantic codes* (SG+/–, SD+/–). As illustrated by Figure 7.1, their continua of strengths also generate a *semantic plane*, with infinite capacity for gradation. The concepts thus combine typology (the four principal codes given by varying '+/–') with topology (the semantic plane), and boundaries (that create four code quadrants) with continua (the axes). By conceptualizing their organizing principles, Semantics thus offers a basis not only for typologizing practices (e.g. Shay 2013) but also for topologically exploring differences *within* types and dynamic processes of strengthening and weakening (SG↑↓, SD↑↓). The concepts thereby move beyond dichotomizing and homogenizing categories, such as abstract/concrete, hard/soft or pure/applied, to embrace differences both between and within different forms.[5] Dynamizing static accounts of knowledge forms is also crucial for capturing practices that unfold through time, such as knowledge-building. The concepts enable research to trace the *semantic profiles* of practices in terms of their positions on a scale of relative strengths, and the associated *semantic range* between their highest and lowest strengths. For example, Figure 6.5 (p.119) contrasted a *flatline* profile of semantic gravity characterizing a low-achieving student essay in school English with the *wave* profile associated with a high-achieving essay. The flatline delineates a much lower *semantic range* of strengths than the wave.

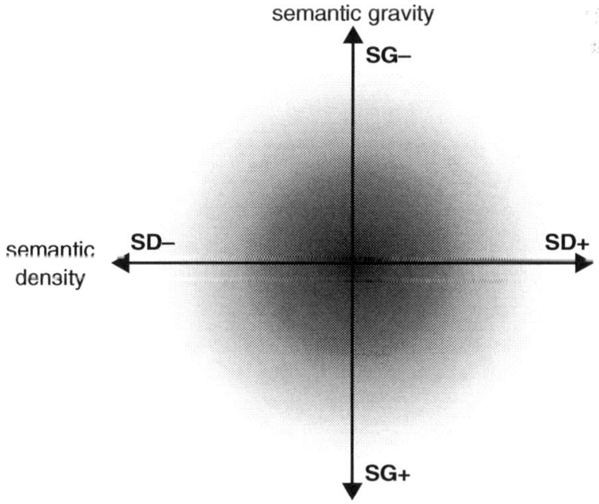

Figure 7.1 The semantic plane

Revisiting Bernstein's typologies, Semantics keeps the ball rolling not only in terms of conceptualizing organizing principles but also by enabling a more integrated account of education. The inherited framework comprises separate concepts for internal and external relations and for theories and fields. In contrast, 'semantic gravity' does not refer to external relations only, nor 'semantic density' to internal relations only (and vice versa), and such reductionism would weaken their explanatory power. As this chapter will illustrate, ***both concepts*** can be used to conceptualize ***both*** internal relations and external relations of knowledge practices (as signalled by the superscript 'i' and 'e' of the chapter's opening motif). They can also be enacted for different levels of analysis, including individual theories (this chapter) and whole intellectual fields (Chapter 8). Moreover, where the inherited models focused solely on production fields (as will this chapter), these concepts can also be used to analyse fields of recontextualization and of reproduction (e.g. Macnaught *et al.* 2013; Maton 2013; Matruglio *et al.* 2013). Moreover, as shown by the example of 'cilia' given earlier, they can trace changes in knowledge practices between these fields, enabling analysis of the effects of struggles and the 'play of ideology' in and beyond education (Chapter 3).

Dimensions

In relation to the Specialization framework unfolded through the book so far, Semantics opens up a second dimension to understanding social fields. Specialization and Semantics refer not to different empirical practices but rather to different organizing principles underlying the same practices (and so can be used together). Both explore the bases of languages of legitimation. Thus, what previous chapters have stated of specialization codes also holds here: a specific semantic code or profile may dominate as the (typically unwritten) 'rules of the game', but may not be transparent, universal or uncontested. Not everyone in the field may be able to recognize and/or realize what is required, there may be more than one code or profile present, and there are likely to be struggles over which is dominant. One can thus describe degrees of code match and code clash, such as among the stances of actors within a field or between pedagogic practices and the dispositions of learners.

Exploring this dimension also advances understanding of the Legitimation Device. Chapter 3 hypothesized the 'epistemic–pedagogic device' to be an incomplete conceptualization of this generative mechanism underlying social fields of practice. Semantics brings to light another aspect. Actors struggle for control of the ***semantic device*** to maximize the legitimacy of the semantic codes or profiles characterizing their own stances. Whoever controls this device establishes the semantic structure of the field. The semantic device is thus one aspect of what is at stake in struggles among actors. Bringing Specialization and Semantics together thereby provides a fuller understanding of the Legitimation Device as an ***epistemic–semantic–pedagogic device*** or what I shall henceforth refer to as an ***ESP device***.

I shall now draw on concepts from both these dimensions to explore cumulative knowledge-building. Substantively, I focus on two modes of theorizing, exemplified by the work of Basil Bernstein and Pierre Bourdieu. Their approaches share sufficient features to make such comparison meaningful: common intellectual foundations; relational and realist frameworks; and conceptualization of similar phenomena (e.g. coding orientation/habitus and arena/field). They are also both approaches on which LCT builds. In turning the tools of LCT onto its own foundations, I further reveal the rationale behind the differing roles they play within LCT (Chapter 1). As discussed earlier, Bernstein's models highlight internal relations (among concepts or ideas) and external relations (such as to data) as significant to knowledge-building but their underlying principles and interrelations remain unclear. I shall, therefore, analyse these relations in turn for both theories before addressing how they combine to enable or constrain cumulative knowledge-building. I should emphasize: my concern is not with the theories *per se* but rather with the *mode of theorizing* each theory represents, and my aim is not to determine which theory is better but to explore how their modes of theorizing offer different resources for knowledge-building.

Internal semantic relations

Bernstein's internal language

The theoretical framework inherited from Bernstein comprises a number of strands at different stages of development. Some remain at a prescient, suggestive but preliminary stage of descriptive typologies, such as knowledge structures, languages of description, singulars/regions/generic modes of academic knowledge, and 'an embryonic outline' (Bernstein 2000: 65) of pedagogic identities. Other strands reach further to conceptualize the generative principles underlying such types and their variation. At this more advanced stage the mode of theorizing is characterized by the development of concepts of successively weaker semantic gravity and stronger semantic density.

Figure 7.2 portrays one such development. It begins with Bernstein's theorization of progressivist pedagogy (1977: 116–156). This analysis first describes six fundamental characteristics of a progressivist classroom, such as control of the teacher over children being implicit (no. 1 in Figure 7.2). These characteristics are then described in terms of three basic features regulating pedagogic relations: 'hierarchy', 'sequencing rules' and 'criteria' (no. 2). The preceding characteristics are described as one possible form of these three features, such as implicit rather than explicit. The features are, in turn, gathered and condensed (no. 3) into a distinction between 'visible pedagogy' (where all three are explicit) and 'invisible pedagogy' (all three are implicit). At this point, the theorization has, in similar fashion to 'knowledge structures', created dichotomous types. It has climbed a semantic scale (SG↓, SD↑) as concepts move away from empirical descriptions and condense a wider range of potential meanings (nos 1–3), but still exhibits stronger semantic gravity and weaker semantic density than achievable by a second kind of theorization.

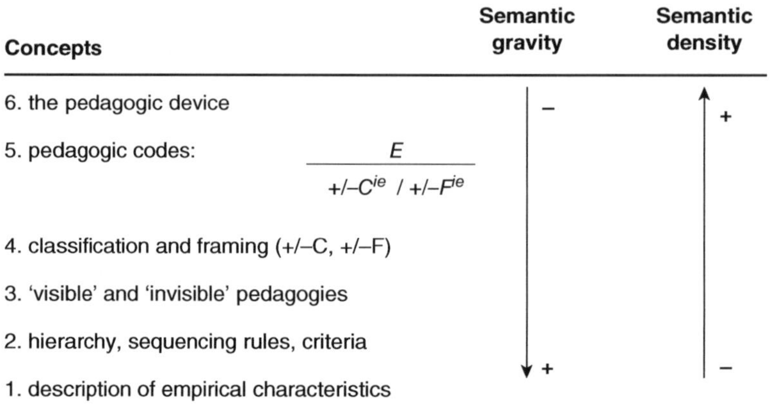

Figure 7.2 The semantic range of Bernstein's code theory

This second kind was realized when Bernstein conceptualized the principles underlying visible/invisible pedagogies in terms of their strengths of 'classification' and 'framing' (no. 4). The original description now becomes one (–C, –F) of four possible modalities (+/–C, +/–F). Three characteristics of this move are salient to our focus here. First, the concepts have become less contextually dependent: they are not necessarily locked onto descriptions of pedagogy: 'classification' refers to the strength of boundaries between contexts or categories, and 'framing' refers to the locus of control within those contexts or categories (Bernstein 1977: 176). Second, this generative conceptualization is of greater generality because it moves beyond the specific case to theorize possible modalities that may never have been actualized or empirically observed (Moore 2013b). Third, higher-order concepts condense a greater range of meanings at lower levels. The concepts of classification and framing incorporate preceding conceptualizations (nos 1–4 in Figure 7.2), which are in turn condensed within a more generalizing concept of 'pedagogic codes' (no. 5), defined as:

$$\frac{E}{\pm C^{ie} / \pm F^{ie}}$$

> where *E* refers to the orientation of the discourse (elaborated): ______ refers to the embedding of this orientation in classification and framing values.
>
> (Bernstein 2000: 100)

Moreover, this concept connects with a number of other strands of code theory, such as work on elaborated and restricted codes (Bernstein 1971), and thence with processes of the differential social distribution of coding orientations and wider issues of social order. The concept 'plugs in' to a wide range of established meanings from concepts and research studies across the framework.

This is now a considerable semantic distance from the description of empirical practices (and requires translations through lower-order concepts to reach the empirical). These processes of weakening semantic gravity and strengthening semantic density ($SG\downarrow$, $SD\uparrow$) are repeated in a further stage when the focus shifts from conceptualizing principles underlying empirical phenomena to conceptualizing what generates those principles in terms of the 'pedagogic device' (Bernstein 1990: 165–218). At this stage the theory reaches a higher degree of abstraction and generality (no. 6), which Bernstein condenses in a highly complex diagram (ibid.: 197) that includes not only a range of levels (from the family through various fields and discourses to the 'international field') and a host of technical terms (such as 'pedagogic code', 'ID' and 'RD') but also relations between them, such as '$\frac{ID}{RD}$', which are in turn interconnected by lines and arrows with other terms. Such complex diagrams offer a synoptic picture of extremely weak semantic gravity and strong semantic density.

The development of the internal relations of this strand of the theory thereby traces a rising semantic profile to higher-order concepts. Each conceptualization raises the question of what in turn gives rise to the principles already theorized, creating vertical extension of the theory to abstractions from abstractions and condensations of condensations. When these relations to lower-order concepts are explicitly defined, it creates vertical abstraction–condensation chains; for example, the definition of 'pedagogic codes' above includes 'elaborated', 'classification' and 'framing'.

This is not always the case: another form taken by development in Bernstein's framework comprises new versions of past concepts aimed at greater generality or condensing a greater range of meanings. For example, 'pedagogic codes' also subsumes such previous concepts as 'positional'/'personal' and 'instrumental'/'expressive' (Bernstein 2000: 89–100). As mentioned above, this semantic code and profile is not present across all strands of Bernstein's framework and relations between concepts are often not made explicit, segmenting strands of the framework. Nonetheless, at its most advanced, internal relations of this *mode of theorizing* aims towards a semantic code of SG^{i}–, SD^{i}+ (where 'i' indicates 'internal relations').

Bourdieu's internal language

The concepts of Bourdieu's 'field theory' are also highly abstract and condensed. 'Habitus', for example, encompasses a wide range of meanings that are relatively context-independent, including 'the *result of an organizing action ... a way of being, a habitual state* (especially of the body) and, in particular, a *predisposition, tendency, propensity or inclination*' (Bourdieu 1977: 214, original emphases). However, it is the *relations* among concepts that determine the semantic structure of an internal language. Many of Bourdieu's concepts are tightly interrelated. For example, the constituent concepts of 'practice' ('field', 'capital' and 'habitus') and those of 'symbolic violence' (including 'pedagogic work', 'pedagogic authority' and 'cultural arbitrary') are defined in terms of each other (Bourdieu 1977;

Bourdieu and Passeron 1977). There are also vertical relations between concepts. The logic of practice, for example, is summarized (Bourdieu 1984: 101) as:

[(habitus)(capital)] + field = practice

This condenses the idea that practice results from relations between one's structured and structuring dispositions (habitus) and one's relational position in a field of struggles (capital), within the current state of play of struggles in that social arena (field). However, these relations are between concepts of equivalent magnitudes of semantic gravity and semantic density.

The concepts are thus more strongly related horizontally than vertically and the mode of theorizing reaches less elevated levels. Vertical relations do not move as far along the semantic continua by, for example, conceptualizing the ***principles*** underlying 'practice'. Instead, such higher-order concepts are created by establishing ***horizontal*** relations between aggregated lower-order concepts (e.g. field, capital, habitus). Similarly, at a lower level, 'habitus' is defined as a 'structured and structuring structure' (Bourdieu 1994: 170) but the principles underlying that 'structure' are not systematically conceptualized: actors' habituses are shown by describing their practices rather than analysed in terms of organizing principles (Bernstein 2000; Maton 2012).

Internal semantic relations in this mode of theorizing are thus characterized by stronger semantic gravity and weaker semantic density than code theorizing. This limits a potential stimulus to theoretical development: answers (e.g. 'habitus'), however suggestive and insightful, do not lead to questions concerning their basis ('what are the organizing principles of habituses?'). This reduces vertical extension of the theory. For example, Bourdieu defines the structure of a 'field' as given by the rate of exchange between its species of 'capital' (status and resources), where their relative values reflect the state of play in struggles among actors possessing those capitals. As Chapter 3 discussed, this raises the question of how their relative status is determined at a particular moment in time, or what exchange rate mechanism actors are struggling over. Bourdieu's response reflects a horizontal mode of theorizing: the limits of the field and of legitimate participation are at once what are at stake in struggles, the ground over which struggles are fought, and what are used in struggles (1994: 143). The field is not only the thing, it is the *only* thing – there is no generative mechanism to be explored and so no higher-order concept to be defined (such as the *Legitimation Device*; Chapter 3). There is thus less vertical extension within the theory. Though exhibiting weaker semantic gravity and stronger semantic density than empirical descriptions, in comparison to code theorizing this modality aims towards a semantic code of $SG^{i}+$, $SD^{i}-$.

External semantic relations

Code theory's external languages

The key external relation of code theory is to the empirical world. Bernstein (2000) insisted that theoretical development is futile if concepts cannot engage with substantive problems. This was not, however, advocating the imposition of concepts onto empirical phenomena nor proclaiming the possibility of an empiricist reflection of reality. Rather, for Bernstein, concepts and data must speak to one another. Three implications of this position for the nature of these relations require noting here. First, it posits relatively strong epistemic relations (ER+) between knowledge and its object as the basis of legitimacy. Second, to enable dialogue between theory and data requires a means of translating meanings across these epistemic relations, what Bernstein (2000) described as an 'external language of description'. This represents the basis for translating theoretical concepts into empirical descriptions, and empirical descriptions into theoretical concepts. Third, once such an external language is established for the specific object being studied, the means of analysis is publicly visible to and reproducible by other researchers. Thus, 'who you are' is downplayed as the basis of legitimacy: relatively weak social relations (SR–) between knowledge and actors. Anyone who understands the theory can see if the analysis is consistent with the data and conclusions borne out by evidence. The external relations of this mode of theorizing are thus characterized by a ***knowledge code*** (ER+, SR–).

For Bernstein, this external language is crucial; he stated that 'a theory is only as good as the principles of description to which it gives rise' (2000: 91). In his own corpus, such languages are more often discussed than provided, something he acknowledged (ibid.: 121). However, neither one author's corpus nor a conceptual framework should be confused with a ***mode*** of theorizing: that Bernstein did not prolifically publish external languages does not mean this mode cannot generate them. Indeed, a variety of external languages for his concepts of classification and framing have been created by other scholars (e.g. Morais and Neves 2001; Morais *et al.* 2004). Similarly, Table 7.1 exemplifies an external language for specialization codes developed during research into the experiences of Chinese students at an Australian university (Chen 2010; Chen *et al.* 2011). Rather than a pre-established matrix or an inductively generated schema, such languages result from repeated movements between theory and data until a means of translation between the two emerges (Moss 2001). Table 7.1, for example, resulted from rather than pre-existed the study. Similarly, the external language for 'semantic gravity' discussed in Chapter 6 (Figure 6.2, p.113) arose from dialogic negotiation between data and theory: the study was conducted first, 'semantic gravity' was later developed in another study, and the coding schema and results of the earlier study were re-analysed using the concept. Fidelity to objects of study (stronger epistemic relations) is fundamental to such external languages. Thus, given an external language acts as a translation device between concepts and the specificities of data, different external languages may be required for the same concept when studying different phenomena. Kilpert and Shay (2013), for example, found the aforementioned external language for 'semantic gravity' limited because of differences in their object of study and so adapted another schema.

Table 7.1 Example external language for specialization codes

	Epistemic relations (ER)				*Social relations (SR)*			
	Concept manifested as emphasis on:		*Indicators*	*Example quotes from empirical data*	*Concept manifested as emphasis on:*		*Indicators*	*Example quotes from empirical data*
Curriculum	content knowledge	ER+	Content knowledge is emphasized as determining form of legitimate educational knowledge.	The information in the textbook – decided by the teacher – was what a study unit was all about.	personal knowledge and experience	SR+	Personal experience and opinions are viewed as legitimate educational knowledge.	[Students] actually come with a whole range of background and experience … what they need is a framework to download that.
		ER–	Content knowledge is downplayed as less important in defining legitimate educational knowledge.	We … show them … digital repositories that they need to go to in order to access those readings that are relevant to their context.		SR–	Personal experience and opinions are downplayed and distinguished from legitimate educational knowledge.	Online discussion is chaotic, and is like you conduct a survey and everyone tells you their opinions. That's all. It's different from a class.
Pedagogy	the teaching of content knowledge	ER+	Procedures for learning content knowledge are explicit to learners and emphasized as determining form of pedagogy.	[The teacher] extracts the best things from what he or she knows and gives this to you in class, and then offers you instructions on the tasks you need to complete.	personal dimension of the learning process	SR+	Individual learners' preferences are explicitly emphasized as determining form of pedagogy.	So negotiate to learn in a way that suits them … it's constructing your own learning in a way that is helpful for you.
			Procedures for learning content knowledge are implicit to learners and downplayed as not significantly shaping form of pedagogy	The teacher only points out the things you need to read.… But as to how to think, how to read and understand, it's your own business.		SR–	Individual learners' preferences are downplayed as not significantly shaping form of pedagogy.	Even if your question is brilliant, the teacher still might not answer you because he or she wants to teach something else first.
Assessment	explicit criteria	ER+	Explicit evaluative criteria are emphasized in judging student performances.	When a Chinese child paints the moon blue, the teacher will correct the child, saying that the moon shouldn't be blue.	self-evaluation	SR+	Evaluation of legitimacy of student performances resides in beliefs of individual learners.	What's valid for you and what's valid for me are two different things, aren't they?
		ER–	Explicit evaluative criteria are less significant in judging student performances.	It's not like learning medicine, you've got to get it right [otherwise] the patient will die. It's not like that. It's more open to interpretation.		SR–	Student performances are judged against shared criteria external to the learner.	I am a 'test-taker.' If the teacher doesn't give me a standard, I don't know what to do.

Source: Chen 2010: 83.

Such external languages are required whenever the internal language conceptualizes organizing principles. Lower-level theorization, such as typologies, produces concepts more dependent for meaning on their empirical objects and thus less capable of being used to analyse and bring together a wider range of problem-situations. Because 'classification' and 'framing' in Bernstein's framework (as well as epistemic relations, social relations, semantic gravity and semantic density in LCT) can be used to analyse a vast diversity of social practices, one needs to establish how they are realized within the *specific* problem-situation being researched. Analysing the semantic codes of the external language illustrated by Table 7.1, for example, shows that relations between concepts and data are thereby characterized by stronger semantic gravity than the theory's internal language. They are 'locked onto' a particular empirical context, in this case educational experiences of students expressed in interview data. Indeed, stronger and weaker epistemic and social relations are realized differently in discussions of curriculum, pedagogy and assessment. The language also exhibits relatively weaker semantic density, with descriptions of the concepts and their realizations within the data that condense less – they are 'locked into' a specific range of meanings. The semantic code of this external language is thus $SG^{e}+$, $SD^{e}-$ (where 'e' indicates 'external relations').

Just as important as its code is its semantic profile, in other words the ways an external language transforms meanings. Reading the epistemic relations and social relations columns in Table 7.1 from right to left, the external language works to: *weaken semantic gravity* by moving away from the concrete specificities of interview transcripts of a particular group of students; and *strengthen semantic density* by condensing a range of experiential meanings from the data into concepts. Reading from left to right, the external language also works to successively *strengthen semantic gravity* by moving from: abstract concepts ('epistemic relations', 'social relations'); to what forms these take in this object of study ('content knowledge', 'explicit criteria', etc.); to how these forms are in turn realized in student recounts of their experiences ('Content knowledge is emphasised...', etc.); and to examples of how these are realized in the data (quotes from students). At the same time condensed concepts are unpacked and specified, successively *weakening semantic density* by filling in more empirical detail and providing pointers to the specific kinds of meanings to be found across the reported data. So, an external language provides a means of moving meaning both up and down the strengths of semantic gravity and semantic density.

Bourdieu's external gaze

Bourdieu also emphasized that his concepts were intended to engage in a dialogue with data, describing them as 'a *temporary construct which takes shape for and by empirical work*' (in Bourdieu and Wacquant 1992: 161, original emphasis). Against empiricism he warned of the dangers of accepting the accounts of participants. Against theoreticism he warned against confusing the model of reality with the reality of the model (Bourdieu 1977: 29) and emphasized differences between 'the *theoretical* aims of theoretical understanding and the practical and directly concerned aims of practical understanding' (Bourdieu 1994: 60). This has parallels with Bernstein's concerns. Where Bourdieu differs is in how he attempts to avoid these problems. For Bourdieu they imply the need for a double 'epistemological break', first from the viewpoints of participants and second from the viewpoint of the detached observer. Crucially, the 'important thing is to be able to objectify one's relation to the object' (Bourdieu 1993b: 53) in terms of the effects of one's relational social positioning. Relations between theory and data are thus typically understood by Bourdieu in terms of the social positions of actors and their situated viewpoints (Maton 2003).

This approach has two key implications for the theory's external relations. First, in this mode of theorizing there are no *explicit* principles of translation between theory and data (no external languages). Instead, Bourdieu attempted to create concepts of sufficient versatility to be flexible enough for any research; as Wacquant argues, 'Bourdieu has not exhibited the "obsessive preoccupation" with achieving relatively unambiguous meaning in his concepts' (in Bourdieu and Wacquant 1992: 35–36). The problem, as Swartz summarizes, is that 'this very appealing conceptual versatility sometimes renders ambiguous just what the concept actually designates empirically' (1997: 109). As has been widely commented, this opens up the possibility of circularity and *ad hoc* explanations, for example: actors make bourgeois choices because of their bourgeois habituses; their bourgeois habituses are shown by the bourgeois choices they make (Maton 2003). Bourdieu acknowledged this possibility and claimed to be 'keenly aware of this danger' (Bourdieu and Wacquant 1992: 129), but did not explicate how it could be avoided except through vigilance. In short, external relations between the theory and data are characterized by relatively weaker epistemic relations (ER–).

Second, instead of an external language, Bourdieu's theorizing emphasizes developing a sociological 'gaze' or habitus: 'a system of dispositions necessary to the constitution of the craft of the sociologist in its universality' (1993a: 271):

> The task is to produce, if not a 'new person', then at least a 'new gaze', a sociological eye. And this cannot be done without a genuine conversion, a *metanoia*, a mental revolution, a transformation of one's whole vision of the social world.
>
> (Bourdieu and Wacquant 1992: 251)

The emphasis here is on stronger social relations between knowledge and actors (SR+). The external relations of Bourdieu's theory are thus characterized by a *knower code* (ER–, SR+).

Where code theory emphasizes the translation of meanings across epistemic relations, field theory emphasizes the translation of meanings across social relations. Bourdieu consistently described his approach in subjective terms: 'gaze', 'mental revolution', 'thinking tools', 'dispositions', etc. This highlights an issue explored in Chapter 5: the epistemic relations that Bernstein's concept of 'grammars' also point to are not the only external relations of knowledge practices. Bernstein would characterize his own and Bourdieu's theories as strong and weak grammars, respectively – a deficit account of the latter. However, that mode possesses stronger external relations of a different kind: ***social relations*** (or what Chapters 4 and 5 temporarily referred to as 'knower-grammars') which relate concepts to data via the gazes of knowers. Every field involves a specialized gaze, the question is of what kind. For example, with a ***trained gaze*** understanding specialized knowledge forms the legitimate gaze rather than the gaze defining legitimate principles and procedures. In contrast, Bourdieu's mode of theorizing is based on a ***cultivated gaze***, where prolonged immersion in a range of contexts under the guidance of a master shapes the knower's dispositions and these ways of knowing define the appropriate procedures of enquiry and means of evaluation. In short, for Bourdieu what matters is learning 'the craft of sociology':

> You have some general principles of method that are in a sense inscribed in the scientific habitus. The sociologist's *métier* is exactly that – a theory of the sociological construction of the object, converted into a habitus. When you possess this *métier*, you master in a practical state everything that is contained in the fundamental concepts: habitus, field, and so on.
>
> (Bourdieu *et al.* 1991: 253)

Where the external relations of code theory represent a knowledge code, those of field theory represent a knower code. However, both share a semantic code of stronger semantic gravity and weaker semantic density ($SG^{c}+$, $SD^{c}-$). The aim of the 'sociological gaze' is to grasp the concrete particularities of meanings in specific contexts. For example, Bourdieu proclaimed that 'one cannot grasp the most profound logic of the social world unless one becomes immersed in the specificity of an empirical reality' (1993a: 271). Where for code theory this means the immersion of the concept through an external language, for field theory it means the immersion of the researcher.

Compared to the explicit translation of external languages, what this cultivated gaze does to meaning is less visible. Any processes of strengthening and weakening of semantic gravity and semantic density are less available for inspection. Rather than exhibiting ***semantic flow*** by tracing continuous movements up and down the range of strengths of semantic gravity and semantic density (Maton 2013), meanings can thus give the appearance of quantum leaps (where the intervening stages are invisible) between different positions on the semantic scale as research publications shift between empirical and theorized descriptions. This profile is often illustrated in Bourdieu's major studies, such as *Reproduction in Education, Society and Culture* (Bourdieu and Passeron 1977) and *Distinction* (Bourdieu 1984), which comprise highly theoretical discussions and empirical descriptions as separate sections or in different fonts. In the work of other scholars, this profile appears more often as unexplicated leaps between concepts and their ostensible empirical realizations.

Cumulative and segmental modalities

Thus far, the internal and external relations of two modes of theorizing (illustrated by code theory and field theory) have been analysed. They have exhibited contrasting semantic codes for internal relations and the same semantic code for external relations but embedded in different specialization codes:

- the internal relations of code theorizing aim towards ***weaker semantic gravity*** and ***stronger semantic density*** (SG^i-, SD^i+) than those of field theorizing; and
- the external relations of both kinds of theorizing exhibit ***stronger semantic gravity*** and ***weaker semantic density*** (SG^c+, SD^c-), but code theorizing is underpinned by a ***knowledge code*** (embodied by external languages of description) while field theorizing exhibits a ***knower code*** (embodied by a 'sociological gaze').

Having analysed the nature of internal and external relations, the question remains of how these codes enable or constrain cumulative knowledge-building.

Cumulative modality

To be intentionally context-independent and condensed, the kind of theorizing illustrated by code theory, which I shall refer to as ***the cumulative modality***, can be summarized as:

$$\frac{SG^i-, SD^i+, SG^c+, SD^c-}{ER+, SR-}$$

This combination of codes enables knowledge-building in two principal directions. As discussed above, its internal semantic code (SG^i-, SD^i+) provides a basis for vertical extension of the theory and for strength in those vertical relations; that is, how context-independent and condensed it can become and how integrated each conceptual stratum is with higher-order and lower-order concepts. Its external semantic code (SG^c+, SD^c-) provides a basis both for the theory to engage with empirical data, ensuring it is not freely floating, and for horizontal extension of the range of substantive problems encompassed by the theory, enabling its use across different contexts. Crucially, however, its underlying knowledge code (ER+, SR–) provides a means of translating meanings between theory and data that creates ***semantic waves*** over time and so enables development of knowledge across those problem-situations.

Put less abstractly, this modality enables knowledge-building because of what it *does* to meanings. Figure 7.3 heuristically portrays three semantic profiles.[6] A theory comprising context-independent and highly condensed concepts but lacking the means to operationalize those concepts and for empirical data to 'speak back' progresses as a ***high semantic flatline*** (A1). Descriptive substantive research lacking such concepts develops over time as a ***low semantic flatline*** (A2).

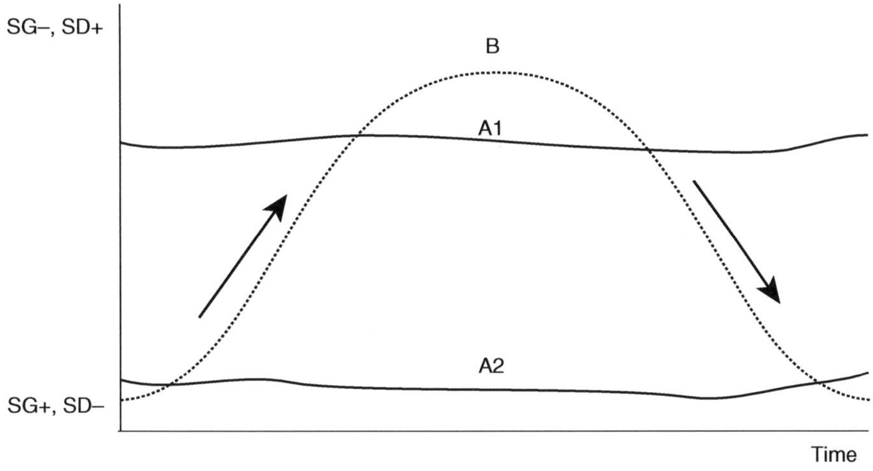

Figure 7.3 Three semantic profiles

In contrast, the cumulative modality traces a *semantic wave* (B). On the one hand, as indicated by the upward arrow, it lifts meanings out of the gravity well of a context through abstracting organizing principles into a condensed language that rises above the concrete particulars of that context. This enables such concepts to be enacted across a wider range of contexts. On the other hand, as indicated by the downward arrow, this potential is realized through the way it concretizes and 'fleshes out' concepts through a dialogue with the particularities of each context. External languages of description show how concepts are realized within specific objects of study. The cumulative modality thereby enables *both* the strengthening and weakening of *both* semantic gravity and semantic density between lower-order and higher-order concepts within the theory, and between theory and data, tracing a wave profile over time. This enables both the decontextualization and the recontextualization of knowledge and so makes possible knowledge-building across different contexts and over time.

The cumulative modality also stimulates knowledge-building in these two directions. Internally, each conceptualization of principles raises the question of what in turn generates those principles, pointing forward to a future moment of theorizing of greater generality, abstraction and condensation. Its external relations, based on a knowledge code, enable dialogue between concepts and data, so new problem-situations may 'speak back', requiring clarification, revision or extension of the theory. Of course, this potential may not be recognized or realized: not all actors possess the requisite semantic coding orientations. For example, some scholars criticize typologies for failing to fit empirical data and abandon them rather than develop the internal language further by conceptualizing the principles underlying such types and developing external languages for their translation. Nonetheless, this mode of theorizing enables the potential for cumulative knowledge-building.

Segmental modality

The kind of theorizing illustrated by field theory, which for contrast I shall refer to as *the segmental modality*, can be summarized as:

$$\frac{SG^i+, SD^i-, SG^c+, SD^c-}{ER-, SR+}$$

This modality, based on a cultivated gaze, represents a considerable advancement on most approaches in sociology and education. Bourdieu's field theory is one of the most powerful and subtle of its kind; its capacity for highlighting issues of significance should not be understated. Nonetheless, the ***kind*** of theorizing exemplified by field theory ***as it currently stands*** has weaker stimuli to knowledge-building than the cumulative modality.

Internally, its stronger semantic gravity and weaker semantic density reflect a tendency for the questions to stop too soon. Although horizontal relations among concepts are strong, vertical extension of the theory is relatively constrained. Externally, a cultivated gaze offers a tacit and indirect means for data to 'speak back' to theory because translations of meaning are via an actor's habitus. In Figure 7.3, this would trace one flatline (as abstract theorizing), then jump to another flatline (empirical descriptions), and back again, without explicit shifts up and down, as illustrated by the bifurcated discourse of many studies. It would also slow development. Bourdieu described the habitus as durable and transposable: it typically takes repeated and lengthy exposure to circumstances for the habitus to significantly change. Thus, to return to Bourdieu's quotes earlier, mastering 'in a practical state' the meanings condensed within the concepts takes time, prolonged experience and intimate pedagogic relations to enable a 'genuine conversion, a *metanoia*, a mental revolution'. Once the theory is 'converted into a habitus', these dispositions are again durable and transposable across contexts. This knower-code means of dialogue between theory and different objects of study is thus slower changing and less direct than (knowledge-code) external languages of description. The results are illustrated by the development of Bourdieu's theory. Though he described his framework as a 'temporary construct', the approach primarily advanced through applying the theory to new topics rather than through the creation of new concepts of greater generality and condensation. Where concepts changed, they did so slowly; 'habitus', for example, evolved from a more cognitive focus to embrace the corporeal but remained fundamentally the same (Maton 2012).

More significantly, cumulative knowledge-building in an intellectual field is a cooperative endeavour and this modality depends on 'sociality' (Chapter 5), the extent to which the cultivated gaze is shared. Unfortunately Bourdieu's sociological gaze is not widely possessed, even among prominent proponents of the theory. Though his concepts are widely used, studies rarely build on each other. Indeed, 'development' of concepts by other scholars has been towards *less* generality and condensation. Researchers restlessly prefix 'habitus' and 'capital' with adjectives ('institutional habitus', 'family habitus', 'gendered capital', etc.) to denote the arena of social life or kinds of actors being studied, locking the concept onto specific contexts. Moreover, contrary to Bourdieu's own proscriptions, studies typically use individual concepts separately, disengaging them from the semantic structure that underpins their range of meanings. 'Habitus', for example, has often been regularly reduced to a synonym for social class background, socialization or organizational culture. While praising Bourdieu's ideas, such scholars have thereby strengthened the semantic gravity and weakened the semantic density of the internal language of the framework, reducing its potential to enable cumulative knowledge-building.

Conclusion

Cumulative knowledge-building requires something for actors to share, an intersubjective element that allows their work to 'play directly into each other'. Whether described as bred into the bones (Parsons), a new gaze (Bourdieu) or 'the sociological imagination' (Mills 1959), a common refrain in sociology is the need for researchers to share an 'adequate working theoretical tradition'. The nature of this tradition, however, remains open to debate. Theories of theories abound. Most models, though, embody a form of theorizing that can neither fully see nor serve as the basis for knowledge-building. Earlier I stated that explaining the form taken by the concepts of Semantics required first introducing and enacting them. We can now begin to see why. Using the concepts highlights how typologies embody stronger semantic gravity and weaker semantic density than topological codes. This is not to dismiss typologies. As Bernstein (2000: 133) wrote of other ideas, this 'does not mean that we abandon such a conceptual syntax but should recognise it for what it is, something good to think with, or about'. Their value lies principally in providing a first step towards conceptualizing organizing principles and offering potential external languages of description for such concepts.

Using specialization codes and semantic codes we can now follow Bernstein's blueprint and keep the ball rolling by describing the structuring of a set of knowledge practices as one of a range of possibilities (ER+/–, SR+/–; SG+/–, SD+/–), some of which may never have been actualized or perceived. Rather than empirical redescriptions of practices, the concepts thus offer a generative theorization of their principles. They can also be used to analyse both internal relations and external relations of practices, at all levels of social fields, as well as processes of change through time. This chapter has examined theories, but studies of curriculum and classroom practice show that these concepts are applicable to fields of production, recontextualization and reproduction. They can thus condense a greater range of meanings across a wide array of different problem-situations. Recent studies using concepts from Semantics have, for example, explored biology and history (Martin and Maton 2013), design studies (Shay and Steyn 2014), engineering (Wolff and Luckett 2013), environmental education (Tan 2013), ethnography (Hood 2014), jazz (J.L. Martin 2013), journalism (Kilpert and Shay

2013), marketing (Arbee 2012), physics (Lindstrøm 2010; Zhao 2012), sociology (Stavrou 2012), and teacher education (Shalem and Slonimsky 2010), as well as beyond education, such as freemasonry apprenticeship (Poulet 2011). The capacity of codes to reach further up the semantic scale (SG–, SD+) thereby provides a basis to see beyond specificities of the concrete particulars of each study and so for the mutual implications of empirical studies of diverse issues to play directly into each other. (Thus the choice of a highly condensed and context-independent motif for this chapter.) By keeping the ball rolling, LCT thus both reveals and embodies the principles for creating ideas at higher levels of abstraction which integrate knowledge at lower levels and across an expanding range of apparently different phenomena.

However, as the analysis of this chapter reveals, weaker semantic gravity and stronger semantic density of a theory's internal language are not enough. The aim is not simply for context-independence and condensation. Such concepts require translation to engage with empirical data – in terms of semantic profiles, what goes up must come down. Where this depends on a cultivated knower code, the tendency of conceptual development may be towards fragmentation and segmentalism of the framework by actors without the requisite gaze. Moves towards empirical descriptions thereby come at the cost of strengthening semantic gravity and weakening semantic density for the theory's internal relations, lowering its capacity for building knowledge across contexts. Moreover, because the workings of this gaze are less visible, such tendencies are difficult to counteract through public discussion. In contrast, external languages of description make explicit the translation of meanings between concepts and their realizations within specific objects of study. This knowledge code enables the possibility of a trained gaze – it makes public the principles of selection, recontextualization and evaluation in relations between theory and data.

However, herein lies an essential tension: no single code is necessarily the answer to every moment of the logics of discovery and demonstration of cumulative knowledge-building. The knowledge code of external languages characterizes the finished product, the results of research. Learning how to create such external languages may require not only explicit principles and procedures but also modelling and apprenticeship. Moreover, one rarely begins research with a completed external language (unless replicating another study) but rather with a gaze cultivated through guided immersion in the theoretical framework and exemplars of studies. (As Chapter 9 would suggest, one begins with a gaze and ends with insight.) Nonetheless, the cumulative modality suggests the aim should be to make this process as explicit as possible. Thus, the successor volume to this book (Maton *et al.* 2014) includes accounts of developing external languages for qualitative research (Chen and Maton 2014), mixed-methods research (Howard and Maton 2014), and praxis (Carvalho *et al.* 2014). Nonetheless, these are not cookie-cutter models: the minute particulars of each study requires learning how to see or listen to, as well as to act on, the specificities of its focus, for which experience is essential.

Turning the tools of LCT onto its foundation frameworks thereby sheds light on the different ways LCT builds on these two approaches. The binary constellations of sociological and educational research (Chapter 8), which set up 'either/or' instead of 'both/and' as default settings for the fields, make it likely the analysis is misread by some scholars as condemning field theory. However, this framework is something good to think with and about. It is also something good to think beyond: rather than dismissing the theory this analysis highlights what it offers and how a different mode of theorizing can develop it further. Bourdieu's field theory models a sociological gaze. Through a prolific series of analyses, Bourdieu showed that to think sociologically is to think in a relational and realist manner about such issues as struggles, status, dispositions and power in social fields. His work sensitizes us to what issues may be significant and how to think about them. Bernstein's code theory at its most advanced additionally shows the basis for creating new conceptual tools, principally 'codes' and 'devices', that enable both these issues to be conceptualized more powerfully and the workings of this sociological gaze to be made more visible, explicit, trainable and accessible. Sociology is both a craft and a science – it needs a gaze but one whose vision is made as explicit as possible. An adequate working theoretical tradition is not only epistemologically powerful but also socially inclusive. By making visible the workings of the gaze, we have a chance to make that gaze more widely available. We can climb on the shoulders of both giants. Not only can we then see further, more of us can do so.

Notes

1 The meanings of '↑' (strengthening) and '↓' (weakening) are the same across all LCT concepts. Thus, 'weakening semantic gravity' is denoted by 'SG↓', though weaker semantic gravity (SG–) is typically placed at the top of semantic planes and scales.

2 Semantic density should not be confused with the linguistic notion of 'lexical density', which concerns numbers of different kinds of words in texts.

3 I am here describing degrees of *epistemological condensation*; commonsense understandings may exhibit stronger *axiological condensation* (Chapter 8). In short, the example does not suggest a deficit model of horizontal discourse, which may exhibit stronger semantic density of a different kind.

4 What kinds of contexts generate stronger or weaker semantic gravity and what kinds of meanings enable different strengths of semantic density is a fruitful area for exploration, for which existing typological studies may prove invaluable first steps. As this chapter emphasizes, typologies and codes are *both* useful; as Chapter 10 highlights, such models may be integrated with LCT.

5 While categories such as abstract/concrete or pure/applied can be redescribed as endpoints of a continuum, their definitions are vague, hotly contested, elide instances with principles, conflate context-dependence and condensation, and remain embedded in dichotomizing discourses that imbue each category with considerable axiological loading (see Chapter 8). In short, they exhibit weaker epistemological condensation, stronger axiological condensation, and a limited range of semantic gravity than the concepts of Semantics. Notably, using categories such as abstract/concrete or pure/applied to analyse categories such as abstract/concrete or pure/applied would offer less insight into their value and limits.

6 This is a simplified representation, with semantic gravity and semantic density inversely related, as they are in the theories analysed here; see Maton (2013) on the diversity and complexity of semantic profiles.

8 Cosmologies

How to win friends and influence people

The truth is no guarantee of belief. Belief is no guarantee of the truth.

Introduction

For the social sciences to progress cumulatively it is not enough to identify practices that enable knowledge-building, they also need to become widely practiced. That a framework for research offers more explanatory power and potential for progress is no guarantee of its adoption. The two theories analysed in Chapter 7 – Bourdieu's field theory and Bernstein's code theory – are cases in point. Over recent years Bourdieu's star has risen in the intellectual firmament and his concepts are now drawn on across a range of disciplines. Yet, the form taken by this theorizing is less conducive to cumulative knowledge-building and most uses are perfunctory, reductive or disengage individual concepts from the wider framework that gives them meaning. In comparison, the mode of theorizing exemplified by code theory enables explanations of a growing range of phenomena to be integrated within an economical framework. However, Bernstein's profile is relatively low and this 'enormous potential for addressing enduring debates and dilemmas within social science and education ... remains largely unrealised' (Power 2010: 239). As Mary Douglas wrote:

> the power and originality of his thinking should have made a much bigger impact. He was firing the first shots in a revolution in the social sciences. That the revolution has still not arrived was no one's fault directly.
>
> (Douglas 2000)

Why, then, has the revolution not arrived – who or what is at indirect fault?

A common explanation blames Bernstein for being obscure. Commentators state that 'many of his readers profess to find his ideas difficult, obscure and elusive' (Atkinson 1985: 6), accuse him of using 'a code of sociologese which is hard to break' (Barcan 1993: 156) or claim his use of imagined examples indicates an inability to engage with empirical data (Power 2010). Bernstein's writings are indeed highly theoretical, with minimal empirical exposition interspersed by complex diagrams of concepts. It is as if substantive objects of study have been reduced for a long time on a low heat, leaving a condensed theoretical description, a kind of conceptual stock cube to which readers must add their own examples. Thus, the bulk of his sociological theory fits into three slim volumes of papers (1977, 1990, 2000). In contrast, Bourdieu presented his ideas in a highly textured, prosaic style, embodied in a large corpus of often heavy books thick with empirical descriptions complemented by tables and graphs of data. Bourdieu wrote as if paid by the word, Bernstein wrote as if paying for the paper and ink himself. Nonetheless, Bourdieu has been similarly criticized as obscure. Commentators note that 'virtually everyone complains about Bourdieu's dense and highly euphemised style' (Nash 2001: 65) and characterize his writing as 'unnecessarily long-winded, obscure, complex and intimidatory' (Jenkins 1992: 10). Employing empirical examples is thus no insurance against a theory being viewed as dense and obscure and, in turn, that image is not fatal to its widespread adoption. As Davies (2010: 35) argues, those describing Bernstein as too difficult are often also 'overdosing on the less than pellucid prose of one or more Grand Masters or more recent structuralist and post-structuralist circumlocutions'.

Obscurity is in the eye of the beholder and everybody is somebody's bore. Claims that a theory is 'obscure' only obscure the issues. It is less that a theory is abstract and dense and more the *form* taken by abstraction and condensation that matters. Chapter 7 analysed the forms taken by abstraction and epistemological condensation in these two theories; here I explore why those forms are valorized differently. However, this issue reaches beyond the two theorists. For example, a study of citations of 'situated learning', from Lave and Wenger (1991), shows very little use to be cumulative and concludes by asking how the text could 'achieve prominence in the literature while directly producing little in the way of cumulative research' (Lang and Canning 2010: 299). This chapter builds on Chapter 7 to explore this issue: why are stronger theories marginal and weaker ideas so prominent in fields like sociology and educational research? This is to shift focus from the theories to the fields in which they are positioned. The combined analysis of both chapters thereby explores how relations between the organizing principles of stances within a field (Chapter 7) and the organizing principles of that field (this chapter) help shape their differing positions.

I begin by briefly recapping how Bernstein's approach helps overcome knowledge-blindness but needs extending to embrace fields where knowledge structures are relatively weak. I describe how previous chapters began this process by conceptualizing ***knower structures*** (Chapter 4) and ***gazes*** (Chapter 5), but themselves raise questions of how practices are related to the gazes of privileged knowers. To explore this issue I introduce concepts for conducting ***cosmological analysis*** of the basis of legitimacy in social fields of practice in terms of: cosmologies, clusters, constellations, condensation and charging. These examine how belief systems or *cosmologies* underlie the ways actors select and arrange *clusters* and *constellations* of stances that, in turn, shape what is viewed as possible and legitimate within a field. Their organizing principles are explored by bringing together concepts from Specialization and Semantics to distinguish epistemological and axiological forms of ***condensation*** whereby stances are imbued with meanings that are then differentially ***charged*** with legitimacy.

Using these concepts, I analyse a portrayal of educational research by advocates of 'student-centred learning' that has dominated the field since the 1990s. First, I highlight how the terms 'student-centred' and 'teacher-centred' represent tightly knit but strongly bounded constellations that obscure other possibilities. Second, I show that dominant valuations of these constellations reflect a knower code by downplaying explanatory power and emphasizing moral virtue. Claims for 'student-centred learning' exhibit ambiguous relations among concepts and to data but relatively strong semantic density of moral meanings – ***axiological condensation*** – that reflects well on their proponents and badly on their perceived opponents. Third, I bring this analysis together with that of Chapter 7 to discuss how cumulative and segmental modes of theorizing are positioned by this ***axiological cosmology*** in ways that suggest knowledge-building must involve morally and politically indefensible practices. I conclude by discussing the capacity of cosmological analysis to not only explore but also change the basis of fields and thereby encourage the wider adoption of cumulative practices.

Stargazing

The conventional sociological approach to questions of intellectual predominance is to focus on *relations to* knowledge practices (see Chapter 1). Echoing Marx's famous dictum that the ruling ideas of any age are the ideas of the ruling class, most approaches explore social power. Bourdieu, for example, argues that the relational positions of practices within a 'field of stances' reflects the relational positions of their sponsoring agents in a 'field of positions' (Chapter 2). Most sociological analyses adopt (typically less sophisticated) forms of this approach, such as foregrounding the role of gatekeepers or shared values of dominant groups. From this perspective there is no reason why any particular ideas and not others serve the interests of dominant groups. They thereby construct knowledge practices as arbitrary epiphenomena, obscuring ***relations within*** knowledge practices that, as previous chapters show, shape social fields.

Bernstein's code theory begins bringing these relations within knowledge practices into view but, I have argued, requires development. The concepts of 'educational knowledge codes' (Bernstein 1977) and 'knowledge structures' (Bernstein 2000) most illuminate fields where knowledge is explicit and strongly bounded but are less enlightening where knowledge is less clear-cut (see Chapters 4 and 5). For example, the ascendance of ideas in 'hierarchical knowledge structures', exemplified by the natural sciences, is said to be motivated by their comparative explanatory power and conceptual economy: stellar theories encompass more phenomena within fewer, more tightly integrated propositions.

However, the model is less clear about the basis of choice among ideas in 'horizontal knowledge structures', exemplified by the humanities and social sciences, where knowledge is less strongly structured and worldly corroboration of ideas is downplayed. What makes ideas shine here?

Previous chapters have begun addressing this issue. Chapter 4 showed that viewing social fields as ***knowledge–knower structures*** avoids the possibility of a deficit model by highlighting that fields with horizontal knowledge structures may also have ***hierarchical knower structures.*** In such knower-code fields the ascendance of ideas or practices is motivated by their capacity to reflect the gazes of legitimate knowers. Chapter 5 deepened this analysis to explore a range of such gazes. However, the question remains as to how stances come to be associated with legitimate knowers and ways of knowing. With standpoint theories this is direct and explicit: actors explicitly valorize a (typically dominated) social group such that anything its members say or do is legitimate. However, while playing a key role in the history of cultural studies (Chapters 2 and 5), standpoint theories have been marginal to most academic subjects, including sociology and education. In these fields relations between practices and the gazes of legitimate knowers are indirect and tacit. Put another way, Bourdieu's ideas and 'situated learning' are not directly and explicitly said to legitimate or be legitimated by specific social groups. Chapter 5 described standpoint theories as exemplifying but one kind of gaze and highlighted the significance of *cultivated gazes* (see also Chapter 6). However, the basis of cultivated gazes in these fields has yet to be explored. How ideas and practices come to be viewed as luminous and widely adopted in the humanities and social sciences thus remains unclear.

This chapter argues there is more at work in fields than the evaluations of explanatory power of hierarchical knowledge structures or the direct expressions of social power highlighted by 'relations to' studies and enacted by standpoint theories. There is also axiological power: ideas and practices have affective effects. However, as Boudon (2008: 349) states, 'axiological feelings – i.e. the feelings that X is good, legitimate, etc. – are both one of the most important social phenomena and one of the least mastered scientifically'. To embrace fields from across the disciplinary map, we thus need a means of explaining the differential valuation of practices that integrates analyses of all these forms of power.

Cosmological analysis

Wondering how a barren approach dominated philosophy for decades, Gellner argued:

> It isn't so much that we need one word for an account of ideas and another for an account of sentiments, but rather we need one word for the clusters of ideas which engender powerful sentiments (and perhaps the other way round).
>
> (Gellner 1959: 2)

Gellner's suggested word was 'ideology', which he described as 'a system of ideas with a powerful sex appeal' (1959: 2). Though the word 'ideology' is encrusted with political meanings and often contrasted with 'science', Gellner's point can be extended to embrace all systems of ideas or practices, including scientific theories: each has more or less 'sex appeal'. Gellner did not propose, however, a word for that which makes one set of ideas and practices sexy and another not so hot. This I shall define as a *cosmology*.[1] Cosmologies are constitutive features of social fields that underlie the ways actors and practices are differentially characterized and valued. A cosmology is the logic of the belief system or vision of the world embodied by activities within a social field. The process whereby a cosmology shapes the hierarchizing of actors and practices within fields works along two principal dimensions encompassing what I shall term the 4-Cs of cosmological analysis: *clustering* and *constellating* of internal relations; and *condensing* and *charging* of external relations.

Clustering and constellating

In terms of internal relations, hierarchization first involves the *clustering* of ideas, practices, beliefs and attributes – or, for brevity, 'stances' – through their association together and contrast with other clusters. These clusters may become arranged into more strongly or weakly integrated *constellations* that are more strongly or weakly bounded from other constellations. The arrangement of constellations shapes what Bourdieu (1991) termed the 'space of possibles': the range and combinations of stances viewed by actors as possible within a field. For example, where stances are tightly associated within two bounded constellations, the adoption of one stance may appear to actors to necessarily entail adoption of other stances within its constellation and rejection of those from the opposing constellation.

The nature of constellations and their arrangement are, of course, neither essential nor invariant. In astronomy a 'constellation' historically referred to a grouping of stars that make an imaginary picture in the sky. For a particular group of viewers, they may appear to have a necessary basis to their coherence but this need not be the case. For example, Pleiades is an open cluster of stars that are gravitationally bound to one another and which appear in the constellation of Taurus, though they have no substantial astrophysical relationship to its other stars. Similarly, constellations are understood here as groupings that appear to have coherence from a particular point in space and time to actors with a particular cosmology. Different cosmologies may generate different constellations. Thus, which stances are included in a constellation, and relations within and between constellations, may vary according to different actors, change over time and be the subject of struggles.

Condensing and charging

In terms of external relations, cosmologies imbue constellations with meanings from beyond the stances. Chapter 7 introduced the notion of *semantic density*, the degree of condensation of meaning within practices. Semantic density may be relatively stronger or weaker along a continuum of strengths: the stronger the semantic density, the more meanings are condensed within practices; the weaker the semantic density, the less meanings are condensed. This condensation may take many different forms. For example, using concepts from Specialization, one can distinguish between:

- *epistemological condensation*, where the condensing of meanings (from other concepts or empirical referents) emphasizes epistemic relations; and
- *axiological condensation,* where the condensing of meanings (from affective, aesthetic, ethical, political and moral stances) emphasizes social relations.[2]

These two forms describe condensation driven by a knowledge code and a knower code, respectively. As defined in the *specialization plane* (Figure 2.1, p. 30), not only are there two further principal codes (élite and relativist) but also epistemic and social relations can be varied along continua of strengths with infinite capacity for gradation. Thus, one can describe a very wide range of different forms, as well as processes of strengthening and weakening each of these forms of semantic density.[3] Put another way, constellations of stars may have more or less astrophysical meaning *and* more or less astrological meaning; similarly, the semantic density of practices may be stronger or weaker epistemologically *and*, independently, stronger or weaker axiologically. Chapter 7 explored epistemological condensation (in the theories of Bourdieu and Bernstein); this chapter explores axiological condensation.

A second feature of external relations is that meanings condensed within practices may be *charged* differently. For example, a social scientific concept condensing a range of political meanings (stronger axiological condensation) may be portrayed positively, neutrally or negatively (along a continuum) in comparison to other meanings. Constellations can thus condense more or less epistemological and/or axiological meanings that are charged positively, neutrally and negatively to different degrees.

Cosmologies

Bringing these internal and external relations together: constellational structure defines a field's space of possibles; condensation imbues its constituent stances, clusters and constellations with meaning; and charging determines their positive and negative valuations. A *cosmology* provides the organizing principles of these processes and thereby shapes which stances have 'sex appeal', of what kind and how much. Every social field of practice has a cosmology, though its form varies between fields and may change over time. Moreover, through the languages of legitimation of their practices actors struggle for control of the Legitimation Device (Chapters 3 and 7) which 'sets' the relative values of legitimation codes within a field and thereby the nature of its cosmology: the basis of 'sex appeal' is thus subject to ongoing struggles.

The organizing principles of a cosmology are manifold; which should be analysed depends on the problem-situation. Varying the strengths of relations in specialization codes (ER+/–, SR+/–) and semantic codes (SG+/–, SD+/–) enables the conceptualization of a wide range of possible cosmologies. However, reflecting the forms dominating educational research, I shall simply distinguish:

- *epistemological cosmologies*, where the 'sex appeal' of stances is based on their comparative explanatory power, such as emphasizing coherence, integration, economy and worldly corroboration; and
- *axiological cosmologies*, where stances are measured in terms of their comparative capacity to place knowers in a good light.

(As mentioned above, these reflect knowledge codes and knower codes, respectively; thus, one can, at its simplest, also describe cosmologies where both explanatory power and knower-reflection are emphasized and where both are downplayed. There are numerous cosmologies to explore.)

In this chapter I shall particularly explore an axiological cosmology. However, cosmological analysis is not confined to knower-code fields. All systems of ideas and practices – scientific, religious, political, moral, aesthetic, athletic, linguistic, etc. – comprise a semantic structure of stances chosen from a potential array, arranged into patterns, condensed with meanings, and charged with valuations. From an infinite number, all these systems identify and name particular stars (as, for example, concepts) and draw relations among them (causal, sequential, associational, compositional, etc.) to create a semantic structure of constellations. This reaches far beyond academia. The industries of advertising and public relations, for example, attempt to condense and charge actors and symbols (Pleiades is the logo of Subaru whose advertising attempts to imbue the symbol with such notions as 'reliability' or 'value for money'). It should be added that these constellations may also be in motion: new stars may be added, new relations among stars drawn, old stars expunged, old relations changed or erased. Meanings may also be added or removed and subject to revaluation. Rather than static knowledge structures, cosmological analysis thus delineates a universe of movement and becoming in which the bases of constellations may be analysed.

Using these concepts I shall now analyse stargazing in educational research. I examine, first, its internal relations, focusing on how dominant portrayals of the field construct its space of possibles. I begin by identifying *central signifiers* around which constellations are constructed, in this case 'student-centred learning' and 'teacher-centred'. I then delineate their respective *associated signifiers*, drawing on descriptions of the field, to show the structure of constellations centred on these terms. Second, I explore the external relations of educational research, using Specialization and Semantics to analyse the basis of condensation and charging of stances. I then relate these analyses to Chapter 7 to explore possible reasons for the differential positioning of theories in the field.

Internal relations: Clusters and constellations

The dominant vision of educational research focuses on two of its most significant terms: 'teaching' and 'learning'. Since the 1990s a range of stances have been constellated around the term 'student-centred learning', 'learning-oriented' or 'learning', and contrasted with another group labelled 'teacher-centred', 'instruction-oriented' or 'teaching'. The resulting constellations are polyonymous and binary: they are known by many names and opposed. However labelled, the ascendancy of 'student-centred learning' (henceforth 'SCL') and eclipse of 'instruction' has been widely heralded. Advocates argue there has been an unprecedented shift in education:

> During the 1990s, we have witnessed a convergence of learning theories never before encountered. These contemporary learning theories are based on substantively different ontologies and epistemologies than were traditional objectivist foundations for instructional design... The past decade, we believe, has witnessed the most substantive and revolutionary changes in learning theory in history ... We have entered a new age in learning theory. Never ... have there been so many theoretical foundations that share so many assumptions and common foundations.
>
> (Jonassen and Land, 2000: iii, v–vi)

Such talk of revolution is not uncommon. Barr and Tagg (1995: 13), for example, declared a 'paradigm shift' from 'instruction' to 'learning': 'This shift changes everything'. Instances of these claims are countless but share several features. First, they highlight the wide range of 'learning theories' embraced by SCL, including: 'problem-based', 'project-based', 'inquiry', 'open-ended', 'constructivist', 'situated', 'authentic', 'discovery', and others. Second, after noting 'considerable disagreement and confusion about what student-centred learning actually is' (Farrington 1991: 16), it is invariably associated by proponents with a series of stances contrasted to 'teacher-centred' ones. For example, as represented in Table 8.1, Jonassen and Land (2000: viii) synthesize a range of literature to offer a list of associated signifiers for 'traditional instruction' and 'student-centred learning environments'. Again, this is not atypical; a list of lists would be prohibitively long. Third, neither the choice of stances nor basis of their 'convergence' are underpinned by an explicitly elaborated framework; for example, though 'constructivism' is

Table 8.1 Teacher-centred and student-centred learning environments (according to Jonassen and Land 2000)

Teacher-centred	*Student-centred*
transmission/acquisition	interpretation, construction
mastery, performance	meaning-making
external reality	internal reality
dualism, absolutism	cultural relativism, perspectival
abstract, symbolic	contextualized, authentic, experiential
individually interpreted	socially negotiated, co-constructed
mind-centred	community-based, culturally mediated
directed	intentional
reductionist	complex, self-organizing
individual	collaborative
idealist, rational	pragmatist
encoding, retention, retrieval	articulation and reflection
internal, mental	social
receptive, reproductive	constructive
symbolic reasoning	situated learning
psychology	anthropology, sociology, ethnography
laboratory	in situ
theoretical	everyday
central processing architecture	distributed architecture
objective, modelable	experiential, interpretive
symbol processor	symbol builder
disembodied	experiential
conceptual, memorial	perceptual
atomistic, decomposable	gestalt
independent	emergent
possessed	distributed
objective, stable, fixed	subjective, contextualized, fluid
well-structured	ill-structured
decontextualized	embedded in experience
compliant	self-regulated

described as influential, it is rarely defined explicitly (Matthews 2000; Tobias and Duffy 2009).

Though the stances listed in Table 8.1 appear disparate foci and lacking cohesion, these constellations reflect an underlying cosmology. To begin exploring this cosmology Table 8.2 reorders the stances of Table 8.1 into groups based on four principles of opposition: abstract–concrete; objective–subjective; individual–collective; and positivism–hermeneutics.

Abstract–concrete

One opposition represents polarized strengths of semantic gravity (Chapter 6). Teacher-centred stances are 'decontextualized', 'abstract, symbolic', 'theoretical',

Table 8.2 Clustered teacher-centred and student-centred constellations

Teacher-centred constellation	*Student-centred constellation*
Abstract	*Concrete*
abstract, symbolic	contextualized, authentic, experiential
idealist, rational	pragmatist
symbolic reasoning	situated learning
laboratory	in situ
theoretical	everyday
objective, modelable	experiential, interpretive
disembodied	experiential
conceptual, memorial	perceptual
decontextualized	embedded in experience
Objective	*Subjective*
transmission/acquisition	interpretation, construction
mastery, performance	meaning-making
directed	intentional
reductionist	complex, self-organizing
encoding, retention, retrieval	articulation and reflection
symbol processor	symbol builder
receptive, reproductive	constructive
objective, stable, fixed	subjective, contextualized, fluid
well-structured	ill-structured
compliant	self-regulated
Individual	*Collective*
individually interpreted	socially negotiated, co-constructed
individual	collaborative
mind-centred	community-based, culturally mediated
internal, mental	social
atomistic, decomposable	gestalt
independent	emergent
possessed	distributed
central processing architecture	distributed architecture
Positivism	*Hermeneutics*
external reality	internal reality
internal, mental	social
atomistic, decomposable	gestalt
dualism, absolutism	cultural relativism, perspectival
psychology	anthropology, sociology, ethnography
laboratory	in situ
objective, modelable	experiential, interpretive

'conceptual', 'disembodied' and 'objective'. In contrast, student-centred stances are 'contextualized' or 'in situ', closer to the 'authentic, experiential' reality of learners, less abstract and more rooted in the 'subjective' and 'everyday'. In defining the centre of gravity, learners are a touchstone: 'experiential' and 'experience' appear in the student-centred constellation four times.

Objective–subjective

The constellations echo the longstanding 'structure versus agency' debate in social science. Teacher-centred stances are constructed as objectivist: the imposition ('directed') of 'stable, fixed', 'objective' external structures onto the minds of 'compliant', 'receptive' and 'reproductive' learners. In contrast, student-centred stances are subjectivist, involving 'interpretation' and 'constructive' 'meaning making' by 'self-organizing', 'intentional' learners. Notably, learners and not teachers (nor both) are identified with subjectivism and agency.

Individual–collective

A third opposition pits 'individual', 'atomistic', 'independent' teacher-centred stances against the 'social', 'community-based', 'collaborative' and holistic ('gestalt') student-centred stances.

Positivism–hermeneutics

The constellations include different ontologies, epistemologies, disciplines and approaches. 'Teacher-centred' is equated with positivistic study of an 'atomistic' and 'external reality' through 'objective' and 'modelable' approaches. 'Student-centred' is associated with hermeneutic study of the inner life of the mind, and adopting cultural relativism, perspectivism and humanistic approaches to provide insiders' perspectives on their everyday experiences within a more holistic view.

The space of possibles

I shall return to the focus of these oppositions when addressing how theories are positioned in the field, below. Here I highlight how this vision of education delimits the range and combinations of possible stances through its construction of relations within and relations between constellations. First, relations among stances *within* constellations are portrayed as necessarily associated. One effect is that actors associated with one stance (such as 'theoretical') are associated with others in the same constellation (such as 'reductionist'), regardless of whether they explicitly discuss, engage in or agree with them. It also obscures differences between practices of research, curriculum construction, and teaching and learning: constellated stances range from ontology to assessment. As Matthews (2000: 161) puts it, constructivism has grown from a theory of learning to become 'a theory of teaching, a theory of education, a theory of educational administration, a theory of the origin of ideas, theory of both personal knowledge and scientific knowledge, and even a metaphysical and ideological position'. The constellations thus embrace the entire arena created by the ESP device (Chapters 3 and 7). Everything is implicated at every point – there is no escaping the constellation.

Second, relations *between* constellations are portrayed as strongly bounded. Though some commentators proclaim a continuum between poles, most discussions highlight only the poles themselves, precluding the possibility of combining stances from both constellations. For example, 'knowledge-centred' stances can be equated with 'teacher-centred', despite being fundamentally opposed to the behaviourist theories of pedagogy and positivist epistemology said to underpin the latter. In a binary constellation, you are either one thing or the other: student-centred or teacher-centred, positivist or anti-positivist, agency or structure, theoretical or experiential, and so on.

External relations: Condensation and charges

The constellations established by the dominant vision of educational research are not equal. For example, a typical account lists a series of 'tenets' for SCL:

> reliance upon active rather than passive learning, an emphasis on deep learning and understanding, increased responsibility and accountability on the part of the student, an increased sense of autonomy in the learner, an interdependence between teacher and learner (as opposed to complete learner dependence or independence…), mutual respect within the learner–teacher relationship, and a reflexive approach to the learning and teaching process on the part of both teacher and learner.
>
> (Lea *et al.* 2003: 322)

Such descriptions condense positive attributes within the 'student-centred' constellation and project negative attributes onto the 'teacher-centred' constellation: active ***rather than*** passive learning, ***deep*** learning, ***increased*** responsibility and accountability, ***increased*** sense of autonomy, interdependence ***as opposed to*** dependence or independence, and the presence of mutual respect and reflexivity. Indeed, these characteristics are typically introduced within a historical narrative of progress from one constellation to the other. To explore the cosmology underlying this differential charging, I shall now discuss epistemological and axiological condensation in this portrayal of the field by exploring its epistemic relations and social relations.

Epistemic relations as articles of faith

Epistemological cosmologies base legitimation on stronger epistemic relations: constellations with 'sex appeal' are those with greater explanatory power, as shown by conceptual integration and worldly corroboration. In contrast, SCL is characterized by a proliferation of segmented terms and downplaying research evidence: weaker epistemic relations. First, as discussed above, SCL is a polyonymous constellation comprising an ever-growing list of approaches. Though its stances are strongly associated with one another, these relations are simply stated rather than explicated. As advocates admit, the 'lack of attention to and consistency in defining the approach has resulted in a plethora of synonyms … and an inability to compare studies or teaching practices directly' (Lea *et al.* 2003: 321).

This extends to the contrasting constellation: 'teacher-centred' is a catch-all term for everything prior to the rise of SCL or constructivism.

Second, the proclaimed benefits of SCL are rarely defined in ways enabling claims to be empirically explored (Tobias and Duffy 2009). Definitions of SCL condense claims about its effectiveness but mostly comprise aims and assertions. Examining the citations used by papers advocating SCL is sobering. Sources cited as if research studies (such as 'Brandes and Ginnis 1986' and 'Cannon and Newble 2000') are often handbooks of teaching practice. Where research-based sources are cited, they typically comprise small-scale studies whose findings are generalized as indicating the success of SCL. Though portrayed as offering evidence for improved *outcomes* in learning, these studies often focus on *perceptions* of staff and/or students concerning motivation and engagement. For example, Lea *et al.* (2003: 322–323), in a brief review echoed by other papers (e.g. O'Neill and McMahon 2005: 33; Foo *et al.* 2009: 31), claim the balance of evidence shows SCL to be more effective than conventional approaches, on the basis of three cited studies. This evidence base comprises: a survey of perceptions of 108 business studies students (Prendergast 1994); action research on a business information technology module which lacks a basis for comparison (Hall and Saunders 1997); and (to quote from the paper itself) a 'small case study' of a psychology course whose 'intention is not to present directly generalizable results' and which concludes that 'we cannot really say that activating instruction *caused* any changes' (Lonka and Aloha 1995: 366, 351, 364; original emphasis).

Confident claims based on flimsy evidence illustrate the relatively weak epistemological condensation within claims for SCL: there is little systematic articulation of how meanings given to terms relate to empirical evidence. Indeed, meta-analyses of studies report greater student control over learning improves motivation but not subsequent learning (Hattie 2009: 193-4). More generally, meta-analyses typically conclude the balance of evidence is not in SCL's favour; for example:

> In so far as there is any evidence from controlled studies, it almost uniformly supports direct, strong instructional guidance rather than constructivist-based minimal guidance during the instruction of novice to intermediate learners. Even for students with considerable prior knowledge, strong guidance while learning is most often found to be equally effective as unguided approaches. Not only is unguided instruction normally less effective; there is also evidence that it may have negative results.
>
> (Kirschner *et al.* 2006: 83-4)

Potential dissonance between claims made for SCL and research evidence against them can be avoided by proponents because its weaker epistemic relations enable strategies of goalpost shifting and reinvention. The first involves discounting negative evidence as referring to other approaches. For example, in response to the conclusion quoted above, Schmidt *et al.* (2007) and Hmelo-Silver *et al.* (2007) argue that problem-based and inquiry learning are dissimilar to discovery learning and thereby exempt. Similarly, maintaining that 'many institutions or educators claim to be putting student-centred learning into practice, but in reality they are not' (Lea *et al.* 2003: 322) raises questions of the purity of the SCL being appraised. Thus, studies showing a form of pedagogy does not enable, for example, deep learning can be said to have not studied SCL, for SCL by definition enables deep learning. The meaning is thus locked into the definition and unshakeable by empirical disconfirmation.

The second strategy is highlighted by the polyonymous nature of the SCL constellation. As a review of studies concludes: 'Pure discovery did not work in the 1960s, it did not work in the 1970s, and it did not work in the 1980s' (Mayer 2004: 18). Despite this, the same ideas repeatedly re-emerged, 'Like some zombie that keeps returning from its grave' (ibid.: 17), with new names. This process of renaming insulates advocates from empirical evidence of failure of previous versions. Moreover, names tend not to last long, as freely floating signifiers possess a limited lifespan: the moral charge runs down as the term gains currency, problematizing claims to newness and radicalism. Thus, the proliferation of names for SCL highlights both its capacity to reinvent itself in the face of repeated evidence of failure and the need to appear new.

In summary, comparative explanatory power appears not to be a decisive factor in the differential charging of constellations in educational research. Positive valuations of SCL are insulated from the paucity of evidence for and considerable evidence against claims made for the approach. Among advocates, SCL is akin to a faith-based religion: belief is everything, including belief there must be evidence supporting the belief. This is often underpinned by a *certainty–complacency spiral* among proponents. Rather than conjectures to be tested, claims are made with little evidential support and repeated unquestioningly as if proven facts. Accumulating citations then give the impression of pointing to extensive research. Repetition of claims thereby iteratively amplifies and reinforces the sense of certainty that they are well-founded. Such complacent, uncritical acceptance of the veracity of claims in turn encourages further certainty, as the number of publications repeating the claims grows. In this way, the epistemic relations of SCL have become articles of faith.

Mediated social relations to knowers

Though exhibiting weaker epistemological condensation, terms such as 'student-centred' and 'teacher-centred' do exhibit relatively strong semantic density, but of a different kind: ***axiological condensation***. At its most explicit, this comprises claims of direct relations with social groups. Accounts often identify 'teacher-centred' with teachers and élite groups previously served by education and 'student-centred' with hitherto marginalized social groups, such as 'mature students, international students and students with disabilities' (Lea *et al.* 2003: 323). More often, however, social relations to knowers are revealed less directly, by the language in which claims are couched.

First, terms used in SCL stances bring connotations from everyday usage that are not changed through technicalization. As shown by systemic functional linguistics, academic discourse has the capacity to reconfigure everyday discourse in ways that fundamentally modify its meanings, through such resources as 'grammatical metaphor' (Halliday and Martin 1993). Since the world is often not as it appears, such transformed meanings are required to enable understandings unavailable to commonsense knowledge. Though social sciences typically use words drawn from ordinary language, these can be epistemologically condensed with meanings that break free of their everyday connotations by defining them precisely in relation to other concepts and to empirical referents; that is, stronger epistemic relations. In contrast, the weaker epistemic relations characterizing definitions in SCL constrain this capacity and provide greater space for commonsense connotations of terms such as 'discovery', 'authentic' or 'situated' to enter academic discourse.

Second, SCL stances are typically introduced in the context of language rich with explicit attitude, using what systemic functional linguists term 'affect', 'judgement' and 'appreciation' (Martin and White 2005; Hood 2010). Advocates declare, for example, 'a need to humanize the online experience with greater compassion, empathy and open-mindedness' that requires 'authentic learning', an approach they claim enables 'deep and lifelong learning' and possesses 'real world relevance and utility' (Herrington *et al.* 2003: 69, 64, 62). Such terms represent axiological charging. Moreover, inauthentic approaches contrasted to 'authentic learning' are presumably cruel, unempathic and close-minded, and offer shallow, short-lived, irrelevant and useless learning. This axiological charging may also take on more overtly social or political forms, such as claims that design-based research is 'socially responsible' (Reeves *et al.* 2005) or widespread self-descriptions of post-structuralist approaches as 'critical theory', in contrast to other approaches that are presumably socially irresponsible or uncritical.

The accretion of meanings around a central signifier such as SCL thereby creates the feeling that stances are politically progressive or conservative, ethically better or worse, and so on. In other words, where constellations generated by epistemological cosmologies represent *structures of meaning* by condensing formal definitions or descriptions of the world, those generated by axiological cosmologies represent *structures of feeling* by condensing orientations of actors to the world. Returning to the four oppositions outlined in Table 8.2, the teacher-centred constellation is constructed as offering the top-down view and distance from everyday experience of an ivory tower, denying the creative agency of actors, embracing individualism, and projecting a mechanistic view of the world – an élitist, dominating, neoliberal and reductive outlook. In contrast, SCL is constructed as providing the 'view from below', emphasizing the subjective agency of creative actors, embracing social and collective endeavours, and projecting a holistic and contextualized view – a populist, liberatory, communitarian and humanist outlook. Moreover, teacher-centred stances are associated with tradition and the past, in contrast to the 'never before encountered ... revolutionary' student-centred constellation (Jonassen and Land, 2000: iii, v–vi).

The structures of feeling condensed within constellations reflect on the actors associated with them. Such axiologically charged terms may become 'bondicons'

(Martin and Stenglin 2006) or totems around which actors rally and which, crucially, also bathe their advocates in a virtuous light. As Bourdieu argues, 'taste classifies, and it classifies the classifier' (1984: 6): your choice of films, furniture, music, clothes and so forth, say something about you. Similarly, a scholar's choice of theory, citations, writing style, figures, titles, punctuation and so forth, offer messages about what kind of person they are by virtue of the axiologically charged constellation to which those stances are assigned. These messages need not be explicit, as moral positioning works through the gazes of actors, semi-consciously, in a similar manner to the way we 'read' people's accents, clothes, physical gait, etc. Such *cultivated gazes* are part of that 'feel for the game' gained through prolonged immersion in a social field of practice (Chapters 5 and 9). Thus, one's intellectual choices classify and they morally classify the classifier. They show whether your heart is in the right place, your aesthetic, ethical, moral or political affiliations correct, and so whether you are one of us or one of them. In other words, the axiological cosmology generates a *hierarchical knower structure* (Chapter 4), a ranking of actors based on how moral, righteous, virtuous, ethical or politically progressive they are considered to be. In such fields, as Montaigne (1580/2003: 338) put it: 'Anything we do reveals us'. (Thus, the choice of a highly condensed and context-independent motif for Chapter 7 assigns me to the dark side.)

Where stances are tightly associated within opposed constellations, such as portrayed by advocates of SCL, this hierarchizing process enables *clusterboosting*, whereby actors appropriate progressive credentials by adopting stances associated with others that are axiologically charged as radical, critical and working for dominated Others, even where the effects of their adopted stances are deleterious to social justice. Conversely, it enables the strategy of *clusterfucking* other actors, ideas and practices through their identification with negatively viewed terms, so they assume guilt by association. (For example, Chapter 7 began with a quote from Talcott Parsons; Parsons was a structural functionalist; structural functionalism is typically described as socially conservative; the ideas of Chapter 7 must be socially conservative. That this chain of irreason is epistemologically unfounded need not matter.) Terms can also become used as a dog whistle: without needing to be made explicit, a position can be implied, and valorization or disapprobation evoked, through the use of other constellated terms. Thus, using the term 'teaching' (or, worse, 'transmission') to refer to pedagogic relations may be viewed as advocating behaviourism, positivism, authorative imposition, disempowerment of students, disengagement from learners' experiences, and conservativism.

Positioning theories: Altitudes and latitudes

Having analysed the cosmology dominating educational research, we can now explore how a theory's capacity for knowledge-building may shape its status within the field. Chapter 7 showed the *cumulative modality* of theorizing enables knowledge-building over time and across empirical phenomena.

Internally, its stronger epistemological condensation and abstraction of meanings enables greater vertical extension of the theory and, externally, languages of description translate between concepts and data from diverse problem-situations. In contrast, the ***segmental modality*** of theorizing has less such capacity by virtue of its weaker vertical relations among concepts and reliance on a cultivated gaze for relating concepts and data. To address why segmental rather than cumulative theories are more widely adopted in educational research, I now focus on how their semantic codes are construed by the field's dominant cosmology in terms of epistemic relations and social relations.

Altitudes: Knowers as objects of study

The cumulative modality of theorizing achieves greater vertical extension towards higher levels of *epistemological* condensation and context-independence. Reaching higher up this *epistemic*–semantic scale also lightens the discourse by reducing lengthy descriptions; for example, Chapter 7 can become:

- Cumulative modality = $\dfrac{SG^i-,\ SD^i+;\ SG^c+,\ SD^c-}{ER+,\ SR-}$
- Segmental modality = $\dfrac{SG^i+,\ SD^i-;\ SG^c+,\ SD^c-}{ER-,\ SR+}$

However, while lightening discourse it raises the price of entry to that discourse: to make sense of this summary requires understanding the symbols and their relations. Whether it is experienced as obscure thus depends on whether actors have that knowledge or the opportunities and desire to acquire it. One reason why more actors do not do so may lie with how this 'height' in the epistemic–semantic scale is construed. In other words, how is this epistemological condensation viewed?

The axiological cosmology dominating educational research constructs epistemic relations in humanistic terms as relations to ***knowers*** as objects of study: both what is studied and how it is studied are anthropomorphized. Theories are then measured according to their perceived distance from the experiences and contexts of these actors: they are allocated to different *altitudes* above the human world. Cumulative theorizing not only achieves greater height in the semantic scale but also acknowledges what Bernstein (2000) termed a 'discursive gap' between empirical and theoretical descriptions and generates external languages of description for traversing that gap (Chapter 7). Thus, code theorizing embraces a fuller semantic range; as studies illustrate (Chapter 10; Maton *et al.* 2014), research can relate dense abstractions and rich empirical descriptions. However, the axiological cosmology dominating educational research associates code theories with the thinner, colder air of higher altitude in two ways. First, its binary constellationality denies the possibility of being both abstract and concrete or able to move between these poles. That code theorizing achieves a higher semantic range is thereby taken to mean it must remain at its highest altitude – it is the uppermost reading on the scale that is foregrounded, and the greater semantic range this entails is obscured. Reviewing Figure 7.3 (p. 143), only the top of the semantic wave is seen. Second, this ***discursive distance*** between conceptual and commonsense meanings is constructed as ***dispositional distance*** between the experiences conveyed and those of non-academic knowers (Chapter 4). As discussed above, these attributes (abstract, disembodied, etc.) are identified with negatively charged constellations, such as 'teacher-centred' and 'positivism'.

In contrast, segmental theories are allocated to a lower, warmer altitude, closer to everyday experiences. This is *not*, however, because they are couched in everyday language or necessarily involve actors. For example, Kitching's analysis of student essays using post-structuralist theory shows how they 'conjure up an unpeopled world of things – often a mechanical or mechanistic world; frequently a world of spatial or geographical things ... But there are no clearly discernible people' (2008: 20–21). Indeed, unlike standpoint theories, the author is removed from the discourse; 'the prose itself appears to have no subject or creator' (ibid.: 21). Yet, segmental theorizing is often associated with 'agency', 'meaning-making', and the lived experiences of subjects. This association is enabled, at least partly, by denying any discursive gap between empirical and theoretical descriptions, which can then appear seamlessly interwoven. For example, much post-structuralist writing comprises allusive, suggestive accounts of empirical phenomena that are redescribed in theoretical terms without explanation of their relations. In other words, they jump from one flatline of Figure 7.3 to the other, and back again. The result is less a dialogue between theory and data than a monologue in which the empirical is subjugated to the discursive rules of the theoretical. Meaning is less transformed by theory than overlaid by theory or the theory-laden interpretation of authors. However, the dominant axiological cosmology constructs this lack of *explicit* transformation of meaning as involving less violence to meaning-making activities in the social world and as less abstracted from concrete, experiential reality.

Latitudes: Knowers as subjects

A second feature of cumulative theorizing is its higher degree of *explanatory latitude*: the capacity for a small number of higher-order concepts to embrace a wide range of phenomena with relative precision. However, the axiological cosmology of educational research constructs these stronger epistemic relations as necessarily lessening ***interpretive latitude*** by offering less space for actors to creatively engage with concepts. Though even the most passing acquaintance with the history of natural science or mathematics reveals the falsity of such a trade-off, this portrayal of cumulative theorizing enables 'its misrepresentation as ... a closed, theoretical edifice of baroque proportions, which allows for no dialogue. Either one accepts it all and becomes a slave to its categories, or one can find no use for it' (Moss 2001: 117). In comparison, segmental theorizing is based on a cultivated gaze for translating between theory and data. For example, Bourdieu's concepts have been described as 'an inkblot test used as a stimulus for the imagination' (Gorard 2004: 9); similarly, concepts such as 'governmentality' and 'biopower' (Foucault) and 'assemblage' or 'machine' (Deleuze) may stimulate thinking but their relations to empirical referents are vague. These weaker epistemic relations are constructed as offering greater interpretive latitude for actors to interpret the theory. For example, reviewing uses of Bourdieu's concept of 'habitus', Reay concludes by quoting herself:

> paradoxically the conceptual looseness of habitus also constitutes a potential strength. It makes possible ***adaptation*** rather than the ***more constricting straightforward adoption*** of the concept within empirical work
>
> (Reay 1995: 357; emphases added)

Reay also twice quotes Bourdieu's claim that 'one cannot grasp the most profound logic of the social world unless one becomes immersed in the specificity of an empirical reality' (1993a: 271). What is meant here by 'adaptation' and 'adoption'? Cumulative theories allow the systematic adaptation of concepts to become immersed in the specificities of an empirical reality through external languages of description. However, Bourdieu's mode of theorizing does not include such languages (Chapter 7). Thus, for Reay, 'adaptation' has a more interpretive meaning and Bourdieu's quote is understood as describing immersion of researchers rather than concepts in an empirical reality. Conversely, 'more constricting straightforward adoption' is used to describe the kind of precision achieved by cumulative theorizing. Reay is thereby positing a trade-off between referential precision and hermeneutic space: weaker epistemic relations are viewed as providing more space for social relations to flourish. Thanks to binary constellationality, interpretive latitude is thus associated with notions of creativity and agency for actors, and explanatory latitude is associated with domination by theory of actors' meaning-making and imposing concepts onto data.

A Faustian pact

To rephrase Bernstein (1977: 157), in fields dominated by axiological cosmologies, theories are less to be examined and explored at conceptual and empirical levels and more to be assessed in terms of their underlying models of humanity and society. To draw on Bourdieu, the *doxa* of such fields, what 'goes without saying', is a Faustian pact: cumulative knowledge-building comes at the cost of losing sight of the human world, constraining creativity, and allying with domination. By virtue of its attributed altitudes, cumulative theorizing is associated with a cold world of knowledge and segmental theories with a warm world of knowers (cf. Gellner 1959). By virtue of its attributed latitudes, cumulative theorizing is viewed as constraining, and segmental theories as enabling creativity and agency.

Thanks to strong associations among stances within each of the field's binary constellations, theories and actors identified with the cumulative modality may then be clusterfucked through identification with objectivist, individualist, positivist and conservative stances, while advocates of segmental theories may clusterboost their humanist and progressive credentials, regardless of the effects of their enacted positions. Bernstein's code theory, for example, has been denounced as offering little space for agency, embodying élitist beliefs, imposing pre-determined conceptual distinctions onto data, ignoring the empirical, and other negatively charged stances, often with little evidence (Atkinson 1985; Davies 2010). However, more often than being explicitly demonized, cumulative theorizing is an Other through which segmental approaches construct their own axiological positivity. Using 'a mobile army of metaphors, metonyms, and anthropomorphisms' (Nietzsche 1873/1954: 42), the binary, axiologically charged constellationality expressed in conventional accounts of the field – such as the 'epistemological dilemma' (Chapter 1) of 'critical' versus 'positivist' – pronounces not that 'there is no alternative' to segmental approaches but rather 'there is only one alternative and it is morally indefensible'. (The irony, of course, is that approaches prone to such essentializing have done much to highlight the effects of Othering elsewhere.) Given the doxic nature of this seductive illusion, it is unsurprising that cumulative theorizing remains marginalized within educational research.

Conclusion

In *The Unbearable Lightness of Being*, Kundera asks:

> What then shall we choose? Weight or lightness? Parmenides posed this very question in the sixth century before Christ. He saw the world divided into pairs of opposites: light/darkness, fineness/coarseness, warmth/cold, being/non-being. One half of the opposition he called positive (light, fineness, warmth, being), the other negative ... Was he correct or not? That is the question.
>
> (Kundera 1984: 5)

Such questions concern every social field of practice. In understanding how they are answered, most sociological approaches highlight social power, neglecting the possibility that some knowledge practices offer more explanatory power than others. Bernstein's model of 'knowledge structures' brings this issue into view but leaves open how these questions are answered in fields such as the humanities and social sciences. In contrast, this chapter suggests that answers in all social fields may be shaped not only by social power and explanatory power but also by axiological power. It has proposed the notion of *cosmologies* as a means of bringing these together to explore the basis of what Gellner described as ideas which engender powerful sentiments and the other way around. This approach views actors' practices as constellating stances in ways that shape the 'space of possibles' of a social field, condensing meanings of various kinds, and charging those meanings in different ways.

Using these concepts shows that in fields where knowledge is relatively weakly structured and worldly corroboration is downplayed, the hierarchization of stances is concerned less with explanatory power or with explicit social claims than with attributed moral virtue. Cosmological analysis thereby avoids a deficit model of such fields as lacking hierarchical knowledge structures; they are also characterized by hierarchical knower structures based on axiological cosmologies. It thereby also reveals how displaying one's credentials as a legitimate knower can be more complex than 'voicing' social categories. Specifically, extending the notion of 'semantic density' highlighted that stances with weaker epistemological condensation may have stronger axiological condensation. This establishes social relations to knowers that are tacit and mediated through axiologically charged constellations of stances, rather than explicit and direct claims to membership of a social group. Possession of a legitimate gaze is then displayed through one's choices of ideas and practices. By adopting the right stances, not only are actors bathed in a better light by virtue of the axiologically charged meanings condensed within them, they also demonstrate their legitimate gaze: they show they recognize the axiological cosmology; in turn, the axiological cosmology recognizes their gaze. The organizing principles of cultivated gazes dominating fields like sociology and educational research thus comprise its specialization and semantic codes – the cultivated gaze is here an axiological cosmology introjected. Of course, actors recognize and/or realize gazes to varying degrees; ascertaining which potential knowers do so depends always on empirical research. Analysing the structure of a field therefore involves exploring the cosmology dominating the field, the gazes of actors, and relations between them.

As this chapter has highlighted, the truth is no guarantee of belief and belief is no guarantee of the truth. Though cumulative theorizing offers greater capacity for building powerful and cumulative knowledge, the cosmology dominating educational research militates against its widespread adoption. First, it is excluded from the 'space of possibles' by the field's binary constellationality – cumulative theorizing cannot be seen as a viable alternative by most actors. Second, its organizing principles are at odds with those dominating the field: the greater (epistemic-)semantic range and knowledge code of cumulative theorizing represent a double code clash with the field's axiological cosmology. In contrast, the lower (epistemic-)semantic range and knower code characterizing segmental theorizing are more closely code matched with those of the field. Stellar status in such fields at least partly resides in how the different altitudes and latitudes associated with these codes are axiologically charged as embodying positive or negative visions of humanity. Thus, the marginal position of approaches such as code theory may result less from being obscure than being obscured, less from being densely presented than being misrepresented.

This analysis resonates far beyond educational research. Similar cosmologies can be found across the humanities and social sciences, giving rise to constellations centred around such central signifiers as 'the two cultures' (Snow 1959), Mode I/Mode II knowledge production (Gibbons *et al.* 1994) and old/new sociologies of education (Young 1971). Despite claims to be 'revolutionary', those projected by proponents of SCL are also of long standing. Berman, for example, explores how the Enlightenment during the early eighteenth century accreted notions of universalism, domination and essentialism, despite being based on 'the perception of empirical diversity and cultural relativity' (2009: 10). These constellations have been reinforced by recurrent waves of an anthropomorphism which holds that human society is a human tale to be told by its participants in a humanist register (Maton 2005b). The resulting constellations are so similar to those of SCL that one could echo Gellner's weary lament:

> This, then, is the familiar overall confrontation: a granular, cold, technical and naturalistic world confronts a holistic, meaning-saturated, identity-conferring, social-humanistic one.
>
> (Gellner 1987: 176)

Though the analysis resonates with research across the humanities and social sciences, cosmological concepts themselves are not restricted to these fields and practices. The dimensions of LCT enable the organizing principles of fields from across the disciplinary map to be explored. Using Specialization and Semantics, for example, highlights not only axiological but also epistemological cosmologies, as well as many other potential modalities. Moreover, cosmological analysis is not restricted to the study of explicit portrayals of intellectual fields: all practices reflect a cosmology. Martin *et al.* (2010), for example, highlight the centrality to the History curriculum in Australia of a wide range of '-isms' that form binary oppositions (such as 'nationalism' versus 'colonialism') in lessons, textbooks and other teaching materials. By analysing the terms clustered in classroom discourse around central signifiers such as these '-isms' and historical actors (for example, Ho Chi Minh and French colonialists), they reveal the axiologically charged constellations created in teaching and learning. This process of, for example, 'being positioned to appreciate the nationalist position and look critically at the colonialist one' (Martin *et al.* 2010: 451), aims to apprentice students into the moral cultivated gaze required to succeed in Australian school History. Cosmological analysis can thus be used to explore knowledge production, curriculum, and teaching and learning practices, embracing the fields of the ESP device and so enabling an integrated account of education (Chapter 3).

Notably, axiological cosmologies often generate binary constellations: SCL, the examples above and dichotomous types mentioned in previous chapters offer polarized oppositions. However, cosmological analysis is not itself binary: it emphasizes the possibly limitless number of stances and their combinations and raises the question of why some stances are chosen, clustered and constellated in particular ways around particular central signifiers, and not other stances, ways and signifiers. Constellations may take many forms. It thereby offers the possibility of making the impossible possible by seeing beyond the current space of possibles. However, as stated at the outset of this chapter, identifying practices that enable knowledge-building does not by itself mean they will become widely practised. How this can be achieved is a serious question, one requiring, *inter alia*, studies of the coding orientations of actors and their social and institutional positions and trajectories. Such analyses are beyond my scope here. Nonetheless, conceptualizing cosmologies highlights what requires change and emphasizes they are socially constructed and subject to ongoing struggles among actors.

Changing the rules of the game is, however, not easy. First, binary constellations reinforce belief in incommensurability, restricting constructive debate. Particular approbation is reserved for actors drawing on stances from opposing constellations in the search for explanatory power; they are, as Douglas (1975: 174) described Bernstein, 'Neither fish, flesh nor fowl ... anomalous beasts'. (LCT draws insights from, among others, field theory and code theory, and so is likely to evoke a plague from both houses.) Rather than asking which theory is better for what purpose, debate is driven towards asking simply which theory is better. Second, axiological cosmologies encourage an obsession with the moral or political meaning of words, problematizing attempts to place the field on a firmer footing. To paraphrase Popper (2003b: 255), no rational argument will have a rational effect on a person who does not adopt a rational attitude. Misology abounds.

However, the humanities and social sciences are not as polarized as their dominant visions project. There is more than one cosmology active in such fields, and not all actors recognize or realize the dominant codes. Moreover, as Bourdieu would argue, the *illusio* of intellectual fields is to build powerful explanations based on reason, rigour, elegance and evidence rather than blind faith. Many actors remain eager to engage with knowledge practices that are both critical of social inequities and constructive in how these can be overcome. It thus remains important to show that good sentiments may make bad sociology (Bourdieu *et al.* 1991: 251) by both unmasking the effects of axiological cosmologies and demonstrating the capacity of cumulative theorizing to provide powerful explanations with practical implications (Chapter 10). In this way, spaces may be opened for ways of working that emphasize explanatory power rather than axiological purity. By advancing from astrology towards astronomy, we will then have a chance of reaching for the stars.

Notes

1 Though theorized differently, my choice of term was inspired by Douglas (1970).
2 'Semantic gravity' can be similarly distinguished into various forms of *gravitation* and *levitation*. For simplicity, this chapter will focus solely on exploring 'semantic density'.
3 Chapter 9 further distinguishes epistemological condensation into ontic and discursive forms, and axiological condensation into subjective and interactional forms.

9 Insights, gazes, lenses and the 4-K model

Fiercely fought struggles and fundamental shifts in fields

'Minor' differences may have major effects.

Introduction

Basil Bernstein was fond of appendices. Often a paper ended with an appendix introducing new ideas that would be developed in future publications. Indeed, he saw each paper as 'the means of discovering what I shall be thinking, not what I am thinking' (2000: 211). This chapter is, in spirit, a Bernsteinian appendix. It sets forth a host of conceptual developments which future publications will elaborate, enact and exemplify further. In covering considerable theoretical ground the chapter becomes conceptually dense and assumes the reader has ingested ideas from previous chapters. So, if your gaze matches the axiological cosmology analysed in Chapter 8, you will gather more ammunition for your animus; and if you opened the book here, you are starting from the wrong place. Nonetheless, I include the chapter because it begins to grapple with questions raised by preceding developments, opens up new directions, and points towards future analyses of greater explanatory power. It thereby embodies the nature of LCT as a work-in-progress (Chapter 10).

The questions addressed by this chapter concern how knowledge and knowers matter for cumulative development. Previous chapters conceptualized social fields of practice as, *inter alia*, *knowledge–knower structures* (Chapter 4) shaped by their *epistemic relations* and *social relations* (Chapter 2). To put it crudely, knowledge-building depends on particular modalities of epistemic relations among stances and between stances and referents (such as concepts and data) that span a greater *semantic range* and trace *semantic waves* over time (Chapters 6, 7 and 8). Knower-building depends on how the *gaze* generated by social relations shapes a field's *sociality* or capacity to integrate and subsume dispositions of actors (Chapters 2 and 5). This understanding of fields, only touched upon here, extends and integrates concepts from Bernstein's code theory, to overcome both the knowledge-blindness endemic to educational research and the knower-blindness to which the theory was potentially vulnerable. Nonetheless, conceptual development involves both problem-solving and problem-raising: these answers raise further questions. Those addressed in this chapter are centred on what appear to be minor differences in epistemic relations and social relations that have, I argue, major effects and which require further conceptual development to fully explore.

Questions of epistemic relations

One set of questions revolve around whether strong relations between theory and data are sufficient for knowledge-building. The inherited framework implies they are. Bernstein defined 'strong grammar' as 'an explicit conceptual syntax capable of *relatively* precise empirical descriptions and/or of generating formal modelling of empirical relations' (2000: 163; original emphasis). Though ostensibly introduced to distinguish among 'horizontal knowledge structures', Bernstein (2000) also used 'grammar' to describe 'hierarchical knowledge structures'. Thus, social realists have suggested all intellectual fields possess degrees of 'grammaticality' and the stronger the better, for unambiguous referents enable competing claims to be compared with evidence, offering a basis for choosing among them (Muller 2007; Moore 2013b). However, the concept of 'grammar' itself exhibits weak grammar: its referents are vague. Pertinently here, Bernstein's definition embraces both 'empirical descriptions' and 'formal modelling' whose relations to the empirical world are unclear. For example, fields described as 'horizontal knowledge structures with strong grammars', including economics and linguistics, are said to 'often achieve their power by rigorous restrictions on the empirical phenomena they address' (Bernstein 2000: 163). This raises questions of the empirical fidelity of 'strong grammars': Is it sufficient for a theory to clearly define its referents, regardless of their relation to the empirical world? What kind of 'power' is achieved by these 'rigorous restrictions'? And at what cost?

The notion of 'grammar' is extended and integrated by the LCT concept of 'epistemic relations', which is additionally applicable beyond intellectual fields, offers clearer means for enactment in research and, as part of 'specialization codes', reveals organizing principles of a greater range of phenomena within a more tightly interrelated set of concepts. However, epistemic relations have received comparatively little attention in the book thus far. Previous chapters principally examine social relations to knowers (see below), a focus reflecting the adage that, like charity, critique begins at home: sociology and educational research are dominated by knower codes. Thus, while extending and integrating 'grammar', the questions posed above have yet to be addressed. Moreover, substantive research using LCT foregrounds these issues. Studies of fields with stronger epistemic relations, including economics, linguistics and physics (see below and Chapter 10), highlight a need to theorize differences *within* knowledge codes. They show that struggles and changes in these fields are not simply among competing explanations of clearly defined evidence, as notions of 'grammaticality' imply. Competition is not just within shared 'rules of the game'; the rules themselves are subject to contestation, such as what kinds of unambiguously defined referents constitute legitimate evidence. Stronger epistemic relations are thus no guarantee of building cumulative knowledge.

This issue also implicates realist theories of education. The axiological cosmology dominating educational research generates binary constellations (Chapter 8) in which realist and positivist stances are indistinguishable: their practices are allocated to the same negatively charged constellation. From this perspective, the conventional realist strategy of emphasizing ontological or epistemological differences between them represents esoteric hair-splitting among fellow travellers. Thus, for realist approaches to become visible requires both revealing the effects of this cosmology (Chapter 8) and distinguishing the organizing principles of their knowledge practices. However, for the inherited model both are 'strong grammars', and for the enhanced framework both exhibit stronger epistemic relations. In short, differences *within* epistemic relations are undertheorized.

Questions of social relations

Exploring the complexity of knower codes is a theme weaving through the book. Consequently, their conceptualization has surpassed that of epistemic relations to identify differences within social relations. Chapter 2 conceptualized standpoint theory as a *social knower code*; Chapters 5 and 6 revealed a range of knower codes underpinned by different *gazes*. Chapter 8 shifted focus from individual gazes to the field by analysing the *axiological cosmology* dominating educational research, one based on a cultivated knower code. These analyses highlight how legitimacy may emphasize categories of knowers (such as gender) and ways of knowing (such as cultivation). They thereby avoid knower-blindness and a deficit model of the humanities and many social sciences.

Nonetheless, while distinguishing within social relations, these analyses raise in turn questions of differences between and within gazes. First, it remains unclear how 'kinds of knowers' and 'ways of knowing' are articulated within social relations to generate different gazes. Chapter 5 placed gazes along a single spectrum of strengths of social relations but did not describe what generates these strengths. Second, substantive studies highlight the possibility that each gaze may, in turn, take different forms. Chapters 2 and 5 explored struggles between advocates of the cultivated gaze of early work in British cultural studies and those propounding social gazes following the feminist 'intervention' of the mid-1970s. Chapter 8, though focused on educational research, suggested that 'critical' and 'post-' theories, which have also come to dominate cultural studies recently, embody another cultivated gaze. Yet, proponents of these newer approaches are highly critical of early cultural studies. Put simply, both early and late cultural studies exhibit cultivated gazes but one foregrounds great works of culture, the other great works of cultural studies, and proponents express their differences as profound. Moreover, substantive studies using specialization codes to examine the curriculum and teaching of History and English (Chapter 10) highlight analogous shifts in the bases of their cultivated gazes, from historical facts to historiography and from literature to literary criticism. Such studies thereby raise questions of conceptualizing the nature and analysing the effects of differences *within* gazes.

Clashes and shifts

These questions of epistemic relations and social relations share a focus on practices the framework currently describes as sharing the same bases for legitimation. That is to say, they highlight something different to *code clashes* and *code shifts*, exemplified in Chapter 4 by the 'two cultures' debate and school Music. The 'gulf of mutual incomprehension' (Snow 1959: 4) said to separate science and the humanities was conceptualized as a code clash between knowledge codes and knower codes. The school Music curriculum in England was shown to involve several code shifts: from knower code at primary schooling, to knowledge code during the early years of secondary schooling, and thence towards élite code for the GCSE qualification. In contrast, the stances mentioned above share specialization codes: realist and positivist approaches emphasize epistemic relations; early cultural studies, standpoint theories and 'critical' theories emphasize social relations. The questions are thus of differences *within* knowledge codes and *within* knower codes, rather than between them. Moreover, in the case of social relations, the above questions highlight a further level of differences within gazes.

This chapter outlines a model for conceptualizing these differences and reveals that, though they may appear fine-grained distinctions, their effects are anything but minor. It does so through elaborating concepts central to the dimension of Specialization. As depicted in Figure 9.1, for knowledge practices these are realized as: epistemic relations between knowledge claims and their objects of study; and social relations between knowledge claims and their subjects. Here these definitions are deepened by analytically distinguishing two components within each of these relations. These components or sub-relations combine to generate modalities of epistemic relations or *insights*, and modalities of social relations or *gazes*. This conceptual development thereby brings to light: *relation clashes* between practices characterized by the same specialization code but with different insights or gazes; and *relation shifts* between insights and gazes where the code remains the same. The effects of such clashes and shifts are illustrated by examples from across the disciplinary map, including economics, linguistics, physics and cultural studies.

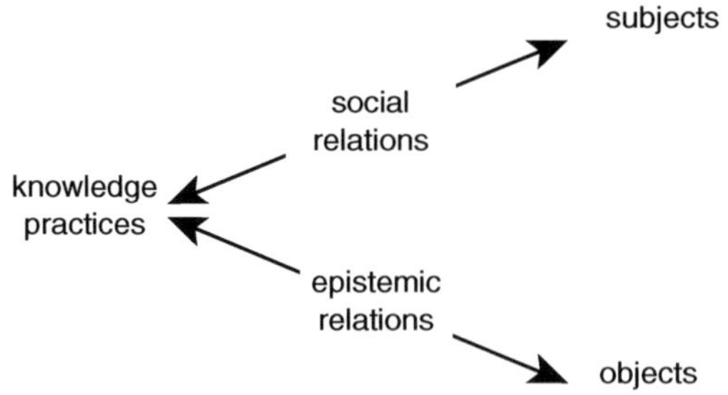

Figure 9.1 Specialization of knowledge practices

For epistemic relations, these brief analyses illustrate that stronger relations to data do not guarantee progress and reveal how different modalities enable and constrain cumulative knowledge-building. For social relations, previous analyses of how different gazes in British cultural studies shape progress (Chapters 2 and 5) are more systematically reconceptualized in terms of relation clashes and shifts. Early and current cultural studies are both shown to exhibit cultivated gazes but based on cultivation into great works of culture and great works of cultural studies, respectively. This difference is explored through introducing a further level of conceptual delicacy that distinguishes the *lenses* that gazes and insights may adopt. Using the example of 'linguistic turns' across the humanities and social sciences, changes of these lenses are shown to have profound effects for practices in intellectual and educational fields. Finally, the four components are brought together to provide a '4-K model' of knowledge practices, comprising relations to knowers, knowing, other knowledges, and the known. I conclude by briefly considering what the concepts introduced in this 'Bernsteinian appendix' may suggest for further substantive research.

Epistemic relations

The concept of ***epistemic relations*** (ER) highlights that practices may be specialized by both ***what*** they relate to and ***how*** they so relate, or by relations to the objects of their focus and to other possible practices. One can thereby analytically distinguish ***ontic relations*** (OR) between practices and that part of the world towards which they are oriented, and ***discursive relations*** (DR) between practices and other practices. As illustrated in Figure 9.2, for knowledge claims these become: ontic relations between knowledge and its objects of study; and discursive relations between knowledge and other knowledges.[1]

Each of these relations can be strongly or weakly classified and framed along continua of strengths to describe how strongly knowledge practices bound and control legitimate objects of study (ontic relations) and legitimate

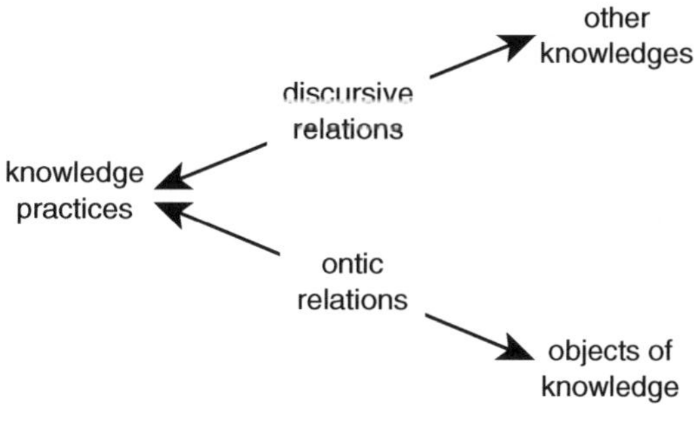

Figure 9.2 Epistemic relations

procedures for constructing objects of study (discursive relations). Each may independently vary in strength, generating the strength of epistemic relations, such that:

$$ER+/- = OR+/-, DR+/-$$

Both can also be strengthened and weakened over time, generating changes to the strength of epistemic relations:

$$ER\uparrow/\downarrow = OR\uparrow/\downarrow, DR\uparrow/\downarrow$$

As shown in Figure 9.3, these continua of strengths delineate an ***epistemic plane*** with four principal modalities or ***insights***:

- Practices characterized by ***situational insight*** relatively strongly bound and control their legitimate objects of study but relatively weakly bound and control legitimate approaches for constructing those problem-situations (OR+, DR–). Simply put, ***what*** one is studying matters but not ***how***. Knowledge practices are thus specialized by their problem-situations, which may be addressed through a range of approaches: procedural pluralism or, at its weakest possible strength of DR, procedural relativism.
- Where practices emphasize ***doctrinal insight***, legitimate problem-situations are not restrictively defined but relations between the legitimate approach and other possible approaches are relatively strongly bounded and controlled (OR–, DR+). Legitimacy flows from using the specializing approach: ***what*** is studied is less significant, ***how*** it is studied matters. This combines theoretical or methodological dogmatism with ontic promiscuity or, at its weakest strength of OR, ontic relativism.[2]
- Practices based on ***purist insight*** relatively strongly bound and control both legitimate objects of study and legitimate approaches (OR+, DR+). Legitimacy is thus conferred by ***both*** 'what' and 'how' – one must use a specific approach to study a specific phenomenon. Using the legitimate approach to analyse other phenomena or using other approaches to study the legitimate phenomenon are both devalorized.
- Practices with ***knower*** or ***no insight*** relatively weakly bound and control both legitimate objects of study and legitimate approaches (OR–, DR–). With different strengths of social relations, these weaker epistemic relations may form part of either a knower code (ER–, SR+), where legitimacy flows from attributes of the subject, or a relativist code (ER–, SR–), where 'anything goes', depending on the strength of social relations. It could thus be described as ***k(no)wer insight***.

These insights begin to reveal the complexity of epistemic relations (or, in old terms, that there is more than one kind of 'grammar' and more than 'strong'/'weak'). Situational, doctrinal and purist insights represent modalities

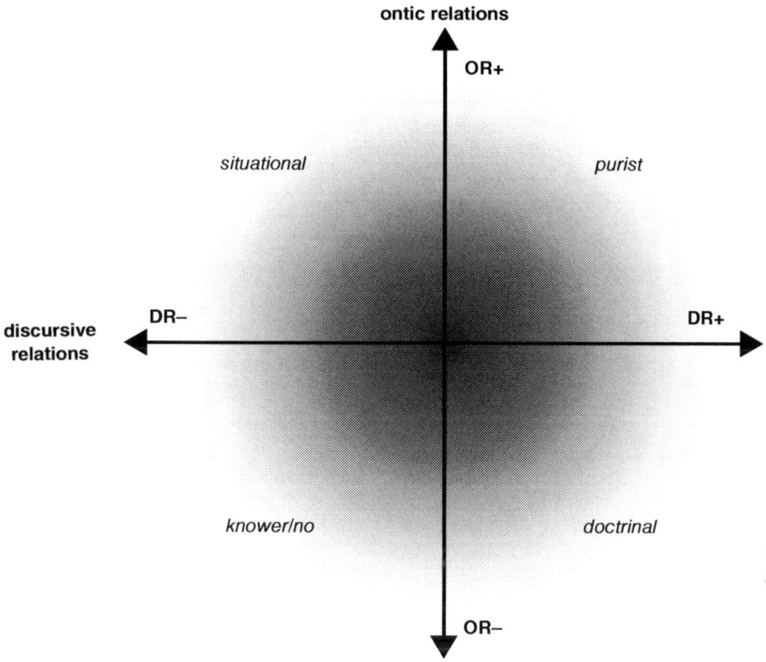

Figure 9.3 The epistemic plane – insights

of *stronger* epistemic relations (ER+); knower/no insight embodies *weaker* epistemic relations (ER–). As with all code concepts in LCT, strengths of ontic and discursive relations are relative and represent continua with infinite capacities for gradation. The above modalities thus embrace a range of possible positions within the epistemic plane, as illustrated by discussing both 'pluralism' and 'relativism' when referring to degrees of weaker relations.

Epistemic relation clashes and shifts

Using these concepts we can explore differences among practices exhibiting stronger epistemic relations and analyse their effects on building powerful and cumulative knowledge. As with specialization codes, the concepts comprising *insights* can be enacted in studies of production, recontextualization and reproduction, embracing all fields of the epistemic–pedagogic device, as well as practices beyond education.[3] To exemplify their usefulness, I shall briefly discuss examples from knowledge-code academic subjects, primarily focused on debates in their production and recontextualization fields, from both the social and natural sciences: economics, linguistics and physics. For illustration, I explore fields including contrastive modalities: ***doctrinal insight*** (OR–, DR+) or 'allegiance to an approach, not to a problem'; and situational insight (OR+, DR–) or 'allegiance to a problem, not to an approach' (to adapt a well-known saying of Bernstein). I illustrate that these insights have ramifications for explanatory power, actors' strategies in struggles, and knowledge-building.

Economics

During the 2000s a variety of approaches, including 'heterodox economics' and 'Post-Autistic Economics' (PAE), gained momentum within the discipline (Lawson 2006; Fullbrook 2007). Though embracing divergent projects, these approaches share opposition to 'orthodox' or 'neoclassical' approaches that have dominated economics for decades. Struggles between heterodox and orthodox economics have been fervently fought, including student protests in France and the United Kingdom during 2000–2001 (Fullbrook 2003b). Yet, proponents of both camps are motivated by knowledge codes: they typically emphasize epistemic relations and downplay social relations as the basis of legitimacy. Their differences lie ***within*** their stronger epistemic relations, in divergent strengths of ontic and discursive relations. In short, their struggle can be understood as an ***epistemic relation clash*** between insights that offer competing visions of the nature of the field.

A defining feature of orthodox economics is belief in the value of mathematical modelling; as a feminist economist puts it:

> To a mainstream economist, theory means model, and model means ideas expressed in mathematical form. ...These models, students learn, are theory. In more advanced courses, economic theories are presented in more mathematically elaborate models. ... They learn that the legitimate way to argue is with models and econometrically constructed forms of evidence ... Claiming that a model is deficient is a minor feat ... What is really valued is coming up with a better model, a better theory.
>
> (Strassman 1994: 154)

Indeed, economists of every kind emphasize that using formal mathematical models is necessary for legitimacy within orthodox economics (Lawson 2006; Fullbrook 2007), such that:

> to get an article published in most of today's top rank economic journals, you must provide a mathematical model, even if it adds nothing to your verbal analysis
>
> (Lipsey 2001: 184)

These ***relatively strong discursive relations*** (DR+) have created a common language for building knowledge, enabling a remarkable degree of cohesion within the field for decades. As the above quotes illustrate, mathematical modelling underpins both training a shared gaze among students and evaluating pedagogic and intellectual progress. Indeed, mainstream economics has formed a powerful orthodoxy: generations of scholars have built a considerable and cumulative body of work that claims knowledge of ever-widening areas of social life. However, the resultant knowledge is now widely portrayed as disconnected from empirical reality. Eminent economists argue the discipline 'has become increasingly an arcane branch of mathematics rather than dealing with real economic problems' (Friedman 1999: 137) and 'is a theoretical system which floats in the air and which bears little relation to what happens in the real world' (Coase 1999: 2).

This apparent contradiction can be understood using the LCT distinction between the *focus* and the *basis* of practices as languages of legitimation (Chapter 2). In terms of *focus,* neoclassical models rigorously restrict the parameters of the phenomena they address and unambiguously define their referents. For example, models limit the variables considered or begin from restrictive assumptions. (A common opening to essay questions when I studied economics at university was 'Take a two country world with two products …'.) However, the *focus* is not the same as the *basis* of legitimation, which give the organizing principles of practices. In terms of *basis,* such models do not correspondingly restrict the phenomena into which legitimate insight is claimed: they exhibit ***relatively weak ontic relations*** (OR–). As critics argue, neoclassical economics often obscures differences between the 'reality' constructed by models (with strictly defined limits and variables) and empirical reality, weakly specializing legitimate problem-situations for the application of its findings. Formal mathematical modelling is legitimated as valid for analysing all economic phenomena, and the results of specific models are portrayed as generating knowledge of unrestricted application to the world, including problem-situations with different conditions to those of the model.

This ***doctrinal insight*** (OR–, DR+) of orthodox economics is portrayed by critics as lost in imaginary worlds and overly policing theoretical principles and methodological procedures (as expressed by its indelicate description as 'autistic' by proponents of PAE). Its power to build cumulative knowledge, they argue, has come at the cost of explanatory power. In contrast, while heterodox economics encompasses divergent approaches, they typically share an emphasis on foregrounding the problems being addressed and the need for greater diversity in theories and methods. For example, writing of university courses, a leading advocate of PAE argued:

> Our view is: courses can no longer focus on TOOLS (maximizing under constraint, finding local and general extrema), but on PROBLEMS (incomes, poverty, unemployment, monetary policy, international trade, European Union, developing countries, immigration, new economy, ecology, etc.). The tools would then be used only to the limit of their relevance for analyzing such problems, and not for their own sake.
>
> (Gilles Raveaud, quoted in Fullbrook 2003a: 30)

Such arguments attempt to re-articulate the epistemic relations of the field by reasserting ontic relations (the explanation of 'problems') and downplaying discursive relations (the use of specific 'tools') as the basis of legitimacy: ***situational*** *insight* (OR+, DR–). (The scale of Raveaud's 'problems' highlights that strengths of ontic relations are not given by size; 'situations' in 'situational insight' are *problem-situations* rather than substantive contexts.)

However, while heterodox economists call for theoretical and methodological pluralism and a return to real-world problems to reinvigorate the discipline's explanatory power, they also highlight a potential cost. As many commentators note (Lawson 2006), the approaches of heterodox economics share little beyond opposition to mainstream economics. The ascendance of situational insight may reconnect to reality but at the cost of problematizing cohesion, professional identity and apprenticeship, fragmenting the discipline.

Struggles between mainstream and heterodox economics thus represent an *epistemic relation clash* between different insights. Their shared specialization code provides a minimum ground state enabling debate, while their different insights offer divergent definitions of achievement in the field. As briefly highlighted here, this struggle for control of the epistemic–pedagogic device between doctrinal and situational knowledge codes is more than a minor matter for the discipline: insights offer potential gains and losses, including explanatory power and cohesion.

Linguistics

Insights are also associated with differing strategies in these struggles, as illustrated by another knowledge-code field, linguistics. The discipline is characterized by long-standing struggles among competing approaches, most notably Chomskyan transformation grammar and systemic functional linguistics (SFL). Two leading systemic functional linguists characterize 'what lies behind the difference' as being that the aspects of language addressed by SFL are 'text-driven':

> the priorities are set by the need to attempt a global understanding of how a grammar works in relation to natural text. In contrast, the aspects given most attention in the current Chomskyan framework are theory-driven: they are selected because of their yield in terms of the theory and there is no reason to attempt a more global coverage.
>
> (Matthiessen and Martin 1991: 14)

This difference is illustrated by their choice of problems and data: SFL focuses on naturally occurring examples of language to explore substantive issues, while Chomskyan research often uses imaginary examples to support arguments aimed at finding solutions to imaginary problems. According to systemicists, phenomena drive the development of theory in SFL (OR+, DR–) and theory drives the choice of foci and exempla in Chomskyan linguistics (OR–, DR+).

This relation clash between situational and doctrinal insights is reflected in their means of argument. Martin, for example, highlights that systemic linguists criticize Chomskyan linguistics for its empirical inadequacy, but Chomskyan linguists employ a 'dismissal genre' that involves 'reductive co-option': 'recasting another's work in one's own terms ... and then rendering it absurd with respect to one's own "in-house" criteria' (1992: 147). SFL work is recast in Chomskyan terms and denounced as flawed according to those terms. In other words, the specialization of the (sacred) theory in relation to other (profane) theories is the key (DR+), rather than the specialization of problem-situations to which the theory is legitimately relevant (OR+). The epistemic logics of engagement with other ideas are thus shaped by the *insights* underlying practices, which may affect explanatory power and cumulative development. Situational insight underlies the recontextualization of concepts from other approaches to help explain a phenomenon, encouraging, for example, inter-disciplinary collaboration to more fully grasp empirical phenomena. In contrast, doctrinal insight underlies the reductive co-option of those concepts to demonstrate the superiority of one's own approach, maintaining theoretical purity at the expense of capturing complex reality.[4]

Physics

Epistemic relation clashes are not confined to social science: another contemporary example lies within theoretical physics. Bernstein (2000) characterized physics as the archetypical hierarchical knowledge structure, illustrated as a triangle with a minimal number of propositions or axioms at the top embracing a maximal number of empirical phenomena at the base (see Chapter 4).[5] Physics currently has two main triangles: quantum mechanics and general relativity. Bernstein's suggestion that such fields 'appear by their users to be motivated towards greater and greater integrating propositions' (2000: 161) is reflected by the current Holy Grail: integration of these theories within a Grand Unified Theory. However, 'the community of people who work on fundamental physics is split' (Smolin 2006: xvii) in a dispute between not merely competing solutions but competing ways of understanding legitimacy in science.

The dominant approach to creating a Grand Unified Theory is string theory, which has rapidly cumulated publications and research degrees. According to many physicists, its ascendency has re-articulated epistemic relations underlying the field. On the one hand, its advocates strengthened discursive relations by proclaiming string theory to be the only legitimate approach to fundamental physics. Smolin, for example, claims:

> Very quickly there developed an almost cultlike atmosphere. You were either a string theorist or you were not ... There was a sense that the one true theory had been discovered. Nothing else was important or worth thinking about.
>
> (Smolin 2006: 116)

On the other hand, ontic relations were weakened by downplaying limitations on the phenomena for which the approach claimed legitimate insight. While involving rigorous restrictions on referents that are defined with mathematical precision, this limited *focus* of the language of legitimation of string theory is not matched by its ***basis***. String theory is often portrayed as unifying all the particles and forces in nature and promising to make clear and unambiguous predictions for all experiments ever (Greene 2005). At the same time, however, it involves complex models of multidimensional worlds that are insulated from experiment. This, critics argue, is not because the theory has outpaced contemporary technological capacity for experiment, but because its proponents move the goalposts whenever facing disconfirmation; Richard Feynman, for example, argued that it produces ***ad hoc*** excuses rather than explanations (Davies and Brown 1988: 194–195). Moreover, though known string theories disagree with observed facts about the world, the approach cannot be disproved by experiment because the large number of possible string theories (as many as 10^{500}) means that other, as yet unknown ones may still hold.

The ***doctrinal insight*** (OR–, DR+) of string theory is portrayed by critics as taking the reality of the model as the model of reality. Though the referents of string theory may be clear and unambiguous, they do not offer a means of deciding among knowledge claims, for the theory defines the world in which it works. For example, the Nobel Prize-winning physicist Sheldon Glashow argues that, despite not showing the theory works or making new, precise and falsifiable experimental predictions, string theorists continue to insist that space is multidimensional 'because string theory doesn't make sense in any other kind of space' (Glashow and Bova 1988: 25). Martin Veltman, a pioneer of the Standard Model of fundamental physics, states more bluntly: 'String theory is mumbo jumbo. It has nothing to do with experiment' (quoted in Farmelo 2009: 438).

Such critics emphasize the need both for closer contact between bold conjectures and the real world through experiments that determine their legitimate limits (OR+), and for greater engagement with alternative theories, such as loop quantum gravity, causal set theory and twistor theory (DR–): ***situational insight***. The result is an ***epistemic relation clash*** within physics, one with potential consequences for the cumulative development of the field, because:

> Those who believe the conjectures [of string theory] find themselves in a very different intellectual universe from those who insist on believing only what the actual evidence supports.
>
> (Smolin 2006: 198)

For many commentators, this relation clash is 'an indication that something is badly amiss' (ibid.), not because competing approaches exist (such diversity of ideas is welcomed) but because there are competing ways of choosing among them.

Insights into knowledge-building

As these debates illustrate, knowledge codes are neither homogeneous nor royal roads to cumulative knowledge-building: stronger epistemic relations do not by themselves guarantee intellectual progress. Cumulative knowledge-building requires both the generation of a diversity of ideas and a shared means of choosing among them, both of which different insights enable and constrain in different ways.

As orthodox economics and string theory illustrate, ***doctrinal insight*** enables knowledge-building, though with costs. By bringing a wide range of phenomena within the purview of a strongly bounded approach, it allows disparate issues to be integrated within an overarching research paradigm. This epistemic basis for status, identity and achievement also enables cohesion among actors. In fundamental physics, for example, critics note that 'you were either a string theorist or you were not', so that 'unlike other fields of physics, there is a clear distinction between string theorists and non-string theorists' with 'a remarkable uniformity of view' among the former (Smolin 2006: 116, 271, 273). A strongly distinct approach provides a clear focus for training noviciates into the legitimate insight and a shared basis for debate. Indeed, by bringing together researchers sharing a common theoretical language, doctrinal insight may generate excitement, innovation and collective purpose. For emerging fields with minimal theory or fragmented by context-dependent models, this can provide much-needed critical mass and integration.

There is, though, a potential price to be paid. The disciplining nature of stronger discursive relations can become a straitjacket. Mainstream economics, for example, is described as:

> relatively open minded when it comes to new ideas but quite close minded when it comes to alternative methodologies. If it isn't modelled, it isn't economics, no matter how insightful
>
> (Colander *et al.* 2004: 10)

Similarly, critics argue string theory has monopolized legitimacy so that 'it is practically career suicide for young theoretical physicists not to join the field' (Smolin 2006: xx). While providing a means of choosing among ideas, doctrinal insight may thus restrict their diversity, with potentially fruitful ideas dismissed because of their origins, regardless of their explanatory potential. Moreover, knowledge-building may come at the cost of increasing disengagement with the real world. The examples discussed above highlight how sponsors of formal models can assume their applicability to open systems and take, as Bourdieu (1977: 29) put it, the reality of the model for a model of reality. It is notable that neoclassical economics, Chomskyan grammar and string theory are all described by their critics as studying imaginary worlds. Moreover, as the examples of these disciplines suggest, doctrinal insight may become subject to the return of the repressed: the real world. The more widely the legitimate approach is applied, the more likely the world 'reacts back' and reveals its lack of validity, encouraging a realist response by disaffected actors within the field and leading to a relation clash. There may thus be a limit to both the explanatory power and the field-building capacity of doctrinal insight.

Situational insight (OR+, DR–) offers a means for opening up debate to new approaches and calling for a return to the real, reinvigorating sclerotic development. Strongly bounded and controlled problem-situations can provide an Archimedean point for debate among actors while procedural pluralism can encourage empirical fidelity to the multifaceted and complex nature of real-world problems. Together these may encourage a proliferation of proposed solutions, such as the diversity of approaches in heterodox economics and alternatives to string theory, as well as genuinely inter-disciplinary collaboration. For example, reflecting situational insight, systemic functional linguists and social realist sociologists are increasingly bringing analyses of language and knowledge together to more fully capture educational practices (see Chapter 10).

However, if its weaker discursive relations become too weak, leading to procedural relativism, situational insight may problematize the capacity of actors to consensually choose among the resulting multitude of ideas. Lacking a well-defined approach for cultivating or training initiates may also lead to increasing segmentation among approaches, fragmenting the field. Similarly, if its relatively strong ontic relations become too strong, resulting in a series of models locked within tightly circumscribed problem-situations, there will be difficulties in integrating understandings of disparate phenomena.

In short, insights have different powers and tendencies, only some of which I have illustrated here. The extent to which they are exercized or realized to enable or constrain cumulative knowledge-building in any particular case remains a matter for substantive research. Nonetheless, this brief discussion highlights that no single insight guarantees cumulative and powerful knowledge-building. For example, situational insight may be valuable for engagements with other approaches while doctrinal insight enables the lessons of such engagements to be recontextualized into the terms of the approach. Moreover, the notion of *profiles,* outlined in Chapter 7 for semantic codes, suggests a key factor may lie with how theories or fields strengthen and weaken their ontic and discursive relations over time. Indeed, a key issue for the health of intellectual fields may be understanding which insights are most valuable for what and when.

Social relations

As previous chapters reveal, the concept of *social relations* highlights that practices may be specialized by knowers in terms of both who they are (such as social categories) and how they know (such as cultivation), or kinds of knowers and ways of knowing. One can thereby analytically distinguish: *subjective relations* (SubR) between practices and the kinds of actors engaged in them; and *interactional relations* (IR) between practices and the ways of acting involved. As illustrated in Figure 9.4, for knowledge claims these become: subjective relations between knowledge and its subjects; and interactional relations between knowledge and practices of knowing by subjects.[6]

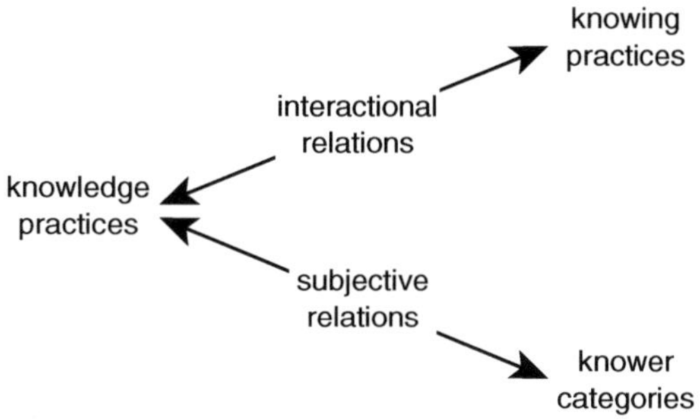

Figure 9.4 Social relations

Each of these relations may be strongly or weakly classified and framed along continua of strengths. They thus describe how strongly knowledge claims bound and control legitimate ***kinds of knowers*** (subjective relations) and legitimate ***ways of knowing through interactions with significant others*** (interactional relations). Both these social relations can take a multitude of forms. There are numerous potential bases for subjectivity – social class, sex, gender, race, ethnicity, sexuality, religion, region, etc. – and thus categories for defining legitimate knowers. Similarly, there are numerous 'significant others' (which may be objects or subjects) and means of interaction that may serve to define legitimate ways of knowing. These are as diverse as therapy with a psychiatrist, external stimuli and the human mind, master–apprentice relations, parent–child interactions, and so forth. (I return to consider implications of this diversity, further below.) The two relations may vary independently in strength, generating the strength of social relations, such as that:

$$SR+/- = SubR+/-, IR+/-$$

Both relations can also be independently strengthened or weakened, generating changes in social relations:

$$SR\uparrow/\downarrow = SubR\uparrow/\downarrow, IR\uparrow/\downarrow$$

As shown in Figure 9.5, these continua of strength create a *social plane* with the four *gazes* outlined in Chapter 5 as principal modalities:

- Where legitimacy is based on knowers possessing a *social gaze*, practices relatively strongly bound and control the kinds of knowers who can claim legitimacy but relatively weakly limit their ways of knowing (SubR+, IR–). For example, standpoint theories base legitimacy on membership of a specific social category (social class, gender, ethnicity, etc.), regardless of knowers' past or present interactions.
- Practices that base legitimacy on the possession of a *cultivated gaze* weakly bound and control legitimate categories of knower but strongly bound and

control legitimate interactions with significant others (SubR–, IR+). These often involve acquiring a 'feel' for practices through, for example: extended participation in 'communities of practice' (Lave and Wenger 1991); sustained exposure to exemplary models, such as great works of art; and prolonged apprenticeship under an acknowledged master.

- Practices that define legitimacy in terms of possessing a ***born gaze*** relatively strongly bound and control *both* legitimate kinds of knowers and legitimate ways of knowing (SubR+, IR+), such as religious beliefs of an act of God towards a chosen person or people, and claims to legitimacy based on both membership of a social category and experiences with significant others (e.g. standpoint theory that additionally requires mentoring by already-liberated knowers in consciousness-raising groups).
- Practices that relatively weakly bound and control both legitimate kinds of knowers and legitimate ways of knowing (SubR–, IR–) are characterized by weaker social relations that, alongside different strengths of epistemic relations, may form part of either a knowledge code (ER+, SR–) underpinned by a ***trained gaze*** that emphasizes the possession of specialist knowledge and skills, or a relativist code (ER–, SR–) that offers a ***blank gaze***.

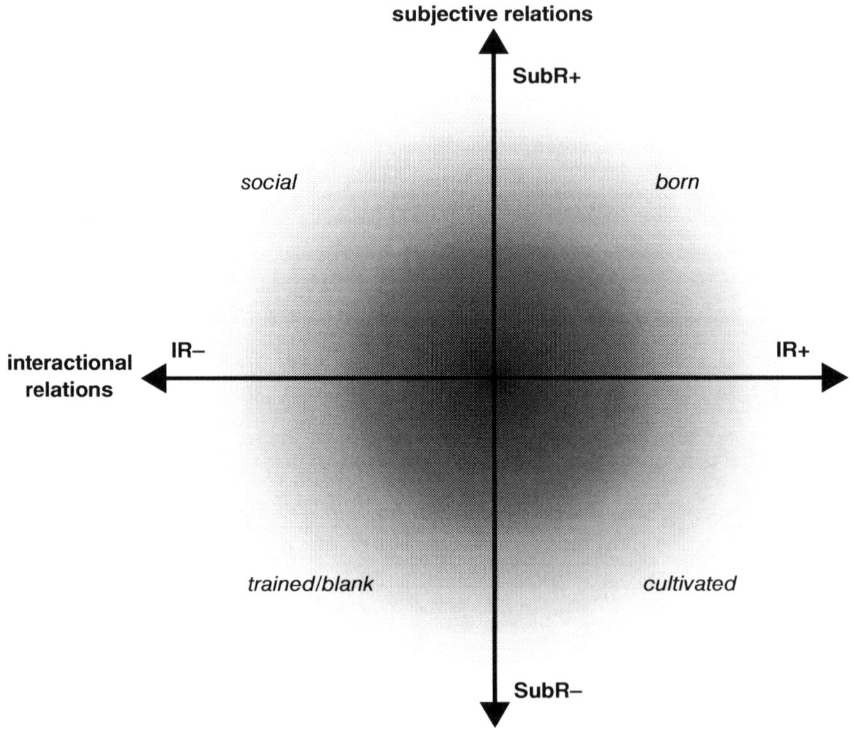

Figure 9.5 The social plane – gazes

Social, cultivated and born gazes represent relational modalities of *stronger* social relations (SR+); the trained/blank gaze represents *weaker* social relations (SR–). All relation strengths are relative, with infinite capacity for gradations, embracing manifold diversity across the social plane.

Social relation clashes and shifts

This conceptualization of gazes enables a deeper understanding of practices exhibiting stronger social relations and their implications for cumulative progress. To illustratively explore these effects, I shall build on analyses of knower codes from previous chapters. First, I briefly reconceptualize the account of British cultural studies from Chapters 2 and 5 in terms of clashes and shifts between cultivated and social gazes, highlighting changes in its subjective and interactional relations. I then extend these analyses in the light of Chapter 8 to show how a new cultivated gaze has come to dominate cultural studies. To explore how this differs to the cultivated gaze underlying the field's emergence – and, more generally, the nature of differences *within* gazes – I then introduce a further conceptual distinction of significance for understanding both gazes and insights: the notion of lenses.

From cultivated to social gazes

From its emergence in the late 1950s to the feminist 'intervention' of the mid-1970s, British cultural studies represented a knower code where legitimacy was predicated on possessing a *cultivated gaze*. The founders of cultural studies mostly came from non-traditional social backgrounds (Hoggart and Williams from the working class; Hall from Jamaica) and had been university educated in literary criticism (Hall at Oxford; Williams and Thompson at Cambridge). In their teaching and publications, they sought to weaken boundaries around and control over the kinds of knowers who could be legitimate – *weaker subjective relations* – by including social groups previously marginalized from education, such as working-class and mature students. In contrast, they maintained relatively strong boundaries around and control over how one can legitimately know – *stronger interactional relations*. During the early 1960s, a key aim was to cultivate critical discrimination among learners through their inculcation into appreciation of great works of culture, where the definition of 'culture' was broadened through extending the techniques of Leavisite literary criticism to study of 'the popular arts' (Hall and Whannel 1964). By the early 1970s this aim became more focused on inculcation into appreciation of great works of cultural studies, thanks to concerted efforts to create a canon of key texts (Chapter 5). Nonetheless, throughout this period cultural studies was underpinned by the notion of a cultivated gaze as key to legitimacy (SubR–, IR+).

In the mid-1970s feminist standpoint theory attempted to re-articulate these social relations. Past work by male scholars was portrayed as reflecting a male gaze, and understanding the experiences of women was held to require a gaze restricted to female scholars, *strengthening subjective relations* (SR↑). In contrast, other dimensions of experience, such as differences in educational background, were downplayed as the basis of legitimacy, *weakening interactional relations* (IR↓). Previous canons, theories and methods were critiqued as reflecting social domination and new, gendered approaches were called for. However, apprenticeship into these approaches was not the basis for a new legitimate gaze; rather, the approaches were said to flow from the pre-existing gaze (once liberated from patriarchal ideology). This *social gaze* (SubR+, IR–) was then echoed, with different social categories, by similar 'interventions' for ethnicity and sexuality.

The struggles within cultural studies initiated by these interventions can now be reconceptualized as *social relation clashes* between cultivated and social knower codes with differing strengths of subjective and interactional relations. As Chapters 2 and 5 demonstrate, these differences were experienced as fundamental. Leading figures in the field attest to the intense nature of struggles and the personal toll they exacted, and social gazes helped shape the institutional and intellectual trajectories of British cultural studies. Paralleling the discussion of insights (above), it is clear that no single gaze guarantees progress; previous chapters suggest each gaze both enables and constrains cumulative development in various ways. For example, cultivated gazes offer greater potential for sociality and thus more inclusive bases for knower- and knowledge-building. However, in this kind of cultivated gaze (see below), the basis of valuations of cultural works have often been portrayed as asocial and ahistorical and located solely within those works, as essential properties. This restricts and ossifies the field by obscuring for new kinds of knowers the possibility of cultivation into a legitimate gaze. Conversely, social gazes offer strategic ways for marginalized actors to carve out institutional and disciplinary spaces in higher education, but their tendencies towards proliferation and fragmentation reduce the sociality of the field, problematize knowledge-building, and leave their sponsors institutionally vulnerable (Chapter 2).

A new cultivated gaze

Chapters 2 and 5 discuss the implications of cultivated and social gazes for knowledge-building by exploring the effects of the *social relation shift* between them in cultural studies during the late 1970s and 1980s. However, that is not the end of the story. Though standpoint theories rose to prominence during this period, they did not completely monopolize the field. Moreover, cultural studies has since come to be dominated by a range of 'post-', 'critical' and deconstructive theories that do not proclaim social gazes. To understand these more recent developments, we can draw on the cosmological analysis of educational research from Chapter 8. This suggested that fields dominated by such approaches are characterized by *axiological cosmologies*. That is to say, the status of such approaches is based less on their comparative explanatory power than on their capacity to reflect sponsors in a virtuous light via the morally or politically charged constellations to which those stances are assigned. Thus, at the level of actors, the stronger social relations of this knower code are based not on 'voicing' social categories (SubR–) but rather on possessing a gaze capable of recognizing and realizing ostensibly 'virtuous' or 'radical' stances. Over recent decades, such stances in cultural studies have included work by an eclectic and changing cast of luminaries, mostly from continental Europe. Some are meteorites that burn brightly but briefly before falling to earth, some are comets which vanish but reappear later, and others represent more longer-lasting stars in the constellations of cultural studies. Knowing what stances are constructed as 'critical' and which of these are ascendant or fading away is part of what Bourdieu called the 'feel for the game' that actors gain through prolonged immersion in a social field of practice. In other words, they reflect stronger interactional relations to significant others (IR+). The basis of legitimacy is thus the demonstration of a ***cultivated gaze***, one gained through exposure to exemplary models.

Prima facie, this cultivated gaze suggests a return to origins, back to where cultural studies began. However, as Chapter 5 highlights, work using 'critical' theories is strenuously opposed to past cultivated gazes, including the left-Leavisite beginnings of the field, distance from which often serves as a proxy measure of progress. Moreover, the 'significant others' of their interactional relations have changed: from great works of culture to great works of cultural studies. This raises questions of how such differences can be captured and their effects for cumulative knowledge-building. I thus now turn to conceptualize differences *within* gazes and, for symmetry, insights.

Lenses

Thus far the chapter has elaborated two conceptual levels of organizing principles. First, I began by conceptualizing knowledge practices in terms of ***specialization codes*** that comprise epistemic relations and social relations. Second, I conceptualized modalities of epistemic relations as ***insights*** and modalities of social relations as ***gazes***, and explored their constitutive relations. I shall now begin to describe a third level of organizing principles: *lenses*. As mentioned above, there are numerous potential categories for subjective relations, and ways of interacting with 'significant others' for interactional relations – the kinds of knowers and ways of knowing underpinning gazes are legion. Similarly, for insights there are numerous potential kinds of objects of study for ontic relations and knowledge practices for discursive relations. Each of these relations is a relation to something; the forms taken by that something represent what I term *lenses*. One can thus describe *lens clashes* and *lens shifts*. Each lens refocuses the gaze or insight in particular ways, helping shape knowledge practices and social fields.

Returning to British cultural studies, a key difference between its early and contemporary cultivated gazes lies with their relatively strong interactional relations, in the 'significant others' that legitimate knowers should be thoroughly acquainted with. The forms these take can be analysed along a number of dimensions. Here, for simplicity of illustration, I shall describe two kinds of lens for cultivated gazes: ***ontic lenses***, where 'significant others' are construed as objects of study; and ***discursive lenses***, where 'significant others' are construed as ***studies*** of objects of study.

Early cultural studies emphasized immersion in exemplary works *of* culture; recent cultural studies emphasizes immersion in exemplary works *about* culture. Of course, a great work of critical appreciation can become viewed as a great work in itself. However, the distinction here refers not to their intrinsic status but rather to ***how they are construed as 'significant others' in cultivating legitimate gazes.*** As discussed, this shift was first heralded in the early 1970s by attempts to create a *Reader in Cultural Studies* comprising key theory and research papers. This process was interrupted rather than halted by standpoint interventions, regained momentum with the growth of undergraduate courses during the 1980s, and by the 1990s 'Readers' and textbooks were being published in ever-growing numbers. While the notion of canons of culture were devalorized, canons of cultural studies proliferated. Thus, though both cultivated gazes are lensed through canonical works, this move from the World to the Word as the 'significant other' for legitimate ways of knowing represents a shift from an ***ontic lens*** to a ***discursive lens.*** They can thereby be redescribed as:

- early cultural studies: knower code–cultivated gaze–ontic lens
- current cultural studies: knower code–cultivated gaze–discursive lens.

Thus, three principal knower codes can be discerned through the history of British cultural studies. As outlined in Table 9.1, the field has been dominated not only by different gazes but also by different lenses. As Bernstein (2000) suggests for horizontal knowledge structures, these shifts represent segmental addition rather than integrating subsumption: the original ontic-cultivated gaze was neither subsumed nor supplanted by social gazes and these, in turn, remain active within the field, though marginalized by the recent discursive-cultivated gaze. This analysis thereby provides further understanding of something not conceptualized in Bernstein's model: the forms taken by segments.

Table 9.1 Social relation shifts within British cultural studies

Period	*Late 1950 – mid 1970s*	*Mid 1970s – 1980s*	*1990s – present*
Specialization code	knower code	knower code	knower code
Social relations	SubR–, IR+	SubR+, IR–	SubR–, IR+
Dominant gaze	cultivated gaze	social gazes	cultivated gaze
Lens (knower categories/ 'significant others')	ontic lens (works of culture)	social lens (gender, ethnicity, sexuality)	discursive lens (theories of culture)
Main approaches	'left-Leavisite' literary criticism, continental sociology	feminism, multiculturalism, post-colonialism, queer theory	post-structuralism, post-modernism, 'critical' theories
Summary of code	ontic-cultivated knower code	social knower codes	discursive-cultivated knower code

This conceptualization raises questions of whether such a lens shift is specific to cultural studies, and whether such third-level changes to organizing principles are significant for knowledge practices. Space precludes extensive discussion but a well-known example provides ample preliminary evidence: the 'linguistic turn'.

'The linguistic turn' – a lens shift

Since the early 1960s, 'linguistic' or 'discursive turns' have been recurrently heralded across many disciplines of humanities and social science. They originate in responses to the post-war rise of science and perceived 'crisis in the humanities' that aimed to maintain the latter's grip on study of the human world by placing language at its centre (Maton 2005b). Influentially, Winch (1958, 1964), echoing the later Wittgenstein, argued that ideas must be understood in terms of their 'meaning' as part of 'language games' within specific 'forms of life'. According to Winch, reality does not generate, structure or constrain language; rather, language makes reality, indeed 'the distinction between the real and the unreal and the concept of agreement with reality themselves belong to our language' (1964: 82). Language was already central to humanist ideas of culture, but from being a key means through which reality is perceived, it became the basis of its construction. From this perspective, knowing how we understand the world is knowing the world itself and so the role of discourse should be foregrounded in analysis. These ideas became extremely influential and have, in various guises, been regularly announced as revolutionizing ideas across the social sciences and humanities. Their influence represents a *lens shift*, from ontic to discursive lenses, as the basis of cultivated knower codes. From emphasizing their objects of study (such as art, literature or history), knowledge practices have shifted towards emphasizing studies or theories of those objects (such as art criticism, literary criticism or historiography) as 'significant others' in cultivating gazes (e.g. Shay 2011). Steiner describes this well-known phenomenon as the rise of 'a culture of the secondary' (1989: 50): the cultural object is replaced by commentary, exegesis and discussion of that object as the basis of cultivation.

The effects of such 'turns' have been extensively discussed elsewhere. In brief, these debates typically highlight how both lenses offer a potential basis for engendering cultivated gazes and enabling sociality in intellectual fields when works are consensually chosen. However, both can also constrain knowledge-building in different ways. Ontic lensing has often downplayed the social and historical contexts for judging exemplars, imputing criteria into works that are held to 'speak for themselves' and whose status is immutable, universal and transhistorical (cf. Chapter 5). This can obscure the active nature of cultivation, and naturalize an ossified canonic list of 'significant others', alienating new potential knowers. In contrast, discursive lensing may tend towards idealism, a retreat from external reality, and insularity by fetishizing intellectual studies at the expense of anything beyond the academy. Again, this may lead to segmentalism, restricting and fragmenting the field.

The 'linguistic turn' illustrates that lens shifts are neither exclusive to cultural studies nor trivial in their consequences. Understanding the effects of these and other kinds of lenses requires further research, not only for interactional relations but also for subjective relations; for example, different categories of legitimate knowers may shape knowledge practices in different ways. Moreover, the notion of lenses is also applicable to ontic relations (kinds of objects of study), and discursive relations (kinds of approaches). Nonetheless, this necessarily brief discussion suggests that fertile future research may lie in exploring the ways different lenses help shape the four relations and thus knowledge practices.

Conclusion: The 4-K model

Answers beget questions. Analyses of previous chapters outlined concepts for analysing practices that overcome knowledge-blindness without succumbing to knower-blindness. In turn, they raised questions of how to account for differences between practices sharing the same specialization codes and, in the case of knower codes, the same gazes. First, differentiating epistemic relations into ontic and discursive relations and conceptualizing their modalities as insights enables different relations between theory and data to be explored in greater depth. This moves us beyond the notion of 'grammar' by distinguishing practices capable of relatively precise empirical descriptions from formal modelling of empirical relations. It shows, for example, that knowledge codes are not all the same and, among other things, enables social realism to adequately describe its own position (situational knowledge code) relative to empiricist modelling (doctrinal knowledge code) with which it is associated in dominant constructions of the intellectual field. Examining the effects of contrastive insights further highlights that unambiguously defining correlates of concepts is insufficient for knowledge-building, and explores the gains and costs of rigorously restricting the empirical phenomena of knowledge claims. Second, differentiating social relations into subjective and interactional relations extends and systematizes the exploration of knower codes and gazes begun in Chapters 2, 5 and 8. These preceding analyses showed that knower-code practices are not all the same; the analysis here conceptualizes the organizing principles underlying gazes to reveal the basis of these differences.

Bringing together these conceptual developments provides an enhanced account of specialization codes as comprising relations between practices and that part of the world towards which they are oriented (ontic relations), other practices (discursive relations), kinds of actors (subjective relations), and ways of acting (interactional relations). As illustrated in Figure 9.6, when applied to knowledge claims this offers a '4-K model' of relations between knowledge practices and the ***known***, ***knowledges***, ***knowers*** and ***knowing***.

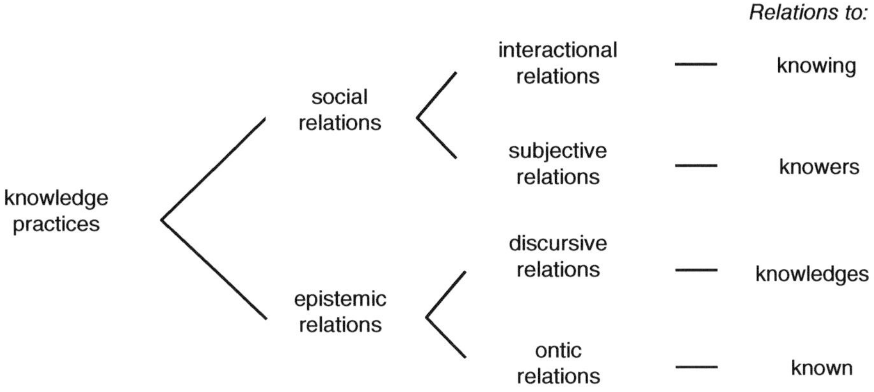

Figure 9.6 The 4-K model of knowledge practices

Using this 4-K model to analyse the *basis* of practices highlighted that specialization codes may be further described in terms of insights and gazes. Moreover, exploring cultivated gazes raised questions of differences *within* insights and gazes, leading to their extension in terms of different *lenses*. As illustrated in Figure 9.7, this gives three levels of conceptual delicacy: specialization codes – insights and gazes – lenses. Put another way, all practices are characterized by both insights and gazes, and both insights and gazes have lenses. The form taken by lenses reflects, I conjecture, an ontic/discursive distinction whose forms vary according to the relation they refract. In terms of social relations, stronger interactional relations have an *ontic lens* or *discursive lens*, and stronger subjective relations may have a *biological lens* or a *social lens* depending on whether legitimate kinds of knowers are defined as biological or socially constructed categories, such as sex or gender, race or ethnicity, etc. Lenses for epistemic relations reflect differences between *empirical* and *technical* (discursively constructed) objects for ontic relations, and between *principles* and *procedures* for discursive relations. Their significance is a matter

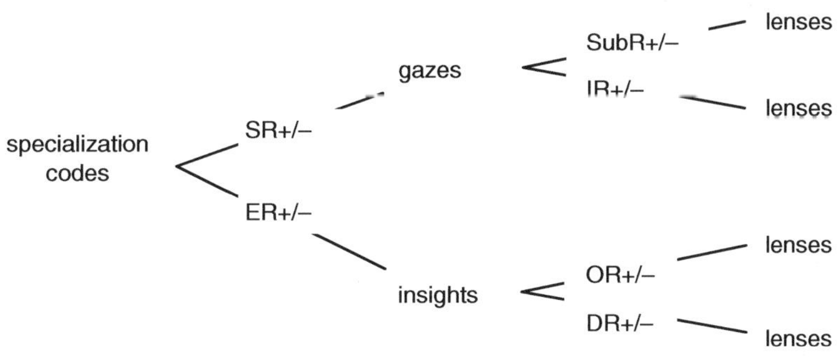

Figure 9.7 4-K model of Specialization

for further substantive research; their conceptual elaboration, as befits a 'Bernsteinian appendix', awaits future publications.

This refining of conceptual delicacy by the 4-K model has several implications. First, it further highlights how specialization codes offer more than dichotomous types. This chapter focused on contrastive insights and gazes for the sake of illustrating their effects. However, varying the strengths of the four relations generates not only a wide variety of potential modalities (typologies of insights and gazes) but also differences and movements over time within those modalities (topologies of Figures 9.3 and 9.5). Moreover, practices may also be characterized by simultaneous epistemic and social relation clashes or shifts. Complex changes can thus be accommodated by the conceptual framework.

Second, the 4-K model has implications for other concepts. For example, Chapter 8 brought together specialization codes with semantic density to distinguish *epistemological condensation* (EC) based on stronger epistemic relations and *axiological condensation* (AC) based on stronger social relations. We can thus now distinguish within EC between *ontic condensation* and *discursive condensation*, and within AC between *subjective condensation* and *interactional condensation*. Thus, the model raises questions of the nature of these processes and their effects for actors, practices and fields. Similarly, the 4-K model can be applied to semantic gravity to distinguish ontic, discursive, subjective and interactional forms of gravitation.

Third, the 4-K model provides a more nuanced understanding of the Legitimation Device (Chapter 3) by exploring further the basis of struggles in social fields. Such finer-grained conceptual distinctions do not, however, necessarily reflect smaller-scale phenomena. Conceptualizing insights, gazes and lenses highlights that, among members of a field, what is shared (specialization code) may provide the basis for intense struggles. The examples of relation clashes and shifts discussed in this chapter show that clashes within codes are just as fiercely fought as clashes between codes, and may represent major schisms over the basis of legitimacy in a field, with the livelihood of actors and the soul of the subject at stake. Similarly, that the effects of 'linguistic turns' are still resonating across the disciplinary map illustrates the significance a lens shift can have for the intellectual landscape.

Last, these examples illustrate how different insights, gazes and lenses have their own powers and tendencies and suggest that no single modality guarantees cumulative progress. The chapter began by summarizing previous chapters as showing relations to knowledge and to knowers matter to how fields develop. The 4-K model elaborates these categories to show that relations to the known, other knowledge, knowers and knowing matter. However, you only need as much theory as the problem-situation requires, no more and no less, and not every problem-situation requires analysis of insights, gazes and lenses. Nonetheless, one impetus to the conceptual development that I have begun to outline in this chapter came from questions raised by scholars using LCT in substantive research (Chapter 10). In turn, a key future issue for research is to explore which gaze or insight enables what kinds of explanatory or institutional gains, when, where and how. As ongoing studies using these concepts are showing, apparently minor differences may have major effects by underlying fiercely fought struggles and fundamental shifts in social fields. God or the devil is indeed in the detail.

Notes

1 These sociological concepts are not philosophical terms; that *ontic relations* are a sub-dimension of *epistemic relations* is *not* to posit ontology as subsidiary to epistemology, or being as secondary to knowing.
2 'Ontic' here refers to that part of the world to which practices are oriented, not being generally or theories of being. Practices exhibiting doctrinal insight do not proclaim reality cannot be known but rather place relatively little significance on what knowledge claims refer to: ontic rather than ontological relativism.
3 I refer to the 'epistemic–pedagogic device' rather than 'ESP device' as I draw on Specialization but not Semantics in this chapter.
4 In realist theories of education, compare the situational insight underlying social realist use of critical realist ideas to explain educational phenomena (Wheelahan 2010; Moore 2013a), with the doctrinal insight underlying Scott's (2010) co-optive reduction of social realism. The latter obscures differences between their objects of study, recasts social realism as philosophy (despite the only cited paper being titled 'Founding the sociology of knowledge'), and devalorizes it as poor ontology.
5 Though defined as typifying 'hierarchical knowledge structures', little if any research has explored physics using the inherited framework. See Lindstrøm (2010), Doran (2010) and Georgiou (2014) for studies of physics using LCT.
6 The quantitative instrument discussed in Chapter 4 included indicators for 'natural talent' and 'cultivated taste' – attempts at capturing the effects of subjective relations and interactional relations *avant la lettre*. See Howard and Maton (2014) for evolved versions of the instrument.

10 Building a realist sociology of education

To be continued …

Much remains to be done. We've only just begu

Introduction

Building knowledge about knowledge-building is a recurrent theme of this book. Chapters have explored a range of enabling conditions for cumulative progress. They have also attempted wherever possible to model that advance by building on established concepts and unfolding a framework through engagements with varied substantive problems. This focus and form foreground questions of how LCT builds on past ideas and how it may be built on in future. Both have been broached before: each chapter begins from established concepts, delineates their extension and integration within new concepts, and alludes to their further development. This chapter foregrounds these issues further by addressing relations to where LCT comes from and where it may be going.

The chapter begins with how LCT extends its foundational frameworks. Focusing on relations to Bernstein's code theory, I discuss how concepts developed in the book resolve past problems, extend and integrate established ideas, and re-animate existing research. Specifically, reconceptualizing what Bernstein called 'the fundamental paradox' illustrates how unresolved issues can be addressed; bringing together theoretical developments from across chapters provides a bigger picture of relations between established and new concepts; and re-analysing an influential study conducted decades before its emergence illustrates how LCT maintains the relevance and can re-invigorate the findings of past research. Together, these demonstrate how LCT aims to extend and integrate past ideas within an economical framework to embrace more phenomena and works to ensure existing research remains active within an extended epistemic community.

Second, the chapter looks forward to directions in which LCT is being developed. Three stimuli are explored: the intrinsic dynamics of the framework, whereby answers themselves raise further questions; substantive research into a rapidly diversifying range of phenomena that is speaking back to the theory; and encounters with other approaches in research studies that shed light on new facets of phenomena. Citing a wide variety of illustrative studies, I discuss how research is analysing evermore forms of knowledge, practices and social fields, using a growing range of methods, and relating to a diversity of other approaches. I highlight some of the questions these ventures are raising for the theory and analyse the cumulative form taken by these developments.

In summary, the chapter explores how the framework helps enable the possibility of cumulative and integrative intellectual development. The chapter concludes by returning to the 'knowledge paradox' of social science with which the book began, and re-emphasizes one of its key recurrent themes: the tentative, provisional and open-ended nature of collectively building a critical, positive and realist account of education and knowledge.

Cumulatively building on firm foundations

For any framework concerned with knowledge-building, the question of relations to established ideas is pertinent. LCT is inspired by diverse influences, from sociology, anthropology, cultural criticism, linguistics, philosophy and political theory. Its most directly foundational frameworks, however, are Bourdieu's field theory and Bernstein's code theory. LCT enjoys cumulative relations to both theories, though these assume different forms.

Chapter 7 discusses how Bourdieu's field theory offers a cultivated sociological gaze but not the conceptual evolution required to democratize access to this gaze. Field theory points to *what* should be analysed: degrees of autonomy of social fields, forms and hierarchies of status, organizing principles of practices, capitals and habituses, etc. However, its current concepts cannot fully enact field theory's strictures as to *how* these should be analysed. Consequently, only someone possessing Bourdieu's gaze can undertake a Bourdieuian analysis. As Chapter 7 shows, a different mode of theorizing is required, one capable of creating concepts that reveal the organizing principles and generative mechanisms underlying practices, habituses, capitals and fields. Thus, LCT integrates the cultivated gaze offered by field theory but retools the framework with concepts capable of achieving its relational and realist promise. Here, relations between inherited and enhanced frameworks are not immediate, direct or explicit, because existing concepts cannot be straightforwardly extended and articulating relations would be prohibitively wordy for this book. An account of how LCT cumulatively builds on field theory thereby requires, as yet, a symptomatic reading.

In contrast, Bernstein's code theory embodies a trained sociological gaze in relational and realist concepts for substantive research. Where field theory offers a new *gaze*, code theory represents a different *insight*. Thus, code theory is the launch site for LCT and relations between frameworks are direct and explicit. It is these relations that I shall focus on here. LCT builds on Bernstein's code theory in three principal ways: enabling unresolved questions to be addressed, extending and integrating concepts to address those questions, and keeping research using inherited concepts active within the developed approach. I illustrate each of these developments in turn.

Resolving problems: The fundamental paradox

Preceding chapters begin from questions raised by Bernstein's framework to offer new concepts for addressing those questions. However, rather than rehearse those contributions, I shall briefly discuss what Bernstein decreed 'the fundamental paradox which has to be faced and explored' (1977: 110). Bernstein introduced this paradox in his seminal paper 'On the classification and framing of educational knowledge', published in the founding text of 'new sociology of education', *Knowledge and Control* (Young 1971), both volumes I (Bernstein 1971) and III (Bernstein 1977) of *Class, Codes and Control*, as well as numerous anthologies. Here Bernstein introduced the concepts of 'collection codes' (strong classification and framing) and 'integrated codes' (weak classification and framing). Exploring how these codes relate to social order, he argued, manifests contradiction, raising a 'question of the problem of order' (Bernstein 1977: 109):

> Collection codes have explicit and strong boundary maintaining features and they rest upon a tacit ideological basis. Integrated codes have implicit and weak boundary maintaining features and they rest upon an explicit and closed ideological basis. The ideological basis of the collection code is a condensed symbolic system communicated through its explicit boundary maintaining features. Its covert structure is that of mechanical solidarity. The ideological basis of integrated codes is *not* a condensed symbolic system, it is verbally elaborated and explicit. It is an *overt* realization of organic solidarity and made substantive through weak forms of boundary maintenance (low insulations). Yet the covert structure of mechanical solidarity of collection codes creates through its specialized outputs *organic solidarity.* On the other hand the overt structure of organic solidarity of integrated codes creates through its *less* specialized outputs *mechanical* solidarity. And it will do this to the extent to which its ideology is explicit, elaborated and closed *and* effectively and *implicitly* transmitted though its low insulations. Inasmuch as integrated codes do not accomplish this, then order is highly problematic at the level of social organization and at the level of the person. Inasmuch as integrates codes do accomplish such socialization, then we have the covert deep closure of mechanical solidarity. This is the fundamental paradox which has to be faced and explored.
>
> (Bernstein 1977: 109–110; original emphases)

This 'tantalizingly brief ... highly suggestive but not developed' argument (Atkinson 1985: 153) employs allusive and shifting terms. Nonetheless, it highlights a 'paradox' whereby one kind of thing appears to generate its opposite. Put simply, pedagogy underpinned by mechanical solidarity (where cohesion arises from similarity among actors) creates organic solidarity (based on relations of interdependence among differentiated and specialized actors), and vice versa. At its simplest: similarity leads to difference and difference leads to similarity.

Despite the imperative that it be faced and explored, Bernstein did not explicitly return to the paradox. It echoes through his corpus, from the suggestion that '[t]he "hidden curriculum" of invisible pedagogies may well be a visible pedagogy' (Bernstein 1977: 143) to the instauration of the necessity for integrated codes to enjoy strong social networks (Bernstein 2000: 11). Bernstein's clarion call has also gone unheeded by other scholars. However, this reflects not the intractable nature of the paradox itself but rather limits of the concepts available for addressing it. Code theory revealed the paradox; to face and explore it required conceptual development. Here I shall draw on Specialization to redescribe and resolve the paradox.

First, Bernstein's 'boundary maintaining features' refers to the organization (classification and framing) of educational knowledge, which can be reconceptualized in terms of ***epistemic relations***. Thus, his opening sentences identify two codes characterized by 'explicit and strong' epistemic relations, and 'implicit and weak' epistemic relations. Second, the undefined notion of 'ideological basis' can be conceptualized as an ***axiological cosmology*** and its nature described in terms of ***social relations***. Doing so reveals that his two codes exhibit 'tacit' (weaker) social relations and 'explicit and closed' (stronger) social relations, respectively. Thus, Bernstein's opening sentences can now be understood as describing two specialization codes:

> Knowledge codes (ER+, SR–) have stronger epistemic relations and weaker social relations (expressing a tacit axiological cosmology).[1] Knower codes (ER–, SR+) have weaker epistemic relations and stronger social relations (expressing an explicit axiological cosmology).

This codifies and integrates the two characteristics Bernstein described for each code. It also brings to light a key issue for resolving the paradox. Though Bernstein focused on 'boundary maintaining features' and 'insulations' of knowledge, by applying classification and framing to knowers, previous chapters have shown that social relations also have boundary maintaining features and insulations.

Next, we can redescribe the paradox itself, in which Bernstein adapted Durkheim's notions of 'solidarity' to foreground issues of integration, cohesion and interdependence. Bernstein stated that the two codes are based (the first covertly) on one form of solidarity but give rise to another. This now becomes: knowledge codes are covertly structured on mechanical solidarity and create organic solidarity; and knower codes are overtly structured on organic solidarity and create mechanical solidarity. Using the new concepts resolves this paradox.

Knowledge codes do not distinguish actors in terms of subjective characteristics and so are not overtly based on similarity. Moreover, as actors are not apprenticed into a dispositionally based gaze, they may remain undifferentiated in terms of personal attributes. However, actors are similar in that these differences are held to have minimal relevance to legitimacy. For example, 'one-size-fits-all' teaching engages all students in similar activities and takes little account of the dispositions of individual learners. In other words, their weaker social relations enable segmented knowers: a ***horizontal knower structure*** of strongly bounded habituses held to exhibit low levels of interdependence, effects and bonds (see Chapters 4 and 5). The ***covert*** structure of knowledge codes may thereby resemble mechanical solidarity. Nonetheless, as actors become successfully inculcated into different knowledge-based specialisms, based on stronger epistemic relations, they (and the knowledges learned) become increasingly differentiated. Apprenticeship into the internally differentiated and interrelated ***hierarchical (educational) knowledge structures*** typically associated with knowledge codes thereby enable specialized identities, roles, activities and beliefs, greater interdependence and extended communities – features of organic solidarity.

In contrast, knower codes downplay the significance of specialised knowledge (ER–) and emphasize personal attributes (SR+) as the basis of legitimacy. They foreground characteristics of actors, measured against ideal knowers at the apex of ***hierarchical knower structures***. Here, differences and relations among individuals ***qua*** knowers are explicitly central to legitimacy, such as pedagogic practices that valorize the experiences, build on the dispositions, and tailor learning to the needs of individual learners. Knower codes thereby ***overtly*** emphasize features resembling organic solidarity. However, they aim to engender a common consciousness among noviciates through inculcation of a ***cultivated gaze*** or revelation of a ***social gaze*** (Chapters 5 and 9). In terms of knowledge specialisms, actors' identities, roles, activities and beliefs are comparatively less differentiated because epistemic relations are relatively downplayed; rather, they are specialized knowers who share ways of acting, thinking and being – features identified with mechanical solidarity. Indeed, the successful maintenance of knower codes depends on maintaining stronger social relations and thus creating similar knowers. This is key to Bernstein's paradoxical problem of order: the ideology of difference (stronger social relations) must be emphasized to maintain a code that generates similarity (through these stronger social relations). If social relations become too weak, knower codes (ER–, SR+) stray too close to relativist codes (ER–, SR–) and order becomes 'highly problematic at the level of social organization and at the level of the person' (Bernstein 1977: 110), because the basis for legitimacy, relation and identity is being eroded.

Thus, similarity and difference are not antinomies nor alternating states. They reflect the effects of the contrastive strengths of epistemic relations and social relations characterizing knowledge codes (ER+, SR–) and knower codes (ER–, SR+). By analysing social relations, we can see that both codes create what Bernstein called 'specialized outputs', and these are differentiated by the relation on which legitimation is based. In short: knowledge codes strongly bound and control knowledges but not knowers, and so produce knowers who, though sharing a ***trained gaze*** (or ***insight***), may have different habituses; knower codes strongly bound and control knowers but not knowledges, and so produce knowers who share similar habituses; and knower codes will be undermined unless they emphasise their social relations. Specialization thus allows the paradox to be faced and explored. Indeed, this issue helped motivate the analyses giving rise to these concepts. Specialization is thus also what results when the 'fundamental paradox' is faced and explored.

Extending and integrating concepts

The 'fundamental paradox' illustrates how LCT draws on Bernstein's concepts which in turn draw on Durkheim's concepts. However, this is not itself a sign of cumulative development: the *form* taken by the concatenation of concepts is crucial. With his model of 'hierarchical knowledge structures', judgements of concepts, and pronouncements on code theory, Bernstein described the form required by cumulative advance and so bequeathed not only firm foundations but also blueprints for future building. Following these guidelines, LCT concepts extend and integrate rather than displace his conceptual tools. This is not to say LCT is the only way code theory can be or has been developed – the framework is pregnant with possibilities. Rather, it simply highlights that LCT is intended to develop code theory in ways compatible with the principles Bernstein laid down.

These relations can be illustrated by Specialization. Bernstein (2000: 155) highlighted three key conceptual landmarks in the development of his framework: 'classification'/'framing', 'the pedagogic device', and 'knowledge structures'. LCT extends and integrates each of these landmarks within, respectively, *specialization codes*, the *epistemic–pedagogic device*, and *knowledge–knower structures* (see Table 10.1, below). First, put simply, by using classification and framing to conceptualize not only knowledge but also knowers, the analytical distinction between epistemic relations and social relations extends and incorporates these concepts within specialization codes (Chapters 2 and 3). Second, the 'pedagogic device' forms the core of the epistemic–pedagogic device that embraces such previously obscured issues as the epistemic logics regulating production fields (Chapter 3). Third, 'knowledge

Table 10.1 Extending and integrating concepts

Inherited code concepts	*LCT(Specialization)*
Educational knowledge codes: +/–C, +/–F	Specialization codes: ER+/–, SR+/–, which abbreviates: ER(+/–C, +/–F), SR(+/–C, +/–F)
Pedagogic device	Epistemic–pedagogic device
Knowledge structures • grammars (strong/weak) • gazes	Knowledge–knower structures • epistemic relations: insights (OR+/–, DR+/–) • social relations: gazes (SubR+/–, IR+/–)

structures' are integrated into a conceptualization of fields as knowledge–knower structures that provides a more expansive understanding of these social universes and especially of the humanities and social sciences (Chapter 4). Furthermore, evocative but elusive notions are systematically conceptualized and integrated into the framework: 'gaze' in terms of modalities of social relations, or *gazes*; and 'grammar' in terms of modalities of epistemic relations, or *insights* (Chapters 5 and 9).

The dimension of Specialization builds on the firm foundations of Bernstein's concepts to offer greater explanatory reach by explaining more phenomena, and greater conceptual economy by doing so within a more integrated and systematic framework. First, they enable previously obscured practices to be analysed, such as élite codes where both epistemic relations and social relations are relatively strong, and relativist codes where both relations are relatively weak. Previously, an exclusive focus on classification and framing of knowledge failed to distinguish élite codes from knowledge codes (both +C, +F of ER), and relativist codes from knower codes (both –C, –F of ER). By additionally conceptualizing social relations, these can be identified. Analyses illustrate the resulting explanatory gains. For example, Chapter 4 showed that distinguishing élite codes helps explain such phenomena as the low take-up of qualifications in school Music. Similarly, Chapter 5 showed how eliding knower and relativist codes problematizes analysis of the arts, humanities and many social sciences: their weaker epistemic relations were interpreted as a lack ('weak verticality', 'weak grammar') leading to the possibility of a deficit model of these fields. By conceptualizing social relations (and so knower structures and axiological cosmologies), the enhanced concepts enable a fuller understanding of fields that are focused more on cultivating knowers than building explicit knowledge structures (Chapters 5 and 8). Specialization thereby also helps overcome knowledge-blindness without succumbing to knower-blindness.

Second, LCT enables conceptual economy and coherence by integrating analyses of practices previously captured by disparate concepts. The inherited framework, for example, conceptualizes classroom practices as 'pedagogic codes' and intellectual fields as 'knowledge structures'. In LCT these are conceptualized as educational and intellectual forms of knowledge–knower structures and their organizing principles interrogated using legitimation codes (specialization codes, semantic codes, etc.), enabling analyses of practices across the fields of the education arena to be integrated (Chapter 3). Similarly, where levels of analysis were addressed with different concepts (such as 'languages of description' for theories and 'verticality'/'grammaticality' for intellectual fields), legitimation codes are fractal and applicable to any level of analysis.

As the discussion thus far illustrates, relations between these established and new ideas take several forms. Some inherited concepts are directly integrated within explicitly extended concepts. As Table 10.1 illustrates, 'classification' and 'framing' live on within epistemic relations and social relations, 'the pedagogic device' within the epistemic–pedagogic device, and 'knowledge structures' within knowledge–knower structures. Other inherited concepts are more suggestive, highlighting an issue but requiring development. What they highlight is then integrated within clearly defined and operationalizable concepts: 'grammar' by modalities of epistemic relations (or insights), and 'gaze' by modalities of social relations (or gazes). Occasionally, cumulative development requires temporary concepts which, like Wittgenstein's ladder, once climbed can be kicked away. Even here, however, such bridging concepts are extensions of the existing framework. Chapter 5, for example, builds on Bernstein's 'grammar' to distinguish 'knowledge-grammars' and 'knower-grammars' as a bridge towards epistemic relations and social relations, which once reached enable these 'grammar' concepts to be dispensed with.

Relations between Bernstein's concepts and LCT concepts are thus dialogic but represent more than a 'conversation' in which past ideas are kept alive through exegetical reinterpretation. They also involve but go beyond 'coalitions in the mind' (Collins 2000) to become coalitions in concepts. Their relations are more direct, vital and organic – it is not just in name that 'code theory' lives on within 'Legitimation Code Theory'. Bernstein's concepts remain a 'real presence' (Steiner 1989) and the firm foundations they provide represent a key fount of support and inspiration. I have attempted to make these relations transparent, but much remains to be done. First, there is more to Bernstein's framework than has been built on by LCT thus far, let alone mentioned in this book. LCT works *within* the problematic and approach of code theory to extend, systematize and integrate existing concepts, rather than claiming to subsume code theory in its entirety. Numerous concepts remain whose fecundity has yet to be fully explored. Second, there is more to LCT than the two dimensions introduced in this book. As Chapter 1 outlines, LCT comprises five dimensions thus far; dimensions other than Specialization and Semantics are also building cumulatively on concepts from code theory to embrace further facets of phenomena. Third, implications of the developments this book does outline have yet to be fully explicated. Specialization codes and semantic codes were explicitly linked to Bernstein's later work on 'knowledge structures' (2000), as the latest reformulation of his ideas. Nonetheless, for scholars familiar with the deep fibres of his framework, these are clearly not the only concepts they build on. As Chapters 2 and 3 show, specialization codes extend Bernstein's 'pedagogic codes' (1977); similarly, semantic gravity and semantic density untangle and conceptualize organizing principles left latent within his earlier work on elaborated/restricted codes (1971). The dialogue with and development of code theory thus holds considerable future potential.

Integrating research

The extent to which theoretical development is cumulative is more than a matter of relations between concepts. It also concerns relations between studies conducted using those concepts. If new ideas render findings from past studies incommensurable with those of new studies, their creation embodies segmental development, proclaims previous work obsolete, and generates a restricted epistemic community (Chapter 3). In contrast, LCT enables both new kinds of studies and the re-analysis of findings from studies using foundational frameworks, keeping past research active and potentially re-enlivened, and thereby enabling an extended epistemic community.

A brief example can be given using research foregrounded by Bernstein (2000: 18–20): Holland's study (1981) of the coding orientations of children from different social class backgrounds. Fifty-eight primary-school students aged 7 were shown twenty-four pictures of food available at the school canteen and asked to 'put the ones together you think go together. You can use all of them or you can use only some of them' (Bernstein 2000: 18–19). In summary, two different kinds of reasons were given by students for their groupings of pictures. One emphasized the student's personal experiences, such as 'I have this for breakfast' and 'I don't like these'; the other emphasized something less personal and more abstract, such as 'They come from the sea' and 'They're vegetables'. Middle-class children tended to use the second form of grouping first and, when prompted to try another ordering, only then used the first form. In contrast, working-class children tended to express only the first rationale.

Bernstein described the researchers' instruction as appearing to be '–C, –F', the primary middle-class response as '+C, +F'; and the working-class (and secondary middle-class) response as '–C, –F'. All three can be redescribed using specialization codes. The instruction appears to be characterized by a knower code (ER–, SR+): Bernstein's '–C, –F' refers to epistemic relations (the absence of indicators that specialist knowledge of this specific object should be drawn upon), to which can be added relatively strong social relations, illustrated by the instruction's repeated references to 'you'. The primary middle-class response represents, relatively speaking, a knowledge code: its basis resides in principles of knowledge. The working-class response represents a personal knower code: its basis resides in individual personal experience. These responses can then be understood as illustrating the capacity of middle-class children to see through the ostensible knower-code instruction to the potential for a task administered by educational researchers in the specialized context of the school to require a knowledge-code response. They offered, as *students*, a knowledge-code response before, when prompted, offering a personalized and experiential knower-code response. The working-class children took the knower code at its face value and responded accordingly. The former interpreted the required code in terms of the contextual demands of education; the latter did not recognize and/or realize the possibility of these demands and offered a code prevalent within everyday life. These reactions resonate with the analysis in Chapter 6 of secondary school English essays which highlights that not all students recognized and realized the need to respond as students of literature, with judgements appropriate to a cultivated gaze, to an essay task that ostensibly solicited personal preferences.

Using semantic codes we can also go further to redescribe the instruction as exhibiting relatively strong semantic gravity and relatively weak semantic density

(SG+, SD−): unspecialized language, anchored in the concrete context of the task. Working-class children echoed this semantic code in their responses. In contrast, middle-class students recognized the potential for the educational setting to require a response further up the semantic scale (more abstract and technicalized): their primary answers exhibited weaker semantic gravity and stronger semantic density, before (after prompting) moving down the semantic scale to more concrete ideas condensing fewer meanings. The responses can thus be understood as also helping to reveal the semantic ranges recognized and realized by children from different social class backgrounds. As Bernstein's theory emphasizes, relations between codes and classes are highly complex, but this highlights how these concepts offer additional insight. Simply put, the different semantic ranges at least partly reflect different degrees of *social levity* or what Bernstein termed relations to 'a specific material base' (2000: 19) and Bourdieu (1984) described as differences of 'distance from necessity'. Again, this resonates with LCT studies of the semantic range required for educational success (Chapter 6; Maton 2013).

Though published decades before the first paper in LCT, the findings of this research thus remain active within and can be related to studies using LCT. Theoretical development has thus not rendered established studies obsolete; indeed, it both allows for their findings to be built upon and offers potential for further analysis. The past remains present, enabling an extended epistemic community. Such re-analysis is one of the least obvious but most productive areas in which much remains to be done. Research grant and scholarship applications typically focus on gathering new data, while the fertility of existing data remains unregistered. There is considerable research using field and code theories, as well as an untapped spring of undertheorized substantive studies in education. Through using the concepts of LCT, their findings could have much more to tell us.

Current and future directions

Having illustrated relations to the past, what might the future hold? Three stimuli to the framework illuminate current and potential directions. First, the intrinsic dynamics of the theory raise questions that necessitate further development. Second, substantive studies extend the framework, speak back to concepts they enact, and illustrate the theory's relevance beyond knowledge and education. Third, encounters with complementary approaches bring to light different facets of phenomena, posing challenges and encouraging the emergence of new ideas. Each of these relationships is stimulating the advancement of LCT in exciting and unanticipated directions.

Intrinsic dynamics

As the framework unfolds, it both offers answers to existing questions and points forward to future moments of theorization by leading, in turn, to previously unthinkable questions. Some of these concern what Bernstein (2000) termed its 'internal language'. For example, the 4-K model (Chapter 9) highlights the need to more clearly theorize ontic, discursive, subjective and interactional forms of condensation and gravitation. Other questions concern 'external languages' and enacting concepts within substantive studies. Though the term 'external' may appear to suggest a secondary role, such languages of description represent a crucial catalyst to development. An external language provides a means for translating between theory and data that other studies can adopt or adapt – to develop an external language is to extend the framework into a new problem-situation. Moreover, they often 'speak back' to the concepts being enacted. For example, it was the development of quantitative instruments that underscored the necessity of conceiving codes topologically as well as typologically (Howard and Maton 2014). Emerging areas of study are highlighting diverse forms of practice requiring external languages that are likely to advance the framework in new directions, including multimodality (imagery and gesture), mathematical symbolism, musical notation, and artefacts, such as laboratory equipment and art tools.

Theoretical development also shines fresh light retrospectively. 'Cosmological analysis' (Chapter 8) clarifies the analytic methodology of previous studies; for example, the study of higher education presented in Maton (2005b) comprises just such an analysis *avant la lettre*. Indeed, one could introduce LCT through the notion of 'constellations' before defining legitimation codes for analysing the organizing principles of their generative 'cosmologies'. Similarly, theorizing 'semantic waves' (Chapter 7, Maton 2013) highlights that profiles can be traced not just for semantic concepts but for all legitimation codes and thus the potential for exploring change through time more fully using, for example, specialization profiles.

A further intrinsic dynamic flows from other dimensions of LCT. Autonomy, Density and Temporality conceptualize further organizing principles of practices and reveal additional aspects of the Legitimation Device (Chapter 3). As yet, limitations of space and time have restricted exploration of these dimensions. Autonomy was introduced in the context of exploring changes in higher education (Maton 2005a). Temporality is being used to analyse schoolteaching in History and Biology.[2] Their relations to past frameworks and value for research are only beginning to be explored. For example, autonomy codes conceptualize principles underlying Bernstein's 'singulars' and 'regions' (1990), and thereby offer insight into, *inter alia*, professional and vocational education. Similarly, temporal codes conceptualize principles underlying Bernstein's 'pedagogic identities' (2000), overcoming problems with enacting this typology in research (Power 2010). As these dimensions are explored, unanticipated questions will be posed to LCT's internal and external languages.

Endless forms most wonderful

'A mandarin madness of secondary discourse infects thought and sensibility', states Steiner (1989: 26); we live in an era characterized by 'imperialism of the second- and third-hand'. Criticism has usurped creation. In social science, such rumination, lacking specific problem-situations as its compass, is often concerned with intellectual lineage and theoretical purity. However, for catalysing intellectual advance, rumination is no substitute for research. Data changes everything. As elaborated in Chapter 1, LCT is a 'theory' in Bourdieu's sense: '"Theories" are research programmes which call not for "theoretical discussion" but for practical implementation' (Bourdieu *et al.* 1991: 255). LCT concepts are developed within and for substantive studies, and reshaped and revised in response to their findings. This research practice represents an important impetus to the directions in which LCT is advancing.

Throughout the book concepts have been developed in the context of substantive studies. However, these have been limited to knowledge practices in education and mostly, though not exclusively, focused on production fields. These foci partly reflect the state of educational research. As argued in Chapter 1, recovering knowledge as an object of study is an important corrective to the knowledge-blindness afflicting the field. They also partly reflect my own research trajectory, which began with intellectual fields before moving onto curriculum and classroom practice (e.g. Maton 2013). Nonetheless, code concepts overcome the gravity well of specific contexts, and LCT is a field activity rather than an individual endeavour. A fast-growing range of studies are using LCT to explore objects of study far removed from the problem-situations discussed in this book, opening up new directions for the framework by embracing evermore knowledges, practices and social fields. Here I shall briefly illustrate some, though by no means all, of these directions and their implications.[3]

Evermore knowledges

While this book focuses principally on the social sciences and humanities, a growing body of research is using LCT to explore the natural sciences. Studies of physics (Lindstrøm 2010; Zhao 2012; Georgiou 2014) and biology (Martin and Maton 2013), as well as inter-disciplinary and applied sciences (Millar 2012; Tan 2013), at school and university are revealing, *inter alia*, ontic and discursive forms of semantic gravity and semantic density and their roles in the successful apprenticeship of students into hierarchical knowledge and curriculum structures.

Other studies are reaching beyond traditional disciplines to explore professional education. Bernstein (1990) described these 'regions' as bringing together 'singulars' (disciplines) on the basis of principles ostensibly drawn from a field of practice beyond the academy. As with other types, 'regions' and 'singulars' represent a valuable first step but require development to conceptualize their organizing principles (see Chapter 7). To explore these principles, research is employing specialization codes and semantic codes in studies of such diverse fields as business studies (Doherty 2010), design (Dong 2008; Carvalho *et al.* 2014; Shay and Steyn 2014), engineering (Wolff and Luckett 2013), jazz (J.L. Martin 2014), journalism (Vorster 2011), marketing (Arbee 2012), nursing (McNamara 2009a, b, 2010a, b, c), Masters degrees (Stavrou 2012), teacher education (Shalem and Slonimsky 2010) and theatre direction (Hay 2012). These studies are uncovering the complex mix of codes characterizing these Janus-faced fields and their effects on, for example, students' capacities to experience cumulative learning. Substantively, this direction of research highlights the need for more studies of vocational training (cf. Wheelahan 2010). Theoretically, it is revealing the limits of Specialization and Semantics, and pointing towards other dimensions of LCT. For example, 'semantic gravity' highlights the significance of context-dependence for understanding regions but raises questions of the contexts giving meaning to regionalized practices. As McNamara (*op cit.*) illustrates, the effects of whether actors, practices and principles are located within or beyond education can be addressed with the dimension of Autonomy by analysing their ***autonomy codes*** (Maton 2005a).

Looking beyond education is highlighting further forms of knowledge. Studies are showing how informal learning may involve tacit instruction of highly metaphorical, allusive and axiologically charged ideas, as found in apprenticeship into freemasonry (Poulet 2010, 2014). Similarly, research involving Indigenous knowledges (O'Brien 2012) highlights the need to deepen understanding of tacit and embodied forms. Such work suggests that while the concept of 'gaze' (Chapter 5) embraces 'ear', 'taste', 'feel' and so forth, these diverse modes may shape knowledge practices in different and as yet untheorized ways. It also highlights areas where more research is needed, including arts, crafts and physical education. Here, work developing Bernstein's code theory to explore apprenticeship (Gamble 2001) and 'body pedagogies' (Evans *et al.* 2010; Ivinson 2012) offers valuable and complementary launch sites.

By embracing evermore knowledges, these and other studies are revealing different facets of phenomena. For example, studies using LCT emphasize the significance of students acquiring a greater ***semantic range*** and the capacity to generate ***semantic waves***, recurrent movements upwards and downwards in semantic gravity and semantic density (Chapters 6 and 7; Maton 2013). Research into different subjects sheds light on different aspects of these movements. Studies of undergraduate physics (Georgiou 2014) reveal that it is not simply 'the higher, the better': students may reach too high up the semantic scale in their work, using ideas that are too generalized or condensed. This 'Icarus effect' suggests one facet of induction into the semantic structure of an academic subject is learning the semantic range appropriate to different levels of education and different problem-situations. Conversely, studies of professional education (Kilpert and Shay 2013) are emphasizing the significance of movements down the semantic scale that appropriately select and enact abstract principles within professional practice. By reaching across the disciplinary spectrum, studies are thereby shedding complementary lights onto phenomena and avoiding reductive stances, such as the valorization of abstraction and condensation.

Practices and praxis

As well as knowledges, studies are embracing evermore practices from production, recontextualization and reproduction fields: research practices, such as forms of writing (Hood 2010, 2011) and ethnographic reporting (Hood 2014); curriculum construction in, for example, English (Macken-Horarik 2011), History (Shay 2011), Geography (Firth 2011), and sociology (Luckett 2009, 2010, 2012); and pedagogic practices, in natural science and humanities disciplines (Martin and Maton 2013), and second language teaching (Sigsgaard 2012).

Research is also addressing evermore kinds of practices *within* each field, including academic literacies and educational technology. Ongoing studies are examining such generic learning skills as 'critical thinking' across a range of subjects (e.g. O'Connor *et al.* 2011). Similarly, research is exploring the use of digital technologies for online learning (Chen 2010), mobile learning (Carvalho 2010) and one-to-one laptop programmes in schools (Howard and Maton 2011). These are both extending the theory to embrace diverse forms of technology and driving the evolution of quantitative instruments to analyse the impact of large-scale policy initiatives. For example, a four-year study of technology integration in schooling includes surveys of up to 80,000 students and 25,000 teachers each year, using instruments enacting specialization codes (Howard and Maton 2014). This is a major methodological step forward for code theory, embracing the explanatory power of mixed-methods. Studying different practices also poses new challenges to the framework. Classroom interaction, for example, foregrounds how students are apprenticed through time into the principles of knowledge-building embodied by subject areas, refocusing attention from static knowledge structures to dynamic processes of knowledge-building, such as semantic waves.

The framework is also being enacted in praxis. Pedagogic interventions are embedding LCT concepts within mobile learning environments (Carvalho *et al.* 2014) and in classroom practice (Martin and Maton 2013). This focus on practical engagement is stimulating new ways of realizing LCT through what can be termed *external languages of enactment*. For example, an intervention in secondary schooling drew on genre-based pedagogies from the 'Sydney School' of linguistics to enact the teaching of 'semantic waves' (Macnaught *et al.* 2013). Such research suggests that the development of languages of enactment will become a key fount of future innovation for the framework.

Beyond education

While Bourdieu's field theory is described as widely applicable, Bernstein's code theory is often viewed as limited to formal education. Yet code theory addresses a broad sociological problematic (Moore 2013b) and has been enacted in studies beyond education (e.g. Daniels 2010). This picture results partly from the centrality of education to Bernstein's concerns. Similarly, this book has focused on formal education. However, a growing number of studies use LCT to explore practices elsewhere, including masonic lodges (Poulet 2010, 2014), museums (Carvalho 2010) and parliaments (Siebörger and Adendorff 2011). Such studies examine not only informal learning but also practices not principally 'educational'; Maton (2005b), for example, employs legitimation codes to analyse architectural design and the layout of buildings.

This research beyond education is posing new questions. Studies of youth justice conferencing in the legal field (Martin 2009; Martin *et al.* 2012), for example, foreground relations between the societal reservoir of 'master identities' (such as class, race and gender) and individuals' repertoires of personae. They also highlight an urgent need to build on, as well as re-analyse, existing research into the coding orientations acquired by actors through socialization in family and peer groups, such as Hasan's landmark study of caregiver–child interactions (2009). While LCT concepts avoid both knowledge-blindness and knower-blindness and can be used to analyse both the codes of contexts and the coding orientations actors bring to them, the specific studies described in previous chapters have not explored the latter. This is a second sense in which knowers need to be brought back into the picture, for the study of knowers' dispositions has been a longstanding area of relative neglect by code sociology and social realism generally. In particular, in recent years little research has examined how different coding orientations are differentially distributed across social groups, in the manner of Holland (1981). Studies exploring relations between students' social class and their semantic range are beginning to open up this area again (e.g. Vitale 2013), but it remains a highly significant area for future research.

Research beyond education highlights how LCT is a framework for analysing more than knowledge. Knowledge practices have been the principal foci for introducing concepts in this book, as part of overcoming knowledge-blindness in sociological and educational research. However, LCT is less a theory of knowledge than a sociology of legitimacy or of possibility (see Chapter 1). It explores what is possible for whom, when, where and how, and who is able to define these possibilities, when, where and how. Put very briefly, social fields of practice are understood as dynamic fields of possibilities; the Legitimation Device is the means of generating and distributing what is and is not possible or legitimate within a field; stances represent possibilities, some recognized, some realized, others latent; organizing principles underlying the variety, constellation, and distribution of possibilities are given by legitimation codes; the structuring of a field is given by relations among those codes; changes in the codes characterizing stances represent changes in the space of possibilities; and actors cooperate and struggle to maximize their status and resources in fields through controlling the Legitimation Device. Practice thereby involves the creation, articulation and contestation of legitimacy in ways that dynamically shape the possible. Put less abstractly, knowledge is just one possible object of study and education just one possible social field of practice for analysis using the explanatory framework of LCT.

Close encounters

The third principal impetus to development comprises different kinds of encounters between LCT and other approaches. First, studies are often using another approach as an ***organizing framework*** and LCT as an ***analytic framework***. Many models offer valuable insights into particular problem-situations but cannot conceptualize their organizing principles – they detail what to analyse but not how.

To acknowledge their limits is not to dismiss such models; often forged in studies of a specific substantive topic, they can provide a first step between data and theory, and between description and explanation. For example, to explore the experiences of Chinese students in Australian higher education, Chen (2010) draws on Berry's 'acculturation' model to organize the study into three principal foci: the 'heritage culture' (dispositions) brought by these students; their current 'host culture'; and relations between the two. Specialization then provides the analytic framework for exploring the organizing principles characterizing each of these sets of practices (Chen and Maton 2014). Similarly, studying change in higher education, Maton (2005b) draws on Archer's 'morphogenetic sequence' (1995) to organize the account into iterations of structure and agency, and uses legitimation codes to analyse the organizing principles of each iteration.

Second, studies are using existing models to generate external languages of description for LCT concepts. 'Semantic gravity', for example, has been enacted by adapting taxonomies of reflective writing (Chapter 6), Bloom's taxonomy of educational objectives (Lindstrøm 2010; Kilpert and Shay 2013), and Kerbrat-Orecchioni's model of language (Richard-Bossez 2012). The original purposes of such typologies should be recognized; for example, they often began as models of knowing rather than of knowledge. However, acknowledging these purposes is not to dismiss their value. Once suitably adapted to the specificities of the study, they can offer a useful means of relating data and theory, enabling more powerful analyses in terms of legitimation codes.

These two kinds of encounters – using existing models as organizing frameworks or external languages – not only utilizes ready-made and topic-sensitive guides to key issues but also enables new research to connect with and build on existing studies. Similarly, using LCT to re-analyse results from research using other approaches – as illustrated in Chapter 6, and by Lamont and Maton (2010) for school Music research – can help extend and integrate an existing body of work, enabling cumulative development rather than segmental displacement of findings.

Third, LCT is increasingly being employed in parallel with other approaches, as complementary ways of exploring a problem-situation. The most sustained encounter of this kind is with systemic functional linguistics (SFL). There is a long tradition of intellectual exchange between Hallidayan linguistics and Bernstein's code sociology, exemplified by the work of Hasan (2005, 2009) on 'semantic variation' and the 'Sydney School' on genre pedagogy (Martin 2012a).[4] However, as Martin (2011) highlights, since the mid-2000s a new phase of inter-disciplinary collaboration and cross-fertilization has begun. This phase involves both kinds of close encounters already described above: SFL points to issues that LCT can analyse, and SFL concepts serve as external languages for LCT, as well as vice versa. These interactions are leading to theoretical innovation in both approaches. For example, the concepts of 'semantic gravity' and 'semantic density' were stimulated by sociological research highlighting the need to explicate organizing principles undertheorized within elaborated/restricted and horizontal/hierarchical types. At the same time, they were also inspired by encounters with linguists using code theory, including Frances Christie, Mary Macken-Horarik, Geoff Williams and J.R. Martin. These concepts are, in turn, leading SFL scholars to consider, for example, the ramifications of axiological condensation for understanding technicality as purely ideational. Such interactions continue the tradition of 'sparking off' the ideas of each other.

What distinguishes current collaboration, however, is the rapid growth of close encounters of the third kind: using both approaches to explore the same data in an integrated analysis. Scholars are increasingly embracing greater bilingualism in studies of education (e.g. Hood 2011; Luckett 2012; J.L. Martin 2013; Martin 2012b; Matruglio 2013; Matruglio *et al.* 2013, 2014; Sigsgaard 2012; Zhao 2012) and beyond (e.g. Tann 2011, Martin *et al.* 2012). This kind of encounter generates greater explanatory power through the capacity of each approach to shed different but complementary light. For example, a collaborative study of secondary schooling (Martin and Maton 2013) highlighted both 'semantic waves' as an attribute of cumulative teaching and the linguistic resources actors marshall to achieve them. It is also becoming a productive source of theoretical advance. During the same study notions of 'cultivated gazes' and 'axiological cosmologies' evoked rethinking of SFL's understanding of History (Martin *et al.* 2010), and SFL insistence on close textual analysis evoked an annotation system equivalent to the 'linguistic graffiti' that provides a shared data-coding language in SFL. Such close encounters can be unsettling – after every discussion of data with Jim Martin, I am certain only that I am certain of nothing. Nonetheless, they bring to light previously unseen facets of problem-situations, pose questions to the framework, and provide a midwife to the birth of new ideas.

Complementarities

The value of close encounters reiterates that no single framework offers a grand unified theory of everything. This is highlighted by adapting the 4-K model outlined in Chapter 9 to explore *focus* rather than *basis*. LCT offers a two-for-one framework: concepts can be employed to explore the *basis* of practices (which is the concern of legitimation codes, code and relation clashes and shifts, etc.) or to highlight their *focus*, that which practices are about or oriented towards. Applying the 4-K model to the *focus* of approaches addressing education and knowledge suggests four principal foci.[5] Psychologically informed and interactional approaches typically focus on ***knowing***, such as processes of learning; most approaches informed by sociology and cultural studies focus on relations to ***knowers***; philosophical approaches principally excavate relations to the ***known*** and the known or knowable themselves; and social realist approaches principally focus on relations among ***knowledges***.

This obviously paints a crude sketch in the broadest of brushstrokes. Nonetheless, it highlights two issues of significance here. First, it warns against subjective, interactional, discursive and ontic forms of reductionism, whereby knowledge practices are viewed as exhausted by analysis of one referent of the '4-K'. This is not to suggest a single substantive study must include analyses of all four, rather it is to avert blindness to the existence of foci other than one's own. For example, the knowledge-blindness of most educational research obscures the referents of discursive relations; conversely, to adopt knowledge-blinkers would be to see nothing but discursive relations, a danger present to social realism. Such blindnesses are a major obstacle to developing an integrative account of education.

Second, it highlights approaches whose complementarities with LCT have yet to be explored. These range from frameworks sharing similar ancestry, such as Mary Douglas (1992) on risk, to those of different heritage, including post-Vygotskian activity theory, which Daniels (2001) has brought together productively with code theory. Key to future encounters are approaches exploring complementary foci in the 4-K. Psychologically informed explorations of learning remain divorced from social realist analyses of what is being learned, though scholars such as Bereiter (2002), drawing on Popper's notion of 'World 3', usefully highlight the need to embrace knowledge as an object of study. We have much to learn from each other. Bluntly put, the taxonomies of knowledge they propose offer little explanatory power, while models of knowing are entirely absent from social realism. Closer encounters with psychology thus represent one of the most promising sources for mutually beneficial future development in our understanding of education. Similarly, encounters with realist philosophy remain underdeveloped. Though social realists illustrate how code sociology and critical realist ontology can be brought together productively (Wheelahan 2010; Moore 2013a), movement in the opposite direction remains limited. Both approaches would benefit from greater dialogue. While discussion of ontological foundations is *not* a precondition for successful and realist research, it would provide a valuable meta-theoretical guide for helping choose among alternative frameworks. Conversely, without explanatory frameworks such as LCT the tenets of critical realism will remain largely divorced from substantive research (see Chapter 1). Each could increase the other's semantic range: towards meta-theoretical articulations of ontology or towards engagement with the empirical. Again, we have much to learn from each other.

Forms of advance

The framework's intrinsic dynamics, substantive studies and encounters with other approaches, are opening up new avenues of advance. Just as significant as the directions that I have outlined above is the form taken by these developments. Following Bernstein's blueprints, LCT aims to embrace the greatest range of phenomena within an economic and coherent framework. Accordingly, as the research above illustrates, each dimension of LCT can be used to analyse:

- diverse practices (curriculum, pedagogy, evaluation, research, attitudes and beliefs, classroom interactions, identities, etc.);
- in diverse social fields (across the disciplinary map, from schools to universities in the institutional map, and manifold fields in everyday life);

- at different levels (social structure, education system, discipline, school, classroom, individual text, clauses within a text, etc.);
- across different national contexts (including, thus far, African, Asian, Australasian, European, North American and Scandinavian countries);
- in conjunction with other approaches (models, taxonomies, SFL, critical realism, etc.); and
- using a range of methods (including documentary analysis, qualitative interviews, and quantitative surveys).

Such flexibility enables widely divergent data and cases to be brought together. In opening up new avenues, research is thus not fragmenting the approach into topic- or data-specific segments.

This integrative potential flows from the framework's semantic range (Chapter 7). External languages of description allow the conceptual and empirical to relate in ways that maintain the irreducible particularity of phenomena, grounding the approach in specific problem-situations. However, research is not merely generating an ever-growing list of types of knowledges, practices and social fields. Such empiricist development typically leads to segmentalism (such as wholly separate concepts for specific kinds of knowledge or praxis), broadening but not integrating the empirical base of a framework. Instead, by analysing the organizing principles of practices as legitimation codes, the theory moves from empirical descriptions, up the semantic scale, towards abstracting, generalizing, interrelating and condensing conceptions. Together, external languages and code concepts enable analyses of diverse substantive phenomena to be brought into relation.

Nonetheless, condensation is not necessarily reductionism. The internal language of description offers high degrees of conceptual delicacy. For example, in specialization codes: 'ER+/–' is given by 'OR+/–, DR+/–'; 'SR+/–' by 'SubR+/–, IR+/–'; and '+/–' by '+/–C, +/–F' (Chapter 9). This can be successively unpacked as follows:

- ER+/–, SR+/–
- ER(OR+/–, DR+/–), SR(SubR+/–, IR+/–)
- ER(OR[+/–C, +/–F], DR[+/–C, +/–F]), SR(SubR[+/–C, +/–F], IR[+/–C, +/–F])

Taking one modality of one relation, 'ER+' thereby refers to 'relatively strong classification and relatively strong framing of ontic relations, and/or relatively strong classification and relatively strong framing of discursive relations'. Considering only the principal modalities, the third line above involves at least 256 different settings. This is a minimum: in LCT the symbols '+' and '–' embrace continua of relative strengths and not binary categories, and each offers an infinite capacity for gradation, along which change can be analysed (↑/↓). Add further levels (in this case, 'lenses') and additional dimensions, and the potential for great theoretical delicacy becomes apparent. Of course, whether such delicacy is required depends on the problem-situation and whether finer-grained distinctions generate greater explanatory power. The point here is that in embracing new phenomena, neither empirical specificity nor theoretical integration need be sacrificed. Thus, properly conducted, research that explores strange new knowledges and seeks out new practices and new fields, may boldly go into the unknown in ways that extend and integrate rather than fragment and segmentalize.

No conclusion

This chapter has barely scratched the surface. Much remains to be explicated concerning relations between LCT and foundational frameworks, substantive research, and complementary approaches. Only the necessity for what Bernstein called 'productive imperfection' prevents expansion without end. However, one chapter is not a field of enquiry, and these issues are being explored elsewhere (e.g. Martin and Maton 2013; Maton *et al.* 2014).

Theoretically, much remains to be discovered through adapting concepts from Specialization and Semantics to explore new problem-situations, there are other dimensions of LCT to explore, there are further dimensions to uncover, and the framework's intrinsic dynamics raise questions of their own. This book is not the whole of LCT and LCT as currently elaborated is not the end of the story. However, as Bernstein noted (2000: 125), a work-in-progress is rarely discussed as such but rather criticized for failing to embrace everything with definitive finality. Nonetheless, LCT is not offered as a universal framework; to repeat Adorno's famous inversion (1951) of Hegel, the whole is the false. Thus the subtitle of the book: '*Towards* a realist sociology of education'. Previously unanticipated questions abound which could not be asked until previous questions had been at least tentatively answered. As Popper argued:

> our progress can best be gauged by comparing our old problems with our new ones. If the progress that has been made is great, then the new problems will be of a character undreamt-of before. There will be deeper problems, and there will be more of them. The further we progress in knowledge, the more clearly we can discern the vastness of our ignorance.
>
> (Popper 1994b: 4)

Knowledge-building is like generating an expanding sphere: its surface area, touching the unknown, grows faster than the sphere itself. Learning what one does not know is one of the prizes of knowledge-building; it is what makes research so exciting, engaging, frustrating ... but never mundane.

Substantively, much remains to be understood about education and knowledge. This book has introduced two dimensions of a toolkit for studying practice. When applied to education, the framework contributes towards enabling an integrative account of education but is not itself that account. Progress is being made but we have little more than raised a corner of the veil. Nonetheless, understanding education and knowledge is crucial for understanding social practice. Returning to the 'knowledge paradox' with which this book began, accounts of social change will always fail to capture their ostensible focus until they overcome knowledge-blindness. Castells (2000) could find 'no compelling reason' for improving on a simplistic and homogenizing definition that distinguished 'knowledge from news and entertainment' (Chapter 1). Such essentialism is self-impoverishing, for little can be said of 'knowledge societies' or 'the information age' until more is known about forms of knowledge or information and the processes of their creation, reproduction, transformation and change. Moreover, in totally pedagogized societies, understanding formal and informal education is crucial to grasping social structures, inequalities and practice. Sociology of education and knowledge is not a mere sub-discipline condescendingly charged with studying classrooms. To paraphrase Bourdieu (1996: 5), a realist sociology of education and knowledge lies at the foundation of a general theory of power and legitimacy. No proclaimed sociology that fails to generate a realist account of education and knowledge, and more generally of possibility and legitimacy, can successfully lay claim to the name. Without such an account, we cannot understand let alone change the world for the better.

Moreover, sociology is not enough. Much remains to be discovered through inter-disciplinary encounters that offer the possibility of a fuller account of education, society and practice. Richard Hoggart (1970) offered a useful mantra: *Speaking To Each Other*. LCT shows this requires more than commitment and goodwill: genuine dialogue requires articulating the legitimation codes underlying our different 'rules of the game' and negotiating code and relation clashes among them. Only then can factional segmentalism be replaced by creative, respectful and rational debate.

Much remains to be done, but this does not mean it cannot be done. That the whole is the false does not resign us to accepting fragments or playing in the ruins. LCT is a critical theory in providing the explanatory power required to critique inequitable social arrangements. However, LCT is also a positive theory in providing for conjectured solutions that are always provisional yet capable of development and improvement. Unlike critical rumination, proclamations of tenets, and theoreticist comparisons of frameworks, this is not easy. Building real knowledge through engagement with real problems and real data requires effort, perseverance, patience and hope. Yet, to paraphrase Walter Benjamin (1919–1922: 356), it is for the sake of those without hope that we are given hope. To only criticize is to but partially fulfil that covenant; it is to forsake hope and those without hope. It is to foreclose the future. 'Hope is the future tense' (Steiner 2011: 21). As shown throughout this book and in evermore studies by a growing community of scholars, LCT is a collective work-in-progress in which we socially produce fallible but real knowledge. Building a realist sociology of education is a task to be continued ...

Notes

1 In LCT terms this is more accurately described as 'expressing an epistemological cosmology' (Chapter 8), but here I am reconceptualizing Bernstein's description of the paradox which focuses on 'ideological basis' only.
2 Maton (2005b), McNamara (2009a, 2010b, c) and Arbee (2012) employ Autonomy, Density, Specialization and Temporality, though the names and definitions of the concepts generating temporal codes have been subsequently refined (see Chapter 1).
3 To keep abreast with research, publications and events, see the LCT website: http://www.legitimationcodetheory.com.
4 On why code theory and systemic functional linguistics work together so fruitfully, see Hasan (2005), Martin (2011) and Matruglio *et al.* (2014).
5 The 4-K model originated simultaneously from analyses of both the *basis* and the *focus* of practices. The latter asked what must be the case about knowledge practices for the diverse array of approaches to education and knowledge to be possible. Here space limits mention to but a few broad-brushed approaches.

References

Adorno, T.W. (1951) *Minima Moralia*, Frankfurt: Suhrkamp Verlag.

Alexander, J.C. (1995) *Fin de Siècle Social Theory*, London: Verso.

Allen, J.D. (1995) 'The use of case studies to teach educational psychology: A comparison with traditional instruction', paper presented at AERA Annual Conference, San Francisco.

Arbee, A. (2012) 'Knowledge and knowers in the discipline of Marketing at the University of KwaZulu-Natal', unpublished PhD thesis, University of KwaZulu-Natal, South Africa.

Archer, M. (1995) *Realist Social Theory*, Cambridge: Cambridge University Press.

Archer, M., Bhaskar, R., Collier, A., Lawson, T. and Norrie, A. (1998) (eds) *Critical Realism: Essential readings*, London: Routledge.

Arnold, M. (1869/1935) *Culture and Anarchy*, Cambridge: Cambridge University Press.

Atkinson, P. (1985) *Language, Structure and Reproduction: An introduction to the sociology of Basil Bernstein*, London: Methuen.

Barcan, A. (1993) *Sociological Theory and Educational Reality*, Sydney: UNSW Press.

Barr, R.B. and Tagg, J. (1995) 'From teaching to learning: A new paradigm for undergraduate education', *Change* 17(5): 13–25.

Becher, T. and Trowler, P.R. (2001) *Academic Tribes and Territories*, Buckingham: SRHE/OUP.

Bell, D. (1973) *The Coming of Post-Industrial Society*, New York: Basic Books.

—— (1976) *The Cultural Contradictions of Capitalism*, New York: Basic Books.

Beniger, J. (1986) *The Control Revolution*, Cambridge, MA: Harvard University Press.

Benjamin, W. (1919–1922/1996) 'Goethe's elective affinities', in M. Bullock and M.W. Jennings (eds) *Selected Writings, Volume 1*, Cambridge: Harvard University Press.

Bennett, S. (2002) 'Learning about design in context', unpublished PhD thesis, University of Wollongong, Australia.

Bennett, S., Harper, B. and Hedberg, J. (2002) 'Designing real-life cases to support authentic design activities', *Australian Journal of Educational Technology* 18(1): 1–12.

Benson, O. and Stangroom, J. (2006) *Why Truth Matters*, London: Continuum.

Bereiter, C. (2002) *Education and Mind in the Knowledge Age*, Mahwah, NJ: Lawrence Erlbaum.

Berger, P.L. and Luckmann, T. (1966) *The Social Construction of Reality: A treatise in the sociology of knowledge*, Harmondsworth: Penguin.

Berman, M. (2009) *The Politics of Authenticity*, London: Verso.
Bernstein, B. (1971) *Class, Codes and Control, Volume I: Theoretical studies towards a sociology of language*, London: Routledge & Kegan Paul.
—— (1977) *Class, Codes and Control, Volume III: Towards a theory of educational transmissions*, second edition, London: Routledge & Kegan Paul.
—— (1990) *Class, Codes and Control, Volume IV: The structuring of pedagogic discourse*, London: Routledge.
—— (1996) *Pedagogy, Symbolic Control and Identity: Theory, research, critique*, London: Taylor & Francis.
—— (2000) *Pedagogy, Symbolic Control and Identity: Theory, research, critique*, revised edition, Oxford: Rowman & Littlefield.
—— (2001) 'From pedagogies to knowledges', in A. Morais, L. Neves, B. Davies and H. Daniels (eds) *Towards a Sociology of Pedagogy*, New York: Peter Lang.
Bhaskar, R. (1975) *A Realist Theory of Science*, London: Verso.
—— (1989) *Reclaiming Reality*, London: Verso.
—— (1993) *Dialectic: The pulse of freedom*, London: Verso.
Biglan, A. (1973a) 'The characteristics of subject matter in different academic areas', *Journal of Applied Psychology* 53(3): 195–203.
—— (1973b) 'Relationships between subject matter characteristics and the structure and output of university departments', *Journal of Applied Psychology* 53(3): 204–213.
Bloom, A. (1987) *The Closing of the American Mind*, New York: Simon & Schuster.
Bloom, H. (1973) *Anxiety of Influence*, Oxford, Oxford University Press.
—— (1996) *The Western Canon*, London: Macmillan.
Board of Studies NSW (2006a) *English Stage 6. Higher School Certificate 2006–2006. Prescriptions: Area of Study electives and texts*, Sydney: Board of Studies.
—— (2006b) *Higher School Certificate Examination 2005, English, Paper 1 – Area of Study: Student answers*, Sydney: Board of Studies.
Boghossian, P. (2006) *Fear of Knowledge*, Oxford: Oxford University Press.
Booker, C. (1969) *The Neophiliacs*, London: Collins.
Boudon, R. (1971) *The Uses of Structuralism*, London: Heinemann.
—— (1980) *The Crisis in Sociology*, New York: Columbia University Press.
—— (2008) 'How can axiological feelings be explained?', *International Review of Sociology* 18(3): 349–364.
Bourdieu, P. (1977) *Outline of a Theory of Practice*, Cambridge: Cambridge University Press.
—— (1984) *Distinction*, London: Routledge.
—— (1988) *Homo Academicus*, Cambridge: Polity Press.
—— (1991) 'The peculiar history of scientific reason', *Sociological Forum* 6(1): 3–26.
—— (1993a) 'Concluding remarks: For a sociogenetic understanding of intellectual works', in C. Calhoun, E. LiPuma and M. Postone (eds) *Bourdieu: Critical perspectives*, Cambridge: Polity Press.
—— (1993b) *Sociology in Question*, London: Sage.
—— (1994) *In Other Words*, Cambridge: Polity Press.
—— (1996) *The State Nobility*, Cambridge: Polity Press.
—— (2000) *Pascalian Meditations*, Cambridge: Polity Press.
—— (2004) *Science of Science and Reflexivity*, Cambridge: Polity Press.
Bourdieu, P. and Passeron, J-C. (1977) *Reproduction in Education, Society and Culture*, London: Sage.

Bourdieu, P. and Wacquant, L.J.D. (1992) *An Invitation To Reflexive Sociology*, Cambridge: Polity Press.

Bourdieu, P., Chamboredon, J-C. and Passeron, J-C. (1991) *The Craft of Sociology: Epistemological preliminaries*, Berlin: Walter de Gruyter.

Bourdieu, P. *et al.* (1999) *The Weight of the World*, Cambridge: Polity Press.

Brandes, D. and Ginnis. P. (1986) *A Guide to Student Centred Learning*, Oxford: Blackwell.

Bransford, J.D. and Schwartz, D.L. (1999) 'Rethinking transfer: A simple proposal with multiple implications', *Review of Research in Education* 24: 61–100.

Bransford, J.D., Brown, A., and Cocking, R. (eds) (2000) *How People Learn: Mind, brain, experience and school*, Washington: National Academy Press.

Brookes, B.C. (1959a) 'The difficulty of interpreting science', *The Listener* LXII: 519–521.

Brookes, B.C. (1959b) 'Letter to the editor', *The Listener* LXII: 783–784.

Bruner, J. (1960) *The Process of Education*, Harvard: Harvard University Press.

Brunsdon, C. (1996) 'A thief in the night: Stories of feminism in the 1970s at CCCS', in D. Morley and K-H. Chen (eds) *Stuart Hall*, London: Routledge.

Burton, L. (1964) 'Film study at a college of art', *Screen Education* 26: 34–43.

Canaan, J.E. and Epstein, D. (1997) (eds) *A Question of Discipline: Pedagogy, power and the teaching of cultural studies*, Boulder, CO: Westview.

Cannon, R. and Newble, D. (2000) *A Handbook for Teachers in Universities and Colleges*, London: Kogan Page.

Carby, H. (1982) 'White women listen: Black feminism and the boundaries of sisterhood', in CCCS, University of Birmingham, *The Empire Strikes Back*, London: Hutchinson.

Carey, J. (2005) *What Good Are the Arts?*, London: Faber.

Carvalho, L. (2010) 'The sociology of informal learning in/about design', unpublished PhD thesis, University of Sydney, Australia.

Carvalho, L., Dong, A. and Maton, K. (2009) 'Legitimating design: A sociology of knowledge account of the field', *Design Studies* 30(5): 483–502.

Carvalho, L., Dong, A. and Maton, K. (2014) 'LCT into praxis: Creating an e-learning environment for informal learning', in K. Maton, S. Hood, and S. Shay (eds) *Knowledge-building*, London: Routledge.

Castells, M. (2000) *The Rise of the Network Society: The Information Age, Volume 1*, second edition, Oxford: Blackwell.

CCCS (Centre for Contemporary Cultural Studies) (1964–1981) *Annual Reports*, Birmingham: CCCS.

—— (1968) *Fourth Report, 1966–1967*, Birmingham: CCCS.

—— (1982) *The Empire Strikes Back*, London: Hutchinson.

Chen, R. (2010) 'Knowledge and knowers in online learning: Investigating the effects of online flexible learning on student sojourners', unpublished PhD thesis, University of Wollongong, Australia.

Chen, R. and Maton, K. (2014) 'LCT and qualitative research: Creating a language of description to analyse constructivist pedagogy', in K. Maton, S. Hood and S. Shay (eds) *Knowledge-building*, London: Routledge.

Chen, R., Maton, K. and Bennett, S. (2011) 'Absenting discipline: Constructivist approaches in online learning', in F. Christie and K. Maton (eds) *Disciplinarity*, London: Continuum.

Christie, F. (1999) 'The pedagogic device and the teaching of English', in F. Christie (ed.) *Pedagogy and the Shaping of Consciousness: Linguistic and social processes*, London: Continuum.

Christie, F. and Derewianka, B. (2010) *School Discourse: Learning to write across the years of schooling*, London: Continuum.

Christie, F. and Humphrey, S. (2008) 'Senior secondary English and its goals: Making sense of "The Journey"', in L. Unsworth (ed.) *New literacies and the English curriculum*, London: Continuum.

Christie. F. and Macken-Horarik, M. (2007) 'Building verticality in subject English', in F. Christie and J. Martin (eds) *Language, Knowledge and Pedagogy*, London: Continuum.

Christie, F. and Martin, J.R. (2007) (eds) *Language, Knowledge and Pedagogy: Functional linguistic and sociological perspectives*, London: Continuum.

Christie, F. and Maton, K. (2011) (eds) *Disciplinarity: Functional linguistic and sociological perspectives*, London: Continuum.

Coase, R. (1999) 'Interview with Ronald Coase', *Newsletter of the International Society for New Institutional Economics* 2(1): 3–10.

Colander, D., Holt, R.P.F. and Rosser, J.B. (2004) *The Changing Face of Mainstream Economics*, Ann Arbor, MI: University of Michigan Press.

Collins, R. (2000) *The Sociology of Philosophies*, Cambridge, MA: Harvard University Press.

Daniels, H. (2001) *Vygostky and Pedagogy*, London: Routledge.

—— (2010) 'Subject position and identity in changing workplaces', in P. Singh, A. Sadovnik and S. Semel (eds) *Toolkits, Translation Devices, Conceptual Tyrannies*, New York: Peter Lang.

Davies, B. (2010) 'Why Bernstein?', in D. Frandji and P. Vitale (eds) *Knowledge, Pedagogy and Society*, London: Routledge.

Davies, P.C.W. and Brown, J. (1988) (eds) *Superstrings: A theory of everything*, Cambridge: Cambridge University Press.

Denby, D. (1996) *The Great Books*, New York: Simon & Schuster.

DfES/QCA (Department for Education and Science/Qualifications & Curriculum Authority) (1999) *The National Curriculum for England: Music*, London: HMSO.

diSessa, A.A. (1993) 'Toward an epistemology of physics', *Cognition and Instruction* 10(2/3): 105–225.

Doherty, C. (2008) 'Student subsidy of the internationalized curriculum: Knowing, voicing and producing the Other', *Pedagogy, Culture and Society* 16(3): 269–288.

—— (2010) 'Doing business: Knowledges in the internationalised business lecture', *Higher Education Research and Development* 29(3): 245–258.

Dong, A. (2008) *The Language of Design: Theory and computation*, London: Springer.

Doran, Y. (2010) 'Knowledge and multisemiosis in undergraduate physics', unpublished Honours thesis, University of Sydney, Australia.

Douglas, M. (1970) *Natural Symbols*, London: Barrie & Rockliff.

—— (1975) *Implicit Meanings*, London: Routledge & Kegan Paul.

—— (1992) *Risk and Blame*, London: Routledge.

—— (2000) 'Basil Bernstein', *The Guardian*, 27 September, http://www.guardian.co.uk/news/2000/sep/27/guardianobituaries.education

Drucker, P. (1969) *The Age of Discontinuity*, New York: Harper & Row.

Durkheim, E. (1912/1967) *The Elementary Forms of Religious Life*, New York: Free Press.
—— (1938/1977) *The Evolution of Educational Thought: Lectures on the formation and development of secondary education in France*, London: Routledge & Kegan Paul.
Edexcel (2002) *Specification: Edexcel Advanced Subsidiary GCE in Music (8501) and Advanced GCE in Music (9501)*, London: Edexcel Foundation.
Epstein, D. (1997) 'The voice of authority: On lecturing in cultural studies', in J.E. Canaan and D. Epstein (eds) *A Question of Discipline*, Boulder, CO: Westview.
Evans, J., Davies, B. and Rich, E. (2010) 'Bernstein, body pedagogies and the corporeal device', in G. Ivinson, B. Davies, and B. Fitz (eds) *Knowledge and Identity*, London: Routledge.
Farmelo, G. (2002) (ed.) *It Must Be Beautiful*, London: Granta.
—— (2009) *The Strangest Man*, London: Faber.
Farrington, I. (1991) 'Student-centred learning: Rhetoric and reality?', *Journal of Further and Higher Education* 15(3): 16–21.
Field, J. (2006) *Lifelong Learning and the New Educational Order*, Stoke-on-Trent: Trentham Books.
Firth, R. (2011) 'Making geography visible as an object of study in the secondary school curriculum', *The Curriculum Journal* 22(3): 289–316.
Foo, Y-W., Taylor, G., Long, J. and Saunders, G. (2009) 'Active learning and active participation in higher education', in M. McManus and G. Taylor (eds) *Active Learning and Active Citizenship*, Birmingham: C-SAP.
Frandji, D. and Vitale, P. (eds) (2010) *Knowledge, Pedagogy and Society: International perspectives on Basil Bernstein's sociology of education*, Abingdon: Routledge.
Frankfurt, H. (2006) *On Truth*, New York: Alfred A.Knopf.
Friedman, M. (1999) 'Conversation with Milton Friedman', in B. Snowdon and H. Vane (eds) *Conversations with Leading Economists*, Cheltenham: Edward Elgar.
Friedman, T. (2005) *The World is Flat*, London: Penguin.
Fullbrook, E. (2003a) 'Two curricula: Chicago vs PAE', in E. Fullbrook (ed.) *The Crisis in Economics – The Post-Autistic Economics Movement*, London: Routledge.
—— (ed.) (2003b) *The Crisis in Economics – The Post-Autistic Economics Movement*, London: Routledge.
—— (ed.) (2007) *Real World Economics: A post-autistic economics reader*, London: Anthem.
Gamble, J. (2001) 'Modelling the invisible: The pedagogy of craft apprenticeship', *Studies in Continuing Education* 23(2): 185–200.
Gellner, E. (1959) *Words and Things*, London: Routledge.
—— (1964) 'The crisis in the humanities and the mainstream of philosophy', in J.H. Plumb (ed.) *Crisis in the Humanities*, Harmondsworth: Penguin.
—— (1987) *Culture, Identity, and Politics*, Cambridge: Cambridge University Press.
Georgiou, H. (2014) 'Putting physics knowledge in the hot seat: The semantics of student understandings of thermodynamics', in K. Maton, S. Hood and S. Shay (eds) *Knowledge-building*, London: Routledge.
Gibbons, M., Limoges, C., Nowotny, H., Schwartzman, S., Scott, P. and Trow M. (1994) *The New Production of Knowledge*, London: Sage.
Gilbert, S.M. (1985) 'What do feminist critics want? A postcard from the volcano', in E. Showalter (ed.) *The New Feminist Criticism*, London: Pantheon.
Glashow, S.L. and Bova, B. (1988) *Interactions*, New York: Warner Books.

Goodson, I.F. (1997) *The Changing Curriculum*, London, Falmer Press.
Gorard, S. (2004) 'Sceptical or clerical? Theory as a barrier to the combination of research methods', *Journal of Educational Enquiry* 5(1): 1–15.
Gouldner, A.W. (1971) *The Coming Crisis of Western Sociology*, London: Heinemann.
Graff, G. (1992) *Beyond the Culture Wars*, London: W.W. Norton.
Greene, B. (2005) *The Elegant Universe*, London: Vintage.
Grenfell, M. (2004) *Pierre Bourdieu: Agent provocateur*, London: Continuum.
Hall, J.A. and Saunders, M.N.K (1997) 'Adopting a student-centred approach to the management of learning: Songs of praise and lessons', in C. Bell, M. Bowden and A. Trott (eds) *Implementing Flexible Learning*, London: Kogan Page.
Hall, S. (1964) 'Liberal studies', in P. Whannel and P. Harcourt (eds) *Film Teaching*, London: BFI.
—— (1971) 'The Centre – history and intellectual development', *CCCS Sixth Report, 1969–1971*, pp.1–6.
—— (1990) 'The emergence of cultural studies and the crisis of the humanities', *October*, 53: 11–23.
—— (1992) 'Cultural studies and its theoretical legacies', in L. Grossberg, C. Nelson and P.A. Treichler (eds) *Cultural Studies*, London: Routledge.
Hall, S. and Whannel, P. (1964) *The Popular Arts*, London: Hutchinson.
Halliday, M.A.K. and Martin, J.R. (1993) *Writing Science: Literacy and discursive power*, London: Falmer Press.
Harcourt, P. (1964) 'Towards higher education', *Screen Education* 26: 21–30.
Harker, R. and May, S.A. (1993) 'Code and habitus: Comparing the accounts of Bernstein and Bourdieu', *British Journal of Sociology of Education* 14(2): 169–178.
Harris, D. (1992) *From Class Struggle to the Politics of Pleasure*, London: Routledge.
Hasan, R. (2005) *Language, Society and Consciousness*, London: Equinox.
—— (2009) *Semantic Variation: Meaning in society and in sociolinguistics*, London: Equinox.
Hattie, J. (2009) *Visible Learning*, London: Routledge.
Hay, C. (2012) '"What is to count as knowledge": The evolving directing programme at the National Institute of Dramatic Art', *Australasian Drama Studies* 60: 194–207.
Herrington, J. and Oliver, R. (2000) 'An instructional design framework for authentic learning environments', *Educational Technology, Research & Development* 48(3): 23–26.
Herrington, J., Oliver, R. and Reeves, T.C. (2003) 'Patterns of engagement in authentic online learning environments', *Australian Journal of Educational Technology* 19(1): 59–71.
Herrington, J., Reeves, T.C., Oliver, R. and Woo, Y. (2004) 'Designing authentic activities in web-based courses', *Journal of Computing in Higher Education* 16(1): 3–29.
Hirsch, E.D. (1987) *Cultural Literacy*, New York: Random House.
Hirst, P.H. (1967) 'The logical and psychological aspects of teaching a subject', in R.S. Peters (ed.) *The Concept of Education*, London: Routledge & Kegan Paul.
Hirst, P.H. and Peters, R.S. (1970) *The Logic of Education*, London: Routledge & Kegan Paul.
Hmelo-Silver, C.E., Duncan, R.G. and Chinn, C.A. (2007) 'Scaffolding and achievement in problem-based and inquiry-learning: A response to Kirschner, Sweller and Clark (2006)', *Educational Psychologist* 42(2): 99–107.

Hoffman, P. (1998) *The Man Who Loved Only Numbers*, London: Fourth Estate.
Hoggart, R. (1957) *The Uses of Literacy*, London: Chatto & Windus.
—— (1963) 'Schools of English and contemporary society', *The Use of English* 15(2): 75–81.
—— (1970) *Speaking To Each Other*. London: Chatto & Windus.
—— (1982) *An English Temper*, London: Chatto & Windus.
—— (2005) *Promises to Keep: Thoughts in old age*, London: Continuum.
Hoggart. R. and Williams, R. (1960) 'Working class attitudes', *New Left Review* 1: 26–30.
Holland, J. (1981) 'Social class and changes in the orientations to meanings', *Sociology* 15(1): 1–18.
Hood, S. (2010) *Appraising Research: Evaluation in academic writing*, London: Palgrave.
—— (2011) 'Writing discipline: Comparing inscriptions of knowledge and knowers in academic writing', in F. Christie and K. Maton (eds) *Disciplinarity*, London: Continuum.
—— (2014) 'Ethnographies on the move, stories on the rise: An LCT perspective on method in the humanities', in K. Maton, S. Hood and S. Shay (eds) *Knowledge-building*, London: Routledge.
Howard, S. and Maton, K. (2011) 'Theorising knowledge practices: A missing piece of the educational technology puzzle', *Research in Learning Technology* 19(3): 191–206.
—— (2014) 'LCT and quantitative research: Evolving an instrument for mixed-methods studies', in K. Maton, S. Hood and S. Shay (eds) *Knowledge-building*, London: Routledge.
Hughes, R. (1993) *Culture of Complaint*, Oxford: Oxford University Press.
Ivinson, G. (2012) 'The body and pedagogy: Beyond absent, moving bodies in pedagogic practice', *British Journal of Sociology of Education* 33(4): 489–506.
Ivinson, G., Davies, B. and Fitz, J. (eds) (2011) *Knowledge and Identity: Concepts and applications in Bernstein's sociology*, London: Routledge.
Jenkins, R. (1992) *Pierre Bourdieu*, London: Routledge.
Jenks, C. (ed.) (1977) *Rationality, Education and the Social Organization of Knowledge*, London: Routledge & Kegan Paul.
Johnson, R. (1983) 'What is cultural studies anyway?', *CCCS Stencilled Occasional Paper*, 74.
—— (1997) 'Teaching without guarantees: Cultural studies, pedagogy and identity', in J.E. Canaan and D. Epstein (eds) *A Question of Discipline*, Boulder, CO: Westview.
Jonassen, D.H. and Land, S.M. (2000) 'Preface', in D.H. Jonassen and S.M Land (eds) *Theoretical Foundations of Learning Environments*, London: Lawrence Erlbaum.
Kant, I. (1790/1951) *Critique of Judgment*, New York: Hafner.
Kenny, M. (1995) *The First New Left*, London: Lawrence & Wishart.
Kermode, F. (1983) *The Classic*, London: Harvard University Press.
Kernan, A. (1990) *The Death of Literature*, London: Yale University Press.
Kilpert, L. and Shay, S. (2013) 'Kindling fires: Examining the potential for cumulative learning in a Journalism curriculum', *Teaching in Higher Education* 18(1): 40–52.
Kirschner, P.A., Sweller, J. and Clark, R.E. (2006) 'Why minimal guidance during instruction does not work: An analysis of the failure of constructivist, discovery,

problem-based, experiential, and inquiry-based teaching', *Educational Psychologist* 41(2): 75–86.

Kitching, G. (2008) *The Trouble With Theory*, Sydney: Allen & Unwin.

Kitses, J. (1964) 'Screen education and social studies', *Screen Education* 22: 19–27.

Knight, R. (1962) 'Film and television study in a training college', *Screen Education* 20: 7–18.

Kolb, D.A. (1981) 'Learning styles and disciplinary differences', in A. Chickering (ed.) *The Modern American College*, San Francisco: Jossey-Bass.

Krathwohl, D.R. (2002) 'A revision of Bloom's taxonomy: An overview', *Theory into Practice* 41(4): 212–218.

Kuhn, T.S. (1962) *The Structure of Scientific Revolutions*, Chicago: Chicago University Press.

—— (1968) *The Essential Tension*, Chicago: University of Chicago Press.

Kundera, M. (1984) *The Unbearable Lightness of Being*, London: Faber.

—— (2000) *The Art of the Novel*, New York: HarperCollins.

Lamont, A. and Maton, K. (2008) 'Choosing music: Exploratory studies into the low uptake of music GCSE', *British Journal of Music Education* 25(3): 267–282.

—— (2010) 'Unpopular music: Beliefs and behaviours towards music in education', in R. Wright (ed.) *Sociology and Music Education*, London: Ashgate.

Lamont, A., Hargreaves, D.J., Marshall, N.A. and Tarrant, M. (2003) 'Young people's music in and out of school', *British Journal of Music Education* 20(3): 1–13.

Lang, I. and Canning, R. (2010) 'The use of citations in educational research: The instance of the concept of "situated learning"', *Journal of Further and Higher Education* 34(2): 291–301.

Lave, J. and Wenger, E. (1991) *Situated Learning: Legitimate peripheral participation*, Cambridge: Cambridge University Press.

Lawson, T. (2006) 'The nature of heterodox economics', *Cambridge Journal of Economics* 30: 483–505.

Lea, S.J., Stephenson, D. and Troy, J. (2003) 'Higher education students' attitudes to student centred learning: Beyond "educational bulimia"', *Studies in Higher Education* 28(3): 321–334.

Leavis, F.R. (1962) *Two Cultures: The significance of C.P. Snow*, London: Chatto & Windus.

Lee, H.D.P. (1955) 'The position of Classics in schools', *Universities Quarterly* 9(2): 135–144.

Lemert, C. (1995) *Sociology after the Crisis*, Boulder, CO: Westview.

Lindstrøm, C. (2010) 'Link maps and map meetings: A theoretical and experimental case for stronger scaffolding in first year university physics education', unpublished PhD thesis, University of Sydney, Australia.

Lipsey, R.G. (2001) 'Successes and failures in the transformation of economics', *Journal of Economic Methodology* 8(2): 169–202.

LiPuma, E. (1993) 'Culture and the concept of culture in a theory of practice', in C. Calhoun, E. LiPuma and M. Postone (eds) *Bourdieu: Critical perspectives*, Cambridge: Polity Press.

Lonka, K. and Aloha, K. (1995) 'Activating instruction: How to foster study and thinking skills in higher education', *European Journal of Psychology of Education* 10(4): 351–368.

Lorde, A. (1984) *Sister Outsider*, Trumansburg, NY: Crossing Press.

Luckett, K. (2009) 'The relationship between knowledge structure and curriculum: A case study in sociology', *Studies in Higher Education* 34(4): 441–453.
—— (2010) 'Knowledge claims and code of legitimation: Implications for curriculum recontextualisation in South African higher education', *Africanus* 40(1): 4–18.
—— (2012) 'Disciplinarity in question: Comparing knowledge and knower codes in sociology', *Research Papers in Education* 27(1): 19–40.
McGuigan, J. (1997) (ed.) *Cultural Methodologies*, London: Sage.
Macken-Horarik, M. (2011) 'Building a knowledge structure for English: Reflections on the challenges of coherence, cumulative learning, portability and face validity', *The Australian Journal of Education* 55(3): 197–213.
Mackerness, E.D. (1960) 'Ignorant armies', *The Universities Review* 33(1): 14–17.
MacKnight, V. (2011) 'Ideal knowing: Logics of knowledge in primary school curricula', *British Journal of Sociology of Education* 32(5): 717–728.
McNamara, M.S. (2009a) 'Academic leadership in nursing: Legitimating the discipline in contested spaces', *Journal of Nursing Management* 17(4): 484–493.
—— (2009b) 'Nursing academics' languages of legitimation: A discourse analysis', *International Journal of Nursing Studies* 46: 1566–1579.
—— (2010a) 'Lost in transition? A discursive analysis of academic nursing in Ireland', *Nursing Science Quarterly* 23(3): 249–256.
—— (2010b) 'Where is nursing in academic nursing? Disciplinary discourses, identities and clinical practice: A critical perspective from Ireland', *Journal of Clinical Nursing* 19(5–6): 766–774.
—— (2010c) 'What lies beneath? The underlying principles structuring the field of academic nursing in Ireland', *Journal of Professional Nursing* 26(6): 377–384.
Macnaught, L., Matruglio, E., Maton, K. and Martin, J.R. (2013) 'Jointly constructing semantic waves: Implications for teacher training', *Linguistics and Education* 24(1): 50–63.
McRobbie, A. (1997) (ed.) *Back To Reality?*, Manchester: Manchester University Press.
Mainds, R. (1965) 'Sixth form', *Screen Education Yearbook 1965*, pp. 99–102
Martin, J.L. (2013) 'On notes and knowers: The representation, evaluation and legitimation of jazz', unpublished PhD thesis, University of Adelaide, Australia.
—— (2014) 'Musicality and musicianship: Specialisation in jazz studies', in K. Maton, S. Hood and S. Shay (eds) *Knowledge-building*, London: Routledge.
Martin, J.R. (1992) 'Theme, method of development and existentiality: The price of reply', *Occasional Papers in Systemic Linguistics* 6: 147–183.
—— (2009) 'Realisation, instantiation and individuation: Some thoughts on identity in youth justice conferencing', *Documentação de Estudos em Linguistica Teorica e Aplicada* 25: 549–583.
—— (2011) 'Bridging troubled waters: Interdisciplinarity and what makes it stick', in F. Christie and K. Maton (eds) *Disciplinarity*, London: Continuum.
—— (2012a) 'Grammar meets genre: Reflections on the "Sydney School"', *Language in Education: The collected works of J.R. Martin, Volume 7*, Shanghai: Shanghai Jiao Tong University Press.
—— (2012b) 'Heart from darkness: Apocalypse Ron', *Revista Canaria de Estudios Ingleses* 65: 67–100.
—— (2013) 'Embedded literacy: Knowledge as meaning', *Linguistics and Education* 24(1): 23–37.

Martin, J.R. and Maton, K. (eds) (2013) *Linguistics and Education: Special issue on cumulative knowledge-building in secondary schooling* 24(1): 1–74.

Martin, J.R. and Stenglin, M. (2006) 'Materialising reconciliation: Negotiating difference in a post-colonial exhibition', in T. Royce and W. Bowcher (eds) *New Directions in the Analysis of Multimodal Discourse*, Mahwah, NJ: Lawrence Erlbaum.

Martin, J.R. and White, P.R.R. (2005) *The Language of Evaluation: Appraisal in English*, Basingstoke: Palgrave Macmillan.

Martin, J.R., Maton, K. and Matruglio, E. (2010) 'Historical cosmologies: Epistemology and axiology in Australian secondary school history', *Revista Signos* 43(74): 433–463.

Martin, J.R., Zappavigna, M. and Dwyer, P. (2012) 'Beyond redemption: Choice and consequence in Youth Justice Conferencing', in F. Yan and J.J. Webster (eds) *Developing Systemic Functional Linguistics*, London: Equinox.

Masuda, Y. (1981) *The Information Society as Post-Industrial Society*, Washington: World Future Society.

Maton, K. (1998) 'Recovering pedagogic discourse', paper presented at Knowledge, Identity and Pedagogy Conference, University of Southampton.

—— (2000a) 'Recovering pedagogic discourse: A Bernsteinian approach to the sociology of educational knowledge', *Linguistics and Education* 11(1): 79–98.

—— (2000b) 'Languages of legitimation: The structuring significance for intellectual fields of strategic knowledge claims', *British Journal of Sociology of Education* 21(2): 147–167.

—— (2002) 'Popes, kings and cultural studies: Placing the commitment to non-disciplinarity in historical context', in S. Herbrechter (ed.) *Cultural Studies*, Amsterdam: Rodopi.

—— (2003) 'Reflexivity, relationism and research: Pierre Bourdieu and the epistemic conditions of social scientific knowledge', *Space & Culture* 6(1): 52–65.

—— (2004) 'The wrong kind of knower: Education, expansion and the epistemic device', in J. Muller, B. Davies, and A. Morais (eds) *Reading Bernstein, Researching Bernstein*, London: RoutledgeFalmer.

—— (2005a) 'A question of autonomy: Bourdieu's field approach and policy in higher education', *Journal of Education Policy* 20(6): 687–704.

—— (2005b) 'The field of higher education: A sociology of reproduction, transformation, change and the conditions of emergence for cultural studies', unpublished PhD thesis, University of Cambridge.

—— (2006) 'On knowledge structures and knower structures', in R. Moore, M. Arnot, J. Beck and H. Daniels (eds) *Knowledge, Power and Educational Reform*, London: Routledge.

—— (2007) 'Knowledge–knower structures in intellectual and educational fields', in F. Christie and J.R. Martin (eds) *Language, Knowledge and Pedagogy*, London, Continuum.

—— (2008) 'Knowledge-building: How can we create powerful and influential ideas?', paper presented at Disciplinarity, Knowledge & Language: An international symposium, University of Sydney, Australia.

—— (2009) 'Cumulative and segmented learning: Exploring the role of curriculum structures in knowledge-building', *British Journal of Sociology of Education* 30(1): 43–57.

—— (2010a) Progress and canons in the arts and humanities: Knowers and gazes, in K. Maton and R. Moore (eds) *Social Realism, Knowledge and the Sociology of Education*, London, Continuum.

—— (2010b) 'Last night we dreamt that somebody loved us: Smiths fans and me in the late 1980s', in S. Campbell and C. Coulter (eds) *Why Pamper Life's Complexities? Essays on The Smiths*, Manchester: Manchester University Press.
—— (2012) 'Habitus', in M. Grenfell (ed.) *Pierre Bourdieu: Key concepts,* revised edition, London, Acumen.
—— (2013) 'Making semantic waves: A key to cumulative knowledge-building', *Linguistics and Education* 24(1): 8–22.
Maton, K. and Moore, R. (2010a) 'Coalitions of the mind', in K. Maton and R. Moore (eds) *Social Realism, Knowledge and the Sociology of Education*, London: Continuum.
—— (eds) (2010b) *Social Realism, Knowledge and the Sociology of Education: Coalitions of the mind*, London: Continuum.
Maton, K., Hood, S. and Shay, S. (eds) (2014) *Knowledge-building: Educational studies in Legitimation Code Theory*, London: Routledge.
Matruglio, E. (2013) 'Negotiating interpersonal stance: The development of literacy in the senior high school years', unpublished PhD thesis, University of Technology, Sydney, Australia.
Matruglio, E., Maton, K. and Martin, J.R. (2013) 'Time travel: The role of temporality in enabling semantic waves in secondary school teaching', *Linguistics and Education* 24(1): 38–49.
Matruglio, E., Maton, K. and Martin, J.R. (2014) 'LCT and systemic functional linguistics: Complementary approaches for greater explanatory power', in K. Maton, S. Hood and S. Shay (eds) *Knowledge-building*, London: Routledge.
Matthews, M.R. (2000) 'Appraising constructivism in science and mathematics education', in D.C. Phillips (ed.) *Constructivism in Education,* Chicago: University of Chicago Press.
Matthiessen, C. and Martin, J.R. (1991) 'A response to Huddleston's review of Halliday's *Introduction to Functional Grammar*', *Occasional Papers in Systemic Linguistics* 5: 5–74.
Mayer, R.E. (2004) 'Should there be a three-strikes rule against pure discovery learning?', *American Psychologist* 59(1): 14–19.
Merton, R. (1957) *Social Theory and Social Structure*, Glencoe: Free Press.
Millar, V. (2012) 'The structuring of knowledge for interdisciplinary teaching in higher education', unpublished PhD thesis, University of Melbourne, Australia.
Mills, C.W. (1959) *The Sociological Imagination*, Oxford: Oxford University Press.
Milner, A. (1994) *Contemporary Cultural Theory*, London: UCL Press.
Montaigne, M. de (1580/2003) *The Complete Essays*, London: Penguin.
Moore, R. (2000) 'For knowledge: Tradition, progressivism and progress in education – reconstructing the curriculum debate', *Cambridge Journal of Education* 30(1): 17–36.
—— (2009) *Towards the Sociology of Truth*, London: Continuum.
—— (2010) 'Knowledge structures and the canon: A preference for judgements', in K. Maton and R. Moore (eds) *Social Realism, Knowledge and the Sociology of Education*, London: Continuum.
—— (2013a) 'Social realism and the problem of knowledge in the sociology of education', *British Journal of Sociology of Education*, 34(3): 333–353.
—— (2013b) *Basil Bernstein: The thinker and the field*, London: Routledge.
Moore, R. and Maton, K. (2001) 'Founding the sociology of knowledge: Basil Bernstein, intellectual fields and the epistemic device', in A. Morais, I. Neves, B. Davies and H. Daniels (eds) *Towards a Sociology of Pedagogy*, New York: Peter Lang.

Moore, R. and Muller, J. (1999) 'The discourse of "voice" and the problem of knowledge and identity in the sociology of education', *British Journal of Sociology of Education* 20(2): 189–206.

Moore, R., Arnot, M., Beck, J. and Daniels, H. (eds) (2006) *Knowledge, Power and Educational Reform: Applying the sociology of Basil Bernstein*, London: Routledge.

Morais, A. and Neves, I. (2001) 'Pedagogic social contexts: Studies for a sociology of learning', in A. Morais , I. Neves, B. Davies and H. Daniels (eds) *Towards a Sociology of Pedagogy*, New York: Peter Lang.

Morais, A., Neves, I. and Pires, D. (2004) 'The what and the how of teaching and learning', in J. Muller, B. Davies and A. Morais (eds) *Reading Bernstein, Researching Bernstein*, London: Routledge.

Morais, A., Neves, I., Davies, B. and Daniels, H. (eds) (2001) *Towards a Sociology of Pedagogy: The contribution of Basil Bernstein to research*, New York: Peter Lang.

Morley, D. (1992) *Television, Audiences and Cultural Studies*, London: Routledge.

Morris, M. (1959) 'The two cultures and the scientific revolution', *Marxism Today* 3(12): 374–380.

Morrissey, L. (2005) (ed.) *Debating the Canon*, New York: Palgrave Macmillan.

Moss, G. (2001) 'Bernstein's languages of description: Some generative principles', *International Journal of Social Research Methodology* 4(1): 17–19.

Muller, J. (2000) *Reclaiming Knowledge: Social theory, curriculum and education policy*, London: RoutledgeFalmer.

—— (2006) 'On the shoulders of giants: Verticality of knowledge and the school curriculum', in R. Moore, M. Arnot, J. Beck and H. Daniels (eds) *Knowledge, Power and Educational Reform*, London: Routledge.

—— (2007) 'On splitting hairs: Hierarchy, knowledge and the school curriculum', in F. Christie and J. Martin (eds) *Language, Knowledge and Pedagogy*, London: Continuum.

—— (2009) 'Forms of knowledge and curriculum coherence', *Journal of Education and Work* 22(3): 205–226.

—— (2012) 'Every picture tells a story: Epistemological access and knowledge', paper presented at Knowledge and Curriculum in Higher Education Symposium, University of Cape Town, South Africa.

Muller, J., Davies, B. and Morais, A. (eds) (2004) *Reading Bernstein, Researching Bernstein*, London: Routledge.

Nash, R. (2001) 'The real Bourdieu: Falsity, euphemism and truth in theories of reproduction', *ACE Papers* Jan: 54–71.

National Union of Teachers (1960) *Popular Culture and Personal Responsibility*, London: NUT.

Neves, I. and Morais, A. (2001) 'Texts and contexts in educational systems: Studies of recontextualising spaces', in A. Morais , I. Neves, B. Davies and H. Daniels (eds) *Towards a Sociology of Pedagogy*, New York: Peter Lang.

Nelson, C. and Gaonkar, D.P. (1996) (eds) *Disciplinarity and Dissent in Cultural Studies*, London: Routledge.

Newsom Report (1963) *Half Our Future*, London: HMSO.

Nietzsche (1873/1954) 'On truth and lies in an extra-moral sense', in W. Kaufmann (ed.) *The Portable Nieztsche*, New York: Viking.

Nietzsche, F. (1968) *The Will to Power*, New York: Vintage

O'Brien, R. (2012) 'Native title and the politics of place and space', paper presented at Theorising Indigenous Sociology Workshop, Sydney.

O'Connor, T., McNamara, M., Ahern, A., MacRuairc, G. and O'Donnell, D. (2011) 'Critical thinking in nursing education', paper presented at Third International Nursing and Midwifery Conference, National University of Ireland, Galway.
O'Neill, G. and McMahon, T. (2005) 'Student-centred learning: What does it mean for students and lecturers?', in G. O'Neill, S. Moore and B. McMullin (eds) *Emerging Issues in the Practice of University Learning and Teaching*, Dublin: AISHE.
Osborne, P. (1997) 'Friendly fire: The hoaxing of Social Text', *Radical Philosophy* 81: 54–56.
Parson, T.S. (1954) *Essays in Sociological Theory*, Glencoe: Free Press.
Peters, R.S. (1967) (ed.) *The Concept of Education*, London: Routledge & Kegan Paul.
Pickering, M (1997) *History, Experience and Cultural Studies*, London: Macmillan.
Plumb, J.H. (1964a) (ed.) *Crisis in the Humanities*, Harmondsworth: Penguin.
—— (1964b) 'The historian's dilemma', in J.H. Plumb (ed.) *Crisis in the Humanities*, Harmondsworth: Penguin.
Popper, K. (1957) *The Poverty of Historicism*, London: Routledge & Kegan Paul.
—— (1959) *The Logic of Scientific Discovery*, London: Hutchinson.
—— (1979) *Objective Knowledge: An evolutionary approach*, Oxford, Oxford University Press.
—— (1994a) *Knowledge and the Body–Mind Problem: In defence of interaction*, London: Routledge.
—— (1994b) *The Myth of the Framework: In defence of science and rationality*, London: Routledge.
—— (2003a) *The Open Society and its Enemies, Volume 1: The spell of Plato*, Abingdon: Routledge.
—— (2003b) *The Open Society and its Enemies, Volume 2: Hegel and Marx*, Abingdon: Routledge.
Porat, M. (1977) *The Information Economy*, Washington: US Dept of Commerce.
Poster, M. (1990) *The Mode of Information*, Chicago: University of Chicago Press.
Poulet, C. (2010) 'Recognising and revealing knowers: An enhanced Bernsteinian analysis of masonic recruitment and apprenticeship', *British Journal of Sociology of Education* 31(6): 793–812.
—— (2011) 'L'apprentissage d'une pratique democratique: L'exemple de la prise de parole en Franc-maçonnerie' unpublished PhD thesis, University of Provence, France.
—— (2014) 'Knowledge and knowers in tacit pedagogic contexts: The case of Freemasonry in France', in K. Maton, S. Hood and S. Shay (eds) *Knowledge-building*, London: Routledge.
Power, S. (2010) 'Bernstein and empirical research', in P. Singh, A. Sadovnik and S. Semel (eds) *Toolkits, Translation Devices, Conceptual Tyrannies*, New York: Peter Lang.
Prendergast, G.P. (1994) 'Student-centred learning in the large class setting', *Journal of Further and Higher Education* 18(3): 48–62.
QCA (Qualifications & Curriculum Authority) (2005) *GCSE Subject Criteria for Music*, London: QCA.
Rata, E. (2012) *The Politics of Knowledge in Education*, London: Routledge.
Reay, D. (1995) '"They employ cleaners to do that": Habitus in the primary classroom', *British Journal of Sociology of Education* 16(3): 353–371.

—— (2004) '"It's all becoming a habitus": Beyond the habitual use of habitus in educational research', *British Journal of Sociology of Education* 25(4): 431–444.
Reeves, T.C., Herrington, J. and Oliver, R. (2005) 'Design research: A socially responsible approach to instructional technology research in higher education', *Computing in Higher Education* 16(2): 97–116.
Richard-Bossez, A. (2012) 'Formes de savoirs et différenciations scolaires à l'école maternelle', paper presented at Seventh International Basil Bernstein Symposium, University of Provence, France.
Rose, D. and Martin, J.R. (2012) *Learning to Write, Reading to Learn: Genre, knowledge and pedagogy in the Sydney School*, London: Equinox.
Rosenberg, H. (1962) *The Tradition of the New*, London: Thames & Hudson.
—— (1970) *The Tradition of the New*, second edition, London: Paladin.
Ross, T. (2000) *The Making of the English Literary Canon*, Montreal: McGill-Queen's University Press.
Salomon, G. and Perkins, D.N. (1989) 'Rocky roads to transfer: Rethinking mechanism of a neglected phenomenon', *Educational Psychologist* 24(2): 113–142.
Sargent, J.R. (1964) 'Economics: The world-be, may-be science', in J.H. Plumb (ed.) *Crisis in the Humanities*, Harmondsworth: Penguin.
Scardamalia, M. and Bereiter, C. (2006) 'Knowledge building: Theory, pedagogy, and technology', in K. Sawyer (ed.) *Cambridge Handbook of the Learning Sciences*, Cambridge: Cambridge University Press.
Schmidt, H.G., Loyens, S.M.M., Van Gog, T. and Paas, F. (2007) 'Problem-based learning is compatible with human cognitive architecture: Commentary on Kirschner, Sweller, and Clark (2006)', *Educational Psychologist* 42(2): 91–97.
Scott, D. (2010) *Education, Epistemology and Critical Realism*, London: Routledge.
Sennett, R. (2006) *The Culture of the New Capitalism*, London: Yale University Press.
Shalem, Y. and Slonimsky, L. (2010) 'Seeing epistemic order: Construction and transmission of evaluative criteria', *British Journal of Sociology of Education* 31(6): 755–778.
Shay, S. (2011) 'Curriculum formation: A case study from History', *Studies in Higher Education* 36(3): 315–329.
—— (2013) 'Conceptualizing curriculum differentiation in higher education: A sociology of knowledge point of view', *British Journal of Sociology of Education*, 34(4): 563–82.
Shay, S. and Steyn, D. (2014) 'Enabling knowledge progression in vocational curricula: Design as a case study', in K. Maton, S. Hood and S. Shay (eds) *Knowledge-building*, London: Routledge.
Showalter, E. (1977) *A Literature of Their Own*, Princeton, NJ: Princeton University Press.
—— (1989) 'A criticism of our own: Autonomy and assimilation in Afro-American and feminist literary theory', in R. Cohen (ed.) *The Future of Literary Theory*, London: Routledge.
Shulman, L.S. (1986) 'Those who understand: Knowledge growth in teaching', *Educational Researcher* 15(2): 4–31.
Sieborger, I. and Adendorff, R. (2011) 'Spatial negotation as recontextualisation in the Parliament of the Republic of South Africa', paper presented at Mobility, Language, Literacy conference, University of Cape Town, South Africa.
Sigsgaard, A-V.M. (2012) 'Who has the knowledge if not the primary knower? Using exchange structure analysis to cast light on particular pedagogic practices

in teaching Danish as a Second Language and History', in Knox, J. (ed.) *To Boldly Proceed*, Sydney: ISFC.

Singh, P. (1993) 'Institutional discourse and practice: A case study of the social construction of technological competence in the primary classroom', *British Journal of Sociology of Education* 14(1): 39–58.

—— (2002) 'Pedagogising knowledge: Bernstein's theory of the pedagogic device', *British Journal of Sociology of Education* 23(4): 571–582.

Singh, P., Sadovnik, A. and Semel, S. (eds) (2010) *Toolkits, Translation Devices, Conceptual Tyrannies: Essays on Basil Bernstein's sociology of knowledge*, New York: Peter Lang.

Smolin, L. (2006) *The Trouble with Physics*, London: Penguin.

Snow, C.P. (1959) *The Two Cultures and the Scientific Revolution*, Cambridge: Cambridge University Press.

—— (1964) *The Two Cultures and a Second Look*, Cambridge: Cambridge University Press.

Stavrou, S. (2012) 'Réforme de l'université et transformations curriculaires: des activités de recontextualisation aux effets sur les savoirs – Les universités françaises et le cas des masters en sciences humaines et sociales', unpublished PhD thesis, University of Provence, France.

Steele, T. (1997) *The Emergence of Cultural Studies*, London: Lawrence & Wishart.

Stehr, N. (1994) *Knowledge Societies*, London: Sage.

Steiner, G. (1989) *Real Presences*, London: Faber.

—— (2011) *The Poetry of Thought*, New York: New Directions.

Strassman, D. (1994) 'Feminist thought and economics; or, what do the Visigoths know?', *American Economic Review, Papers and Proceedings*: 153–158.

Swartz, D. (1997) *Culture and Power*, London: University of Chicago Press.

Tan, M. (2013) 'Knowledge, truth, and schooling for social change: Social realism and environmental education in science classrooms', unpublished PhD thesis, Ontario Institute for Studies in Education, University of Toronto, Canada

Tann, K. (2011) 'Semogenesis of a nation: An iconography of Japanese identity', unpublished PhD thesis, University of Sydney, Australia

Taylor, I., Walton, P. and Young, J. (1973) *The New Criminology*, London: Routledge & Kegan Paul.

Thompson, E.P. (1963) *The Making of the English Working Class*, Harmondsworth: Penguin.

Thornton, S. and Gelder, K. (1996) (eds) *The Subcultures Reader*, London: Routledge.

Tobias, S. and Duffy, T.M. (eds) (2009) *Constructivist Instruction*, Abingdon: Routledge.

Touraine, A. (1971) *The Post-Industrial Society*, New York: Random Books.

Turner, G. (1990) *British Cultural Studies*, London: Unwin Hyman.

Tyler, W. (2001) 'Crosswired: Hypertext, critical theory, and pedagogic discourse', in A. Morais, L. Neves, B. Davies and H. Daniels (eds) *Towards a Sociology of Pedagogy*, New York: Peter Lang.

University of Birmingham (1964–1974) *Report of the Vice-Chancellor and Principal for the Calendar Year*, Birmingham: University of Birmingham.

—— (1975–1989) *Annual Reports and Accounts*, Birmingham: University of Birmingham.

Villani, A. (1999) *La guêpe et l'orchidée*, Paris: Belin.

Vitale, P. (2013) 'Seeing beyond the local context: The understandings of slavery and the slave trade of students in Reunion Island schools', *International Studies in Sociology of Education*, 23(4).

von Glasersfeld, E. (1995) *Radical Constructivism: A way of knowing and learning*, Washington, DC: Falmer Press.

von Hallberg, R. (1984) (ed.) *Canons*, Chicago: University of Chicago Press.

Vorster, J. (2011) 'Disciplinary shifts in higher education', in G. Ivinson, B. Davies and J. Fitz (eds) *Knowledge and Identity*, London: Routledge.

Watson, J.G. (1977) 'Letter to the Editor: Cultural studies and English studies', *Times Higher Education Supplement*, 29 July (301): 5.

Wheelahan, L. (2010) *Why Knowledge Matters in Curriculum: A social realist argument*, London: Routledge.

Wilczek, F. (2002) 'A piece of magic: The Dirac equation', in G. Farmelo (ed.) *It Must Be Beautiful*, London: Granta.

Williams, G. (2001) 'Literacy pedagogy prior to schooling: Relations between social positioning and semantic variation', in A. Morais, L. Neves, B. Davies and H. Daniels (eds) *Towards a Sociology of Pedagogy*, New York: Peter Lang.

Williams, R. (1958) *Culture and Society: 1780–1950*, Harmondsworth: Penguin.

—— (1961) *The Long Revolution*, London: Chatto & Windus.

—— (1968) 'Different sides of the wall', *The Guardian*, 26 September.

—— (1989) *The Politics of Modernism*, London: Verso.

Willis, P. (1977) *Learning to Labour: How working-class kids get working-class jobs*, London: Saxon House.

Winch, P. (1958) *The Idea of a Social Science and its Relation to Philosophy*, London: Routledge & Kegan Paul.

—— (1964) 'Understanding a primitive society', *American Philosophical Quarterly* I: 307–324.

Wolff, K. and Luckett, K. (2013) 'Integrating multidisciplinary engineering knowledge', *Teaching in Higher Education* 18(1): 78–92.

Women's Studies Group, CCCS (1978) *Women Take Issue*, London: Hutchinson.

Wright, H.K. (1998) 'Dare we de-centre Birmingham? Troubling the "origin" and trajectories of cultural studies', *European Journal of Cultural Studies* 1(1): 33–56.

Young, M.F.D. (1971) (ed.) *Knowledge and Control: New directions for the sociology of education*, London: Routledge & Kegan Paul.

—— (2000) 'Rescuing the sociology of knowledge from the extremes of voice discourse', *British Journal of Sociology of Education* 21(4): 523–536.

—— (2008) *Bringing Knowledge Back In: From social constructivism to social realism*, London: Routledge.

Young, M.F.D. and Muller, J. (2007) 'Truth and truthfulness in the sociology of educational knowledge', *Theory and Research in Education* 5(2): 173–201.

Zhao, Q. (2012) 'Knowledge building in physics textbooks in primary and secondary schools', unpublished PhD thesis, Xiamen University, China.

Index

Note: Page numbers for figures and tables appear in bold.